## COMMUNITY ENGAGEMENT IN HIGHER EDUCATION

*Edited by Dan W. Butin*

This series examines the limits and possibilities of the theory and practice of community engagement in higher education. It is grounded in the desire to critically, thoughtfully, and thoroughly examine how to support efforts in higher education such that community engagement—a wide yet interrelated set of practices and philosophies such as service-learning, civic engagement, experiential education, public scholarship, participatory action research, and community-based research—is meaningful, sustainable, and impactful to its multiple constituencies. The series is by its nature cross-disciplinary and sees its readership across the breadth of higher education, both within student and academic affairs.

**Dan W. Butin** is an associate professor and founding dean of the School of Education at Merrimack College and the executive director of the Center for Engaged Democracy. He is the author and editor of more than seventy academic publications, including the books *Service-Learning in Theory and Practice: The Future of Community Engagement in Higher Education* (2010), which won the 2010 Critics Choice Book Award of the American Educational Studies Association; *Service-Learning and Social Justice Education* (2008); *Teaching Social Foundations of Education* (2005); and, most recently with Scott Seider, *The Engaged Campus: Certificates, Minors, and Majors as the New Community Engagement* (2012). Dr. Butin's research focuses on issues of educator preparation and policy, and community engagement. Prior to working in higher education, Dr. Butin was a middle school math and science teacher and the chief financial officer of Teach For America. More about Dr. Butin's work can be found at http://danbutin.org/.

*The Engaged Campus: Certificates, Minors, and Majors as the New Community Engagement*
  edited by Dan W. Butin and Scott Seider

*The Challenges and Possibilities of Engaged Learning: Experience in the Academy*
  by David Thornton Moore (forthcoming, 2013)

# Previous Publications

Dan W. Butin

*Service-Learning in Theory and Practice: The Future of Community Engagement in Higher Education* (2010)

*The Education Dissertation: A Guide for Practitioner Scholars* (2010)

*Service-Learning and Social Justice Education: Strengthening Justice-Oriented Community Based Models of Teaching and Learning* (2008)

*100 Experiential Learning Activities for Social Studies, Literature, and the Arts, Grades 5-12f. Service-Learning in Higher Education: Critical Issues and Directions* (2008)

*Teaching Social Foundations of Education: Contexts, Theories and Issues* (2005)

*Service-Learning and Social Justice Education: Strengthening Justice-Oriented Community Based Models of Teaching and Learning* (2005)

Scott Seider

*Shelter: Where Harvard Meets the Homeless* (2010)

*Character Compass: How Powerful School Culture Can Point Students Toward Success* (2012)

# The Engaged Campus

## Certificates, Minors, and Majors as the New Community Engagement

Edited by
*Dan W. Butin*
and
*Scott Seider*

palgrave
macmillan

First published in 2012 by
PALGRAVE MACMILLAN®
in the United States—a division of St. Martin's Press LLC,
175 Fifth Avenue, New York, NY 10010.

Where this book is distributed in the UK, Europe and the rest of the world,
this is by Palgrave Macmillan, a division of Macmillan Publishers Limited,
registered in England, company number 785998, of Houndmills,
Basingstoke, Hampshire RG21 6XS.

Palgrave Macmillan is the global academic imprint of the above companies
and has companies and representatives throughout the world.

Palgrave® and Macmillan® are registered trademarks in the United States,
the United Kingdom, Europe and other countries.

ISBN: 978–0–230–33881–4 (HC)
ISBN: 978–0–230–33882–1 (Pbk)

Library of Congress Cataloging-in-Publication Data

The Engaged Campus: Certificates, Minors, and Majors as the New
Community Engagement / edited by Dan W. Butin, Scott Seider.
    p. cm.—(Community engagement in higher education)
    ISBN 978–0–230–33882–1 (pbk.)—ISBN 978–0–230–33881–4 ()
    1. Community and college—United States. 2. Service learning—United
States. 3. Education, Higher—Curricula—United States. 4. Education,
Higher—Aims and objectives—United States. I. Butin, Dan W. (Dan Wernaa)
II. Seider, Scott.

LC221.E52 2012
378.1'03—dc23                                                    2012001872

A catalogue record of the book is available from the British Library.

Design by Newgen Imaging Systems (P) Ltd., Chennai, India.

First edition: August 2012

10 9 8 7 6 5 4 3 2 1

Printed in the United States of America.

# Contents

## Part II    Reflecting on the Future of
## Community Engagement

# Foreword

This important book emerges at a time of difficult choices. Most of higher education is facing hard times. Now, more than ever, it matters that, rather than add on yet another set of options that drain resources, we give our thought, time, energy, and money to efforts to improve higher education with regard to its most capacious, enduring, defining purposes.

The problem, of course, is that we may be less clear, or more divided than ever about what those capacious, enduring purposes for education should be. Is our purpose, as we hear all the time, only or primarily to "keep America competitive in a globalizing world"? Is it, as so many students genuinely need it to be, preparation for a good job? If so, there is nothing unique for education to do; via research and training, it is to be a means for economic interests and should be shaped to serve them better (an effort that is indeed being made). However, if we believe there is a capacious if specific calling for higher education that argues for its remaining a largely self-monitoring profession with recognized value to the public good, on what grounds do we do so?

Primary among those with creative, not merely defensive, responses to these questions are those working in engaged education, and this is one clear reason they have been so strikingly successful thus far. In a time of shattered national narratives, the authors in this book (along with their colleagues in the United States and around the globe) speak eloquently of educating, not just for citizenship, but also for a rich civic and community life for all; for the aspirational idea of democracy; for personal, social, and political responsibility; for a more just and equitable world—in many ways, of educating for an engaged and thus more fully realized life for as many as possible. Here then, I believe, is the spirit of the great democratic movements that opened education and much else to long-excluded and devalued people and peoples as participants, as leaders, thereby initiating transformations still to be fully understood.

More specifically, and most importantly for our moment in the ongoing movement to democratize education, engaged education, service-learning in all its guises, brings *action* into the concerns of the academy, which has long sheltered itself from the risks, indeterminacy, controversy, and passions of *praxis*. The "merely practical," or even the "applied," has been devalued; the arts and virtues of action have been marginalized, if not ignored.

It may well be, then, that this movement challenges us to call forward, clarify, and begin suggesting responses to the next phase of transformative work as we continue reinventing education that can know itself to be truer to its own values, when it is more rather than, as it has been for so long, less democratic. That is, might we understand experiential learning and active research (et al.) not only as useful enough to be added on to higher education, but as ways to realize both basic and aspirational educational purposes more fully?

I do not think that, in response to such a need, we can just recur to traditional claims that we "prepare students for citizenship." When, as we are doing now, we actually stop to think about it, we realize, first, that nothing was actually done to practice citizenship (except sometimes in the extracurriculum, which maintains the old split between knowledge and action), and second, that, if provided, such preparation would very likely have been as narrow (if not as searingly, dangerously negative) as the prevailing notions of the political have become (i.e., concerning only political parties, elections, et al.). Were such notions to be defined as central to higher education, the problem would be similar to that now posed by the dominance of economic needs and interests—the threat of reducing higher education to training programs for aspiring politicians or citizenship schools.

In academia—which, it is crucial to remember, is our focus—the case that serving democracy is among the purposes that make up a mission needs to be understood in such contexts as conservation and renewal of knowledge, cultures, and arts and values that enrich the present through their connections to the past, and its responsibilities to the future. That, after all, is why education has over time been formalized and, in would-be democracies, required and/or publicly supported. It keeps us from having to start from scratch with every generation in our shareable quests for better, more meaningful, more just, and happier lives. In closer-in terms, the case for serving democracy has had to connect it intimately to teaching, learning, and research in fields ranging from physics to sociology, environmental studies to art, design to philosophy, criminal justice to literature, African-Africana studies to architecture.

Here, we encounter the stubborn reality that the meanings and ideals of democracy cannot just be added on to disciplines, pedagogies, and systems to which they have long been alien as conventionally understood. It is not surprising that, not far beneath the surface, many faculty still find them to be so. *Democracy* is a famously difficult notion even within its usual meaning frameworks, and all the more so when carried over to educational institutions where, as in families, authority (of knowledge, experience, responsibility) has long seemed an appropriate, even defining (if not uncontested) relation. I imagine that few if any who make a case for "democratic education" escape having to assure faculty that they are not being told to renounce their hard-earned authority, and in particular, that democratic education does not mean we will now be voting on which facts are "true," which theory sound, or which practice is effective and safe. These are not (or not always or only) individual notions held onto by authority-anxious teachers. Difficult epistemological as well as political and ethical issues arise when we bring action and knowledge into equal relation and expect them to play well together.

Anything that involves giving academic credibility to praxis—to *action*—is radical, and goes to the roots of long-dominant meaning, evaluation, and social systems.

Here, we could turn to philosophers (among those that would be useful are the Pragmatists, including Du Bois and Jane Addams); radical educators (Freire and Maxine Greene, again, among others); some political theorists, psychologists, sociologists, and historians of education. We are not the first to remember that "active" as a modifier for "learning" ought to be redundant, nor the first to try to demonstrate why that is so (consider the work that has been done at The Evergreen State College, Goddard, or Antioch). But in this book, we can also see what we are learning afresh, for today, from a rich array of the practices of engaged in many kinds of schools. After all, like other movements for the social good, this one is also animated primarily by on-the-ground, practical purposes—ending long-enduring practices that are now judged harmful, improving our ability to act effectively, and creating better systems—while raising questions of meaning, purpose, justification, implication, as is being done intensively right now. All this work can be considered experimental; higher education in general should be learning from it.

So, where are we now when we ask, What does this jumbled set of programs that take students off campus to get them doing things bring to the core purposes of higher education?

First off, I have to note what it does not do: it does not replicate the growing number of applied-scholarship fields. Engaged learning may not yet always be integrated with standard discipline-based courses, but it also has not been formalized in ways that give it separate, discrete standing. Applied fields do stand apart from their "pure" counterparts. There *is* applied ethics, but it is not normative ethics or meta-ethics, just as art history is not studio art, and political science is not obligated to practice students in the arts and techniques of politicking. These divisions are not just the result of silly academic territoriality. It is neither trivial nor simply the mark of overspecialized academics that it is difficult to figure out how action relates to theory in mutually illuminating ways, throughout inquiry as well as teaching.

Still, when we focus on engaged education, interesting things happen. For example, we realize that it is risky to teach theories without analyzing the circumstances from which they arose, the purposes they served, the effects they had. Students who learn a theory without such contexts might well think it right simply to apply it in times and places and to people who might be seriously violated by it (need I remind anybody of what the theories of eugenics led to in practice?). Before, during, and after all learning experiences, there is a need to reflect, to connect what happens to concepts, and theories, but also to memories and feelings. Through such learning, concepts and theories will shift, at least a bit, as well, as they are thus brought into conversation with fresh examples.

Indeed, *reflection* has become a major concept, and practice, in service-learning. It is striking that projects that are primarily focused on action are reminding us of what ought to be evident: there is no learning without reflection. (Members of an English department once told me that they remembered that they should ask students to reflect on their experiences of learning, wherever they take place, because of the people in the service–learning program on their campus.)

Some rationales that suggest criteria other than "put what we know to use by applying it" are also on offer (although they differ in depth and capaciousness). Depending on the program, experiences are said to serve primarily civic learning as well as preparation for citizenship, psycho-social development, job training, social justice, and the development of democratic capacities such as informed empathy. But, despite radical differences in how such purposes are actually understood, *serving democracy* does indeed seem to be an umbrella that shelters many projects.

We're back where we started, it seems. However, there are some oddities that it is time to note. I think they take us somewhere deeper, closer to where we want to go.

It is usually assumed in claims that engaged education is education for democracy that democracy either cannot or should not be served on campus, nor its arts practiced there. There is nothing subtle in noticing that, even when it does not burst forth from authority-challenged faculty, the assumption is that students need to go off campus, that they need to do something different from what goes on in class, in particular. Time and again, in discussions about civic education I hear that the students need to "go out" to have experiences of (some would say "with") people in circumstances it is assumed they have gotten this far in life having never encountered.

But this is an outdated and peculiar assumption that is truer to the time before the earlier phases of the movements to realize democracy. Faculty come from many different backgrounds now, as do administrators, staff, and students. As one student said after sitting silently through a meeting in which the university's civic-learning initiatives were being evaluated, "You all seem to have no idea whatsoever of what it took for my extended family to get me here, on campus, and now you want to shove me back out. That's weird. And anyhow, you know, the people and communities you want me to go experience? That's my home. It's *you*, this university, that I have no experience of."

Neither just going off campus nor doing so to have experiences (as if anyone arrived without such things), or having cross-class or—race or—cultural experiences suffices to reconfigure relations between knowing and doing, between thinking and acting.

The question recurs: What, then, are we doing if we are only adding *doing something somewhere else* on to—what? Learning? Is that not also something we do, actively? It's weird— the old division but no less potent.

Let us, then, cut to the chase: how is action *intrinsically* significant for all learning? Again, this is not a question I can or should try to answer here (tempted as I am to try). It is a question we need to ask as together we think about all the projects—experiments, as I see them—in engaged learning that we do not wish to relegate to mere add-on status, that we do wish to develop for their genuinely transformative potential.

This book provides rich material for such reflections. Among other things, service-learning programs are evidently increasingly run by scholars long involved in interdisciplinary, active, engaged research who are now also seasoned in the complexities of service-learning. From such scholars, we already have literature that connects experiential learning with, say, political theory, history, and sociology as well as interdisciplinary fields such as peace and justice studies, gender studies, environmental studies. This literature can be taught. There is transformational conceptual work there if we will take the time and trouble to pull it together and think it through such that it can startle us into fresh thought.

There is a still more obvious source of content for minors and majors that promises to bear rich epistemological as well as pedagogical fruit. Appropriately, it emerges from the practices of civic learning as they have been reflected on, conceptualized, taught, rethought, and engaged with various theoretical traditions. An example: it is not new, but it is deeply challenging for all teachers to consider that it is *always* significant that students ought to be prepared, both theoretically and practically, to become, however temporarily, a part of the lifeworlds, the meaning and value systems, of others. This, after all, is something every single one of us does throughout life: we leave our private lives to join with others, strangers at first, to do our work, to act as citizens, to read a book, enjoy the arts, learn a new theory, travel.

We do not yet know how to discern, name, or frame such intellectual arts of relation and action (there may be more clarity about techniques that are useful; a number of projects exist to provide training in them). We have words and terms— *reflexive thinking, reflection, judgment, imaginative empathy, attentiveness,* and the *experiential, conceptual precipitate of action over time with thoughtful others, practical wisdom* are among my own—but it is premature to settle on any. We are learning as we experiment with engaged education, and that is precisely as it ought to be if we are to truly change the meaning systems that have long severed learning from doing, and thinking and knowing from acting.

Still, we are also coming to know in fresh ways why and how acting matters for all learning. There are many examples—this book is a trove of them—but one that is crucial, and so I repeat it with respect for all the service-learning practitioners who also care about it, is that students who go 'out to learn' need to keep thinking once they are placed and when they are done. Discussion, supervision, and journal-keeping all serve the reflection that not only is necessary for real learning but may also stave off the disaster of thoughtlessness.

As a student of Hannah Arendt's, I leave that as my last word, adding only this: if we can, finally, work with our students to learn to *think what we are doing*— wherever we are, whatever we are engaged in—we may finally manage to keep too many theories from being dangerous if directly applied, too much action from being dangerously mindless.

This long moment, in which we try to bring acting and thinking into play with each other, is very important to movements aspiring to the fullness promised by democracy. There is a great deal to learn and to change, but also to hope for.

ELIZABETH MINNICH
Association of American Colleges
and Universities

# Acknowledgments

Many of the chapters that make up this volume emerged from annual summer conferences held in summer 2010 and 2011 entitled "The Future of Community Engagement in Higher Education," hosted jointly by Merrimack College's Center for Engaged Democracy and Boston University's Center for Character and Social Responsibility. We would thus like to acknowledge the generous support for these conferences extended by Merrimack College and Boston University, and particularly Hardin Coleman, Carol Crossen, Amy Moeller, and Sarah Novick for their generosity of time, effort, and guidance. We would also like to acknowledge the contributions and feedback on earlier drafts of these chapters offered by over 200 professionals—academics, administrators, students, and community partners— who came from every corner of the United States as well as Ireland, Canada, and South Africa to participate in the conferences and to share best practices and brainstorm common challenges related to the institutionalization of community engagement in such academic programs. Additionally, we would like to thank Burke Gerstenschlager and Kaylan Connally at Palgrave Macmillan for their administrative support, their belief in the vision and value of this project, and, yes, their patience throughout the publication process.

This edited book, from Dan's perspective, would not have been possible without Scott's tireless guidance, organizational acumen, and scholarly ballast. This book, I believe, truly grapples with new and important issues at a fundamentally precarious moment in the trajectory of higher education. It takes time, wisdom, and thoughtfulness to think through and organize a group of scholars and scholarly ideas into a coherent framework and dialogue. Scott has been key in making this happen. On a more personal level, this book grows out of my steadfast belief that our growth as scholars, students, and citizens is grounded in difficult and deliberate dialogues, actions, and reflections. My friends, many of whom may or may not know it, have thus contributed greatly to who I am and what I write and care about. Thank you Ian, Margie, Pablo, Lauren, Guy, Susan, Scott, Peter, John, Brian, Kim, Elizabeth, and Bill. And underneath, making even that possible, are Gitte, Michaela, and Matthias. Thanks to all.

This edited book, from Scott's perspective, emerged from the vision of community engagement in higher education that Dan Butin has been championing for more than a decade now. Through both the 2010 and 2011 conferences, and now this volume, it has been a privilege to play a supporting role as Dan challenges the place of community engagement within the university and does his part to nurture the majors, minors, and certificate programs that are beginning to sprout in universities across the United States and beyond. On a personal level, I am grateful to my colleagues and students at Boston University for allowing me to do work that feels so engaging and gratifying and to my wife, Amanda Seider, for her unwavering love and partnership.

# When Engagement is Not Enough: Building the Next Generation of the Engaged Campus

*Dan W. Butin*
Merrimack College

## *Introduction*

The community engagement movement, I suggest, has reached an "engagement ceiling." It is thus time to develop a blueprint for the next generation of the engaged campus. It is a chance to seed a second wave of scholarship and activism for the long-term sustenance of civic and community engagement in higher education. This book provides a model for doing so.

Namely, it chronicles a new intellectual movement within higher education: the construction of dozens of academic programs—certificates, minors, and majors—focused on community engagement, broadly construed. Such academic programs are a natural and important outcome of a generation of scholarship and activism in higher education that has seen the ideas of civic engagement, campus-community partnerships, and translational research become commonplace. Yet, until now, there has been little systematic inquiry about or a conceptual framework for understanding the multiple yet disparate programs that have developed at colleges and universities across the country. This book makes visible the powerful models already in place and provides an opportunity for readers to thoughtfully and constructively engage with the challenges and possibilities of what such programs offer to the field.

The academic programs profiled and analyzed in this book are at the forefront of educating undergraduates into both the difficulties and possibilities of community engagement. They are also on the cutting-edge of rethinking what the community engagement movement should look like in higher education. For this movement, as I will argue below, is at a critical juncture. Even as the notion of "engagement" becomes embraced and commonplace across the academy, there is an expanding gap between the rhetoric of possibility and the on-the-ground reality of fostering a civically-engaged and meaningfully-collaborative campus.

The rise and expansion of academic programs focused on community engagement does not suggest or imply the displacement or undermining of existing practices such as service-learning offices or the Carnegie Foundation's "community engagement" classification. Rather, it is a both/and argument for acknowledging, analyzing, and supporting a parallel intellectual movement of academic programs committed to the same key principles and social action of community engagement.

It is, though, of paramount importance to understand this shift. For it offers, for the first time, an academic space from which it becomes possible to critique, explore, develop, and build a different model of what an engaged campus might look like. It offers a space that, I contend, has been sorely missing and which, if nurtured, may provide a key ballast for the forthcoming challenges and opportunities of community engagement in the academy. This book traces this development from its theoretical roots to its current pragmatic practices to the potential next steps of policy, strategy, and vision.

As such, in the rest of this introductory chapter, I position the development of these academic programs within the larger frame of the current state of the community engagement movement. This provides an entrance into the heart of the book, where key individuals in existing academic programs tackle critical issues and document their specific practices vis-à-vis particular institutional histories and cultures. They provide important perspectives and make visible key challenges and the impact of powerful certificate programs, minors, and majors. In so doing, they demonstrate how they have truly embraced and enacted community engagement in their programs and across their institutions in deliberate, sustained, and powerful ways. These are critical insights that will impact how we think about the role of service-learning and community engagement on our campuses and what we can do to insure its legitimate and long-term success.

The final section of the book offers four external perspectives from "critical friends"—Peter Levine at CIRCLE, Elizabeth Minnich at AAC&U, Elizabeth Hollander at Tufts and past-president of Campus Compact, and Ariane Hoy, Mathew Johnson and Bobby Hackett at the Bonner Foundation—on the nature and development of these academic programs. These individuals have been an instrumental part of the rise and spread of the community engagement movement, and Scott and I are honored to have their perspectives about this new academic movement.

At the heart of this book is the idea that, following on de Tocqueville's evocative phrase, the "apprenticeship of liberty is never easy" (Barber, 1985; Butin, 2012). Namely, none of us are born with the skills, knowledge, and disposition to be thoughtful, active, and engaged citizens. While a formal postsecondary education is surely not the only or perhaps even the most efficacious model for building such a citizenry, it is indeed one of the few structured and systematic ways that we as adults—and those that we teach—have for thinking through and engaging with the complexities of community engagement. In fact, bringing the idea of the external community into the center of academic scholarship and teaching offers a unique melding of theory and practice whereby each stands in productive tension with the other, offering immense possibilities for public scholarship and reflective practice (Paul, 2006).

It of course must be noted that this vision of the "disciplined" inquiry of a subject seemingly so wedded to community action may be disappointingly deflationary, particularly for those committed to a revolutionary model of social change (Butin, 2006a, 2006b). We cannot, so it seems, immediately and completely transform either the academy or our communities. But, to be honest, this was never a possibility so much as a rhetorical straw man argument for the value of civic and community engagement. And once we let go of such rhetorical turns, it becomes possible to embrace that what the academy offers is a truly transformative opportunity to train a new generation of students, faculty, and administrators into deep, sustained, and impactful community engagement practices, policies, and philosophies. This, I believe, is what truly constitutes the engaged campus and, ultimately, what this book is about.

### The Community Engagement Movement—Expansions, Undersides, and The Next Generation of Practice

The community engagement movement—composed of a loosely interrelated set of programs, practices, and philosophies such as service-learning, civic and community engagement, public scholarship, and community-based research—has become an assumed and expected part of the higher education landscape. Using a starting point of the late 1980s—Campus Compact was founded in 1985, Ernest Boyer's *Scholarship Reconsidered* was published in 1990, and the Corporation of National and Community Service was begun in 1992—it can easily and legitimately be claimed that the vocabulary of engagement and campus-community linkages has become commonplace in higher education within a single generation (Benson & Harkavy, 2007; Boyer, 1990; Campus Compact, 2000; Saltmarsh, Hartley & Clayton, 2009).

Most faculty, for example, believe that working in and with the community is an important component of the undergraduate education experience; National Survey of Student Engagement (NSSE) has deemed service-learning one of the key means by which to engage in "deep learning"; and the Carnegie Foundation for the Advancement of Teaching has institutionalized and incorporated its "community engagement" voluntary classification into its standard five-year review cycle, allowing hundreds of institutions to demonstrate the breadth and depth of their community partnerships and community engagement (Dalton & Crosby, 2011; DeAngelo, Hurtado, Pryor, Kelly & Santos, 2009; Driscoll, 2009; Kuh et al., 2008; Pryor, Hurtado, Saenz, Santos & Korn, 2007).

This is a powerful testament to the individuals who, in the early 1970s, tirelessly transformed a set of loosely-organized ideas, practices, and initiatives into a national discussion for the necessity of the reaffirmation and reinvigoration of the civic purposes of higher education (Hoy & Meisel, 2008; Stanton, Giles & Cruz, 1999). An immense apparatus—of national nonprofit organizations, federal and state agencies, campus-based curricular and co-curricular offices, philanthropic foundations, and community-based organizations, groups, and corporations—has grown to oversee, manage, guide, and support several billion dollars in federal, state, and private funding; hundreds of thousands of undergraduate students; tens of thousands of faculty; and more than a thousand colleges and universities all seemingly committed to the public good.

And by all outward appearances, such success is only growing stronger. For example, the US Department of Education (USDOE), in partnership with the Association of American Colleges and Universities (AAC&U), has recently launched a high profile multiyear "national effort on civic learning and democratic engagement in higher education" (National Task Force, 2012). Their report—*A Crucible Moment: College Learning and Democracy's Future*—argues that "[w]ith this report [we call on] the higher education community—and *all* its stakeholders—to embrace civic learning and democratic engagement as an undisputed priority.... That will require constructing educational environments where education for democracy and civic responsibility is pervasive, not partial; central, not peripheral" (National Task Force, 2012, p. 6).

Even if we acknowledge that such rhetorical positioning has been promulgated for the better part of a generation (e.g., AASCU, 1992; Boyer, 1990; Brukardt, Holland, Percy & Simpher, 2004; Saltmarsh et al., 2009), it is noteworthy that the report and its central champions have leveraged literally hundreds of initiatives across colleges and universities towards such prioritization (USDOE, 2012). There thus appears to be a notable confluence: ever more research evidence accrues of the positive impact of service-learning and community engagement on a wide range of students' cognitive, social, and dispositional factors (Antonio, Astin & Cross, 2000; Eyler, Giles, Stenson & Gray, 2001; Finley, 2011; Novak, Markey & Allen, 2007); ever more institutions embrace the "community engagement" moniker (Carnegie Foundation, 2011; Campus Compact, 2010); ever more students and faculty assume and expect their institutions to be socially conscious and outwardly centered (Pryor et al., 2011). It is no wonder the federal government has embraced this seemingly singular opportunity to support and push forward the agenda of civic empowerment and renewal.

Yet even as the public face and the upward narrative of community engagement are embraced, there are troubling signs of internal malaise. A wide variety of analyses within the community engagement field, for example, suggest that there continues to be a lack of conceptual clarity, research rigor, or impact of outcomes (Ang, 2006; Brabant & Braid, 2009; Cheney, 2008; Cruz & Giles, 2000; Dempsey, 2010; Dorn, 2011; Hartley, 2009; Head, 2007; Keen & Hall, 2009; Schwartzman & Henry, 2009). Case studies abound of community engagement projects gone awry, of opportunities missed, and of partnerships failed (e.g., Barge, 2006; Cheney, 2008; Dempsey, 2009; Hart, 1998; Himley, 2004; Hogan, 2002; Israel et al., 1998; Winter et al., 2006).

In one respect, this is business as usual in an academic endeavor as complex and multifaceted as campus-community partnerships. The demise of community engagement is certainly not on the horizon: most critical analyses are piecemeal and across many disciplines and areas of inquiry; the definitions and delimitations of what "community engagement" really "is" frustrates simple cross-case analysis or synthesis of key variables and practices; the conclusions of such studies are usually far from conclusive; and almost all such studies are grounded in an amelioristic vision of tinkering with and thus improving the field, negating any opportunity to step outside of the field for a broader and more critical perspective. We are thus far, far away from any sort of "death knell" of the community engagement movement.

But in another respect, such critiques signal an "underside" to the community engagement movement that is rarely acknowledged or further investigated. In fact, if we open the conceptual frame, it becomes clear that a broad range of theoretical arguments in the last quarter century—those within, for example, feminist, critical, postcolonial, poststructuralist, and critical race theorizing—have questioned the grounding for just about every single assumption, enactment, and orientation of "community" and "engagement" (Adorno, 1973; Balibar, 1994; Haraway, 1988; hooks, 1981; Moraga and Anzaldua, 1983; Mouffe, 1992; Spivak, 1988; Young, 1986; see Butin, 2010, for a more detailed analysis). From the reification of "the other" to a problematic ethical foundationalism to a distressing cultural voyeurism to a middling conceptual framework for organizational and community change, the community engagement movement currently lacks the depth of scholarship necessary to provide a solid base for its embrace across higher education.

Yet as Joseph (2002, p. xxxi) astutely notes, none of this critical work has dampened the drive to embrace an ongoing upward narrative: "Before any progressive or resistant reimagination of community will be efficacious, we need to account for the relentless return of the dominant discourse and practice of community. What is the motor driving this discourse ever onward, despite our best efforts to shift it?" Indeed, what makes us continue to embrace and extol the current theory and practice of community engagement so seemingly diffuse and so seemingly without sustained critique?

A partial answer, I suggest, lies in the very heart of the literature affirming and embracing the community engagement movement. Namely, the current model of engagement is premised on and driven by the overarching leitmotif of the transformation of higher education. I have referred to this as the service-learning-as-social-movement argument (Butin, 2011), one that has as its goal the embrace of civic and community engagement across all disciplines and practices in higher education. I should be clear that this vision, in and of itself, is not the problem. The problem is that such a goal positions the community engagement movement as a seemingly external and transformational social movement attempting to remake the internal and nontransformational academic work of the academy.

Such a positioning is problematic on a host of conceptual and strategic levels: it sets up a false dichotomy between the internal and external realms of the academy; gives this binary an unsupportable moral valence of external as socially-just activism versus internal as inchoate status quo; and suggests, through a process of goal displacement, that the institutionalization of the "external" community engagement movement within the "internal" academy becomes the key outcome of such a movement. In so doing—in positioning itself solely and only as a nonacademic social movement coming from the legitimate outside to transform the outdated and insular inside—the community engagement movement becomes seemingly immune to critical examination (see, e.g., Simons, 1970; Stewart et al., 1989, for the conceptual underpinnings of this rhetorical strategy).

In so doing, in preventing the opportunity for internal debate, critique, and revision, such a positioning inadvertently undermines the long-term ability of community engagement advocates within the academy to sustain their practices (see Butin, 2011). For without "academic homes" such as the certificates, minors, and majors detailed in this book, it becomes difficult to develop and sustain safe spaces for critical reflection and action over extended periods of time not beholden to external grant funding, individual force of will (be they presidents, faculty, or community partners), or political pressures.

And with the fundamental changes in American higher education (e.g., Abbott, 2001; AAC&U, 2007; Bousquet, 2008; Musselin, 2007; Slaughter and Rhoades, 2004), I would argue, community engagement as a social movement is no longer either obvious or tenable as a powerful practice all across the academy. The reasons for this are complex, intertwined, and not easily changeable given the long-term economic retrenchment sweeping across higher education: the expanding demographics of "nontraditional," part-time, commuting students; the outsourcing of labor to contingent and adjunct faculty; and the "wickedly" complex and contested problem of engaging with (much less solving) community issues enmeshed within multiple racial, political, economic, social, and historical realities.

If the goal of the first generation of scholars and activists was to transform higher education, the real issue today is how to move beyond what many see as a "stalled" movement. For example, Finley (2011), in a review of the literature on civic engagement for AAC&U, suggests that the key challenge for the civic engagement field is "not so much a dismissal of service-learning as it is a global questioning of the foci of the multitude of service-learning programming which tend to forefront social connectedness among peers, faculty, and community, rather than democratic skills. At the core of this challenge and central to the divisions within the civic engagement literature, is the lack of a common definition or conceptual language for 'civic engagement'" (p. 2). Finley (2011) thus concludes that "civic engagement is a term that lacks a cohesive definition within higher education . . . [and in practice] is as multi-form and disparate as its definition" (p. 20).

Interestingly, the notion of a "stalled" movement due to the lack of terminological clarity and isolation of programs is directly traceable to a key white paper produced by the Kettering Foundation (Saltmarsh et al., 2009) that suggested that there was a "sense of drift and stalled momentum" because of "imprecise and even conflicting language" within the movement, a "highly fragmented and compartmentalized" set of networks, and a "remarkably apolitical" civic agenda (p. 1; pp. 4–5). The Kettering report concluded with a call for reframing the discussion to one of "democratic engagement" which, through "second order" transformational change, actually "holds the promise of transforming not only the educational practice and institutional identity of colleges and universities but our public culture as well" (Saltmarch et al., 2009, pp. 12–14).

The attempt by the USDOE, AAC&U and others, to restart and rejuvenate the community engagement movement is thus, wittingly or not, an attempt to rebuild a social movement through a defining narrative with clear goals and even clearer definitions. The problem from my perspective, though, is that this a more-of-the-same type of attempt to push harder, to generate greater visibility for and to expand even more funding, resources, and energy into a strategic positioning—community engagement as an overarching skeleton key to transform higher education—that has reach its apex. This apex, I suggest, is not so much about a lack of clarity or conflicting language; instead, it is a lack of critical space and opportunity to delve deeply, carefully, and systematically into what community engagement—like any complex and contested real-world practice that links the college classroom with the community—actually means and how it is enacted. This is what I have called for as the "disciplining" of service-learning, and what this book is about: the institutionalization of community engagement in higher education within academic certificates, minors, and majors.

## The Rise of Academic Programs in Community Engagement

I thus want to suggest that there may be another means by which to fruitfully examine the current state of civic and community engagement in higher education: at the level of practice. Namely, the last decade has seen the rise of dozens of new academic programs centered around notions of community engagement, broadly defined. Certificate programs, minors, and majors have popped up at institutions as varied as Mary Baldwin College, the University of Illinois–Chicago, Guilford College, and the University of California, Los Angeles. The academic programs have titles such as "Community and Justice Studies," "Civic Leadership," and "Public Policy and Community Service." They join more established academic programs such as University of California, Santa Cruz's longstanding Department of Community Studies and Providence College's Public and Community Service Studies major (Center for Engaged Democracy, 2011; see also Hoy & Meisel, 2008).

What all of these programs share is the core principle of the academy as providing an academic space for scholars and students to investigate the complexities of a particular area of inquiry thoroughly and thoughtfully. In each case, there are dedicated faculty members attached to each program doing the deliberate, careful, and critical work that is necessary for any successful academic program: advising students, creating introductory courses, questioning the quality of the capstone experience, reaching out to colleagues across the institution and community members outside of it for perspective and feedback and collaboration, advocating for additional tenure-track lines, and questioning whether what they do is ultimately of value and relevance to its critical stakeholders.

Such seemingly mundane practices, are, in fact, key to the daily practices and rituals (Meyer & Rowan, 1977) that build up to structure, solidify, and maintain a field's relevance and legitimacy. They structure and systematize otherwise disparate and ephemeral passions and practices. I am thus not suggesting that we wipe our hands, shut the classroom door, and walk away from the pressing societal problems that colleges and universities must indeed be a part of solving. Rather, we must reframe our terminology to accept that community engagement must also become an intellectual movement. If the next generation of scholars, students, and community members are to have a chance in fostering deep, sustained, and ultimately powerful campus and community collaborations, then we must embrace a second wave of criticality toward the scholarship of engagement.

By this I mean what other movements, such as Women's Studies and Black Studies, have accomplished in the last 30 years. They have created, through majors and minors and interdisciplinary concentrations and research centers, a means to influence and impact the knowledge production and dissemination of their respective areas of study. They have succeeded in the impressive accomplishment that it is no longer possible to speak simply or "obviously" about what feminism or blackness "is," either within their respective fields or across the academy, or, for that matter, in the larger world.

This, then, is the face of the next generation of the community engagement movement in higher education. It is the critical work that cannot take for granted the practice and philosophy of community engagement. For community engagement is a complex and contested practice that claims to engage in "border crossing" and as such engages issues of power, race, and class. It is a practice that has real-world ethical, legal, and political implications for what our undergraduates actually do out there; and it is a philosophy of practice that is seemingly at the heart of a liberal arts education. As such, what we do with, for, and in the community must be open to the same type of scrutiny as any other legitimate academic practice. And it needs to be done in academic spaces that foster the very qualities we are looking for in the community partnerships we espouse: deep, sustained, and impactful reflection, engagement, and action. That is an intellectual movement.

In the end, of course, this is not an either/or proposition. The academy must embrace both the community engagement and the critical academic spaces. To have engagement without the criticality is to succumb ultimately to a cheerleading mentality for a thin-skinned social movement unable to withstand the academy's critique. To have disciplined academic inquiry without a deep and sustained experiential community-based component is to succumb to an ineffectual model of "hallway activists" where theory and practice are disjoined and disjointed and where the thick skin of academic debate cannot feel or see the needs of the community all around it. But without the next stage, without the second wave of critique within academic spaces, the next generation of the engaged campus will be ever more imperiled. The programs highlighted and examined in this book thus offer a unique moment to rethink and rework our longstanding notions of the engaged campus.

## References

Abbott, A. (2001). *The chaos of disciplines*. Chicago: University of Chicago Press.

Adorno, T. (1973). *Negative dialectics*. Trans. E. B. Ashton. New York: Seabury Press.

American Association of State Colleges and Universities (1992). *Stepping forward as stewards of place: a guide for leading public engagement at state colleges and universities*. Washington, DC: AASCU.

Ang, I. (2006). From cultural studies to cultural research: Engaged scholarship in the 21st century. *Cultural Studies Review, 12*(2), 183–97.

Antonio, A. L., H. S. Astin, & C. Cross. (2000). Community service in higher education: A look at the faculty. *The Review of Higher Education, 23*(4), 373–98.

Association of American Colleges and Universities (AAC&U). (2007). *College learning for the new global century*. Washington, DC: AAC&U.

Balibar, E. (1994). *Masses, classes, ideas: Studies on politics and philosophy before and after Marx*. New York: Routledge Press.

Barber, B. (1985). *Strong democracy: Participatory politics for a new age*. Los Angeles: University of California Press.

Barge, J. K. (2006). Dialogue, conflict, and community. In J. Oetzel & Ting-Toomey (eds.), *The handbook of conflict management* (pp. 517–44). Thousand Oaks, CA: Sage.

Benson, L. & Harkavy, I. (2007). *Dewey's dream: Universities and democracies in an age of education reform*. Philadelphia: Temple University Press.

Bousquet, M. (2008). *How the university works: Higher education and the low-wage nation*. New York: New York University Press.

Boyer, E. L. (1990). *Scholarship reconsidered: Priorities of the professoriate*. Stanford, CA: Carnegie Foundation for the Advancement of Teaching.

Brabant, M. & Braid, D. (2009). The devil is in the details: Defining civic engagement. *Journal of Higher Education Outreach and Engagement, 13,* 59–87.

Brukardt, M. H., B. Holland, S. L. Percy, & N. Simpher, on behalf of Wingspread Conference Participants. (2004). *Wingspread statement. Calling the question: Is higher education ready to commit to community engagement?* Milwaukee: University of Wisconsin-Milwaukee.

Butin, D. W. (2006a). The limits of service-learning in higher education. *The Review of Higher Education, 29*(4), 473–498.

———. (2006b). Disciplining service-learning: Institutionalization and the case for community studies. *International Journal of Teaching and Learning in Higher Education, 18*(1), 57–64.

———. (2010). *Service-learning in theory and practice: The future of community engagement in higher education*. New York: Palgrave.

———. (2011). Service-learning as an intellectual movement: The need for an "Academic Home" and critique for the community engagement movement. In Trae Stewart & Nicole Webster (eds.), *Problematizing service-learning: Critical reflections for development and action*. Information Age Publishing.

———. (2012). Rethinking the "apprenticeship of liberty": The case for academic programs in community engagement in higher education. *Journal of College & Character, 12,* 4.

Campus Compact. (2000). Presidents' declaration on the civic responsibility of higher education. Providence, RI: Campus Compact.

———. (2010). 2009 service statistics: Highlights of Campus Compact's annual membership survey.

Carnegie Foundation (2011). *All classified community engagement institutions*. Available at: http://classifications.carnegiefoundation.org/descriptions/2006_2008_CE.pdf.

Center for Engaged Democracy. (2011). *Academic programs in community engagement*. Available at: www.merrimack.edu/democracy. Accessed November 10, 2011.

Cheney, G. (2008). The ethics of engaged scholarship. In J. L. Simpson, J. K. Barge, & P. Shockley-Zalabak (eds.), *Journal of Applied Communication Research, 36,* 281–88.

Cruz, N. I., & D. E. Giles, Jr. (2000). Where's the community in service-learning research? *Michigan Journal of Community Service Learning, 7,* 28–34.

Dalton & Crosby. (2011). Core values and commitments in college: The surprising return to ethics and character in undergraduate education. *Journal of College & Character, 12,* 2.

DeAngelo, L., Hurtado, S., Pryor, J., Kelly, K., & Santos, J. (2009). *The American college teacher: National norms for the 2007–2008 heri faculty survey*. Los Angeles: Higher Education Research Institute, UCLA.

Dempsey, S. E. (2009). NGOs, communicative labor, and the work of grassroots representation. *Communication and Critical/Cultural Studies, 6*(4), 328–45.

Dempsey, S. E. (2010). Critiquing community engagement. *Management Communication Quarterly, 24*(3), 359–390.

Dorn, C. (2011). From "liberal professions" to "lucrative professions": Bowdoin college, Stanford university, and the civic functions of higher education. *Teachers College Record, 113*(7), 1566–96.

Driscoll, A. (2008). Carnegie's community-engagement classification, intentions and insights. *Change, 40*(1), 38–41.

Eyler, J., Giles, D., Stenson, C., & Gray, C. (2001). *At a glance: What we know about the effects of service-learning on college students, faculty, institutions and communities, 1993–2000*. Washington, DC: Learn and Serve America National Service Learning Clearinghouse.

Finley, Ashley. (2011). *Civic learning and democratic engagements: A review of the literature on civic engagement in postsecondary education.* Available at: http://www.civiclearning.org/SupportDocs/LiteratureReview_CivicEngagement_Finley_July2011.pdf

Haraway, D. (1988). Situated knowledges: The science question in feminism and the privilege of partial perspectives. *Feminist Studies, 14*(3), 575–99.

Hart, R. P. (1998). Introduction: Community by negation—An agenda for rhetorical inquiry. In M. J. Hogan (ed.), *Rhetoric and community: Studies in unity and fragmentation* (pp. xxv-xxxviii). Columbia: University of South Carolina Press.

Hartley, M. (2009). Leading grassroots change in the academy: Strategic and ideological adaptation in the civic engagement movement. *Journal of Change Management, 9*(3), 323–38.

Head, B. W. (2007). Community engagement: Participation on whose terms? *Australian Journal of Political Science, 42*(3), 441–54.

Himley, M. (2004). Facing (up to) "the stranger" in community service learning. *College Composition and Communication, 55*(3), 416–38.

hooks, b. (1981). *Ain't I a woman: Black women and feminism.* Cambridge, MA: South End Press.

Hogan, K. (2002). Pitfalls of community-based learning: How power dynamics limit adolescents' trajectories of growth and participation. *Teachers College Record, 104*(3), 586–98.

Hoy, A. & Meisel, W. (2008). *Civic engagement at the center: Building a democracy through integrated cocurricular and curricular experiences.* Washington, DC: AAC&U.

Isreal, B.A., Schulz, A.J., Parker, E.A., & Becker, A. B. (1998). Review of community based research: Assessing partnership approaches to improve public health. *Ann. Rev. Public Health, 19*, 173–202.

Joseph, M. (2002). *Against the romance of community.* Minneapolis: University of Minnesota Press.

Keen, C. & Hall, K. (2009). Engaging with difference matters: Longitudinal college outcomes of 25 co-curricular service-learning programs, *Journal of Higher Education, 80*(1), 59–79.

Kuh, G. (2008). *High-impact educational practices: What they are, who has access to them, and why they matter.* Washington, DC: Association of American Colleges and Universities.

Meyer, J. & B. Rowan. (1977). Institutional organizations: Formal structure as myth and ceremony. *American Journal of Sociology, 83*(2), 340–63.

Moranga, C. & Anzaldua, G. (1983). *This bridge called my Back: Writings by radical women of color.* New York: Kitchen Table Press.

Mouffe, C. (1992). Feminism, citizenship and radical democratic policies. In: J. Butler & J. W. Scott, (eds.), *Feminists Theorize the Political.* New York and London: Routledge.

Musselin, C. (2007). Transformation of academic work: Facts and analysis. In M. Kogan & U. Teichler (eds.), *Key challenges to the academic profession*, 175-90. Kassel, Germany: UNESCO Forum on Higher Education Research and Knowledge.

National Task Force on Civic Learning and Democratic Engagement. (2012). *A Crucible moment: College learning and democracy's future*. Washington, DC: Association of American Colleges and Universities.

Novak, J. M., Markey, V., & Allen, M. (2007). Evaluating cognitive outcomes of service learning in higher education: A meta-analysis. *Communication Research Reports, 24*(2), 149–57.

Paul, E. L. (2006). Community-based research as scientific and civic pedagogy. *Peer Review, 8*(1), 12-15.

Pryor, J. H., S. Hurtado, V. B. Saenz, J. L. Santos, & W. S. Korn. (2007). *The American freshman: Forty year trends*. Los Angeles, CA: Higher Education Research Institute.

Saltmarsh, J., Hartley, M., & Clayton, P. (2009) *Democratic engagement white paper*. Boston, MA: New England Resource Center for Higher Education (NERCHE).

Schwartzman, R. & Henry, K. B. (2009). From celebration to critical investigation. *Journal of Applied Learning in Higher Education, 1*, 3–23.

Simons, H. W. (1970). Requirements, problems, and strategies: A theory of persuasion for social movements. *Quarterly Journal of Speech, 41*(1), 1–11.

Slaughter, S., & G. Rhoades. (2004). *Academic capitalism and the new economy*. Baltimore, MD: Johns Hopkins University Press.

Spivak, G. C. (1988). Can the subaltern speak? In C. Nelson & L. Grossberg (eds.), *Marxism and the interpretation of culture*. Urbana, IL: University of Chicago Press, pp. 271–313.

Stanton, T., D. Giles, and N. I. Cruz. (1999). *Service-learning: A movement's pioneers reflect on its origins, practice, and future*. San Francisco: Jossey-Bass.

Stewart, C, Smith, C.A., & Denton, R.E. (1984). *Persuasion and social movements*. Prospect Heights, Ill: Waveland Press .

US Department of Education (USDOE). (2012). *Advancing civic learning and engagement in democracy: A road map and call to action*. Washington, DC: USDOE.

Winter, A., Wiseman, J., & Muirhead, B. (2006). University-community engagement in Australia. *Education, Citizenship and Social Justice, 1*, 211–30.

Young, I. M. (1986). The ideal of community and the politics of difference. *Social Theory and Practice, 12*(1), 1–26.

# PART I

## Engagement in Action

CHAPTER 1

# Theory Matters: Articulating a Theoretical Framework for Civic Engagement

*Tracey Burke, Tara Palmer Smith, and
Diane Hirshberg*
University of Alaska, Anchorage

In May 2011, the University of Alaska Anchorage (UAA) awarded its first Certificates in Civic Engagement. The time is ripe to reflect on the development of the certificate program and on directions for improvement and growth.

The Certificate in Civic Engagement is a 30-credit program intended to complement students' disciplinary majors by adding a civic perspective to their studies. In the five years it has been offered at UAA, it has faced several challenges and has not reached its expected audience. Yet it has also produced some surprising opportunities and experiences for both students and faculty. Together, the authors played numerous roles in the development and launching of the program. In this chapter, we share what we have learned since program planning began in 2005 and offer our reflections on our experiences for the benefit of other civic engagement programs.

The certificate is now at a transitional point, with new leadership and an expanded pool of committed faculty. We find ourselves in the difficult and unsettling position of having to rethink much of our previous work and make significant structural changes as a result. However, we also find that we laid a foundation; we are not starting over. We hope that others who are developing similar programs learn from our experiences, avoid our mistakes, and make intentional choices about the theoretical and structural underpinnings of their programs.

There must always be a balance between grand design on the one hand, and making things work within a local context on the other. Because it was funding, rather than a strategic vision, that prompted our creation of a formal civic engagement program, we failed to achieve that proper balance. The original certificate was not well-theorized, and not having a strong conceptual basis for the program, we made many decisions based on little-examined assumptions and expedience. This affected numerous dimensions of the certificate, including our approach to publicizing the program; administrative issues, such as location within the academic structure of the university and staffing expectations; and even the structure of the program. We are currently revisiting our learning outcomes, program structure, and outreach. In the process, we have found that we intuitively included some unusual and valuable program features. We have also identified aspects of the program that are not in keeping with our intentions or student needs. We are now articulating the rationale for the program's content and structure, and while we continue to respond to local circumstances, we do so from a stronger foundation.

What follows is a brief account of the certificate's development, followed by a statement of our conceptual framework and reflections on the effects of the lack of theory interacting with a variety of curricular, administrative, and outreach issues.

In brief, our recommendations are as follows:

1) Have the conceptual discussions first, before developing the program. A well-developed, common theoretical foundation is critical.
2) Create a clear, shared understanding of the program among potential students, faculty and advisors as part of launching the program.
3) Implement a program structure that facilitates student acquisition and co-creation of knowledge, the development of community among the students, and a clear path to the completion of the program.

## A Brief History of the UAA Certificate

### Origins

UAA created its Center for Community Engagement and Learning (CCEL) in 2000. The center's early emphasis was on faculty development related to community-based research and service-learning. Service-learning gained legitimacy as a pedagogy among the faculty and generated enthusiasm among students, but there was a haphazard quality to how courses or sections of courses included the service-learning component and to when the service-learning component was offered.

It was in this context that the CCEL director in 2005 won funding from the Bonner Foundation supporting the development of civic engagement academic programs (see Meisel, 2007). CCEL was awarded enough money to assign a faculty member to create a civic engagement curriculum, in regular consultation with the director and a vice-provost, subject to periodic review by the CCEL advisory board, made up of UAA faculty and members of the community.

We saw ourselves as responding to a cadre of students who had already sought out service-learning classes. We assumed these service-learning courses would constitute the "middle" of a program and that therefore our task was to create bookend experiences for these students. We developed a new introductory course, an internship, and a capstone project, and we provided a structure for the other courses students should take. The program would come together with an integrative program port-folio in which students would document achievement of program goals and reflect on the totality of their major and certificate studies. As a certificate, the program would be recorded on academic transcripts as a separate credential, in contrast to minors at our university.

From the beginning we took for granted that the certificate must be integrally connected with a major degree program, and we thought the certificate should complement almost any major. Poverty and environmental sustainability had been identified in the Bonner funding proposal as substantive foci for our program. Both areas were thematically related to many of the service-learning courses being offered, and both were relevant in some way to most disciplines.

We worked hard to make the program flexible enough to be practical for most students while emphasizing students' co-creation of knowledge as they constructed their program plans. Thus, in addition to the bookend courses, the original 30-credit certificate required courses that were all offered through other departments. Rather than provide a predetermined menu of courses, we permitted students to choose any applicable course available at the university. We expected that students would work closely with advisors to develop individualized, coherent programs of study, jointly identifying five courses in which service-learning was a required or preferred com-ponent. Moreover, students whose majors required internships and capstones were permitted to use those classes for the certificate so long as they included an approved "civic" element. The introductory course was therefore the only class all certificate students had to take. The portfolio was listed as a graduation requirement but not specifically integrated into any course(s).

One of the odd circumstances shaping the certificate was that during this period, the CCEL was housed within a unit outside of Academic Affairs, which meant that it could not sponsor a curricular program. Because the certificate's development was supported by time-limited funding, there was an urgent need to resolve the question of what its administrative home would be, and the outcome was largely a matter of convenience. The certificate was adopted by the College of Health and Social Welfare, now the College of Health (CoH). This made sense in some ways; a significant number of the faculty involved with the CCEL came from this college, and other units, such as the College of Arts and Sciences, were not well positioned to launch new programs.

Our location in CoH has meant that the lines of authority were very muddy. The CCEL director does not work in the CoH, even though its dean has mostly let the center's leadership run the certificate. One might call this "benign neglect," except that it has included the CoH's failure to allocate resources for the program. Philosophically, CoH administration supported the certificate's existence, but we were not a priority. We also wonder if the certificate's placement within a college for the helping professions limited the perceived audience for the certificate, despite our inclusive aspirations. Faculty in other units may have dismissed the program as being for do-gooders or may have simply thought the program was less welcoming to their students. At the same time, faculty in CoH professional programs that already saw themselves as community-based may not have appreciated the civic value of the certificate (see Burke, 2011).

## The Early Years

The certificate received final approval in fall 2006, and the introductory class has been offered every semester since. However, initial enrollments were quite low. Fairly quickly, we restructured the course so that it could fulfill a social sciences general education requirement, making it more appealing to students who were uncommitted to the full certificate. Also, we shifted one of the core emphases of the certificate from poverty to the broader area of human rights.

Through this period, staffing was unstable. No full-time faculty were assigned to the program; in the first three years, the introductory course was taught by two faculty members and a postdoctoral fellow, each with different theoretical and practical approaches. The position of program chair defaulted to the CCEL director; faculty were designated as department members without any formal process. Program governance nominally fell to the CCEL advisory council, but there was little genuine decision making about the certificate's operations, other than implementing some minor curriculum modifications. There were several attempts to bring in a broader group of faculty and to establish clear mechanisms for selecting and approving outside courses to fulfill the certificate requirements. This was, however, only a service activity. Long-term commitment was compromised and the curriculum work languished. Given the lack of certificate students and broad faculty involvement, there was little sense of urgency to further examine the structure of the certificate.

At the same time, funding was limited and unstable. The CCEL won a small grant for innovative programs to support the postdoc, and center funds were periodically but inconsistently diverted to certificate needs.

At the end of three years, we had an academic program in an administrative home of convenience, with no funding and no faculty lines. Despite heavy programmatic reliance on advising, no one was formally identified as (or paid to be) an advisor. We had one consistently under-enrolled introduction course, a smattering of nonmajors enrolled in the internship and capstone courses, a handful of students who were considering but not committed to the certificate, and no certificate graduates. During this uncertain time, the funding for the postdoc expired, and the CCEL director retired.

## Period of Transition

The vacuum left by the departure of the CCEL director and the expiration of the postdoc galvanized faculty to become more actively involved in the day-to-day operations of the center and the certificate. Upper-level administrators declined to appoint an acting director but did support using funds from the director's salary for course releases. In regular consultation with a representative of university administration and the center's one staff member, and with the help of an unusually active advisory board, the authors effectively ran the center and the certificate for a year.

We provided or managed the center's core faculty-development activities, taught the certificate courses, and advised (prospective) certificate students. We redirected center activities to focus more on students. The previous faculty-development strategy was successful in creating faculty interest in, and even long-term commitments to, service-learning and community-based research, but it had not brought in certificate students.

The introductory course became our focal point. The course was now a university-wide social sciences general education requirement as well as the "front door" to the certificate. We reasoned that if we had higher numbers of students in the introductory course, there would be a greater pool of students who might move into the full program. The cadre of students already seeking service-learning classes had evaporated, if in fact it had ever existed. At the very least, we were not getting the word out to them.

We devoted considerable energy to reaching out to different constituencies. We encouraged advisors to premajor or undeclared students to steer them to the introductory course as a general education class. We also reached out to fellow faculty to educate them about certificate and how the certificate could complement their programs and majors. The most dramatic reward for these efforts was the decision by faculty in the university's new Environment & Society (E&S) major in to include the civic engagement introductory course and internship as degree requirements. We have seen a steady flow of E&S students into the introductory course and a pool of likely certificate students. Indeed, the majority of the earliest certificate graduates were E&S majors. In addition, the early childhood education program included the introductory course as one of several options for meeting a program requirement, and the (criminal) justice program, which requires its students to minor in a different field, added the certificate as a minor option. And more faculty have began telling their students about the class.

Most importantly, we talked to students. We conducted a series of focus groups with students who had taken the introductory course, which helped us understand some strengths and weaknesses of the course and the certificate (see also Burke et al., 2010). Most described their experiences in the introductory course as vivid, relevant, and transferable; yet, no one had enrolled in the certificate at the time of the study. When we asked them why, they talked about the program's institutional invisibility and the academic challenges to timely completion—problems we now see as symptoms of our lack of conceptual clarity. The focus groups did, however, confirm our suspicion that the introductory course provoked interest in the certificate, such that outreach for the course should increase program numbers.

These efforts led to a dramatic increase in introductory course enrollments. But now many students were (and are) taking the course for reasons other than an expressed interest in civic engagement. We can no longer frame the course simply as a platform for the certificate program, and the course continues to develop. Much has happened since a new CCEL director started in August, 2010. While the program continues to evolve in exciting ways, we turn now to our reflection on and analysis of the lessons we learned during its creation, early years, and first significant transition.

### *Articulating our Theoretical Framework*

As we noted earlier, the theoretical base for the certificate was insufficiently developed. A particular definition of *civic* was implicit in our vision, but until very recently, we had not articulated it. We have learned that this fundamental concept must be explicitly defined so that other decisions can be explained and defended.

Prior to creating the certificate, key individuals had participated in a faculty book group on *Educating Citizens: Preparing America's Undergraduates for Lives of Moral and Civic Responsibility* (Colby et al., 2003), discussing the principles of civic engagement that underlay our consideration of the certificate. But we did not deliberate on civic engagement, community engagement, and service-learning in our curricular planning. We did use the terms, however, and in retrospect we can define them. We saw service-learning and community-based learning as pedagogical strategies. We saw the term "community engagement," used in the center's name, as an umbrella term for community–campus partnerships.

Most importantly, we saw university-based civic engagement as an approach to or an attitude toward all academic disciplines. We viewed civic engagement as a lens for focusing on the public aspects of academic or professional knowledge and learning. We did not presume to establish a new discipline, but rather to clarify the role all disciplines play in a democratic society. Likewise, we never saw the certificate as a way for students to "major in service-learning" (Butin, 2010a). Service-learning can be a very powerful strategy for teaching and learning civic lessons, and we did expect to attract students seeking service-learning courses. Indeed, the focus-group participants who expressed the most interest in the certificate were those who were already highly involved in service-learning. But it was students' attraction to classes with a civic dimension that we wanted to build on, not the notion that service-learning was itself a content area to be mastered.

We can say now that Erhlich's (2000) definition of the term in his anthology *Civic Responsibility and Higher Education* captures our meaning well: *civic engagement* "means working to make a difference in the civic life of our communities" (p. vi). The word *civic*, on the other hand, encompasses "all social spheres beyond the family, from neighborhoods and local communities to state, national, and cross-national arenas" (p. xxv). In the same volume, Boyte and Kari (2000) advocate for a definition of *citizens* that draws from the "public work" tradition of democracy: "[p]ublic problem-solvers and co-producers of public goods" (p. 40). In thinking about our certificate, then, the programmatic marriage of the certificate and other majors makes sense: in offering a *civic* program, we were trying to help students surface the community-oriented "so whats" of their chosen fields. The comment of one student in a focus group captures the kind of civic learning we hope to foster. After taking the introductory course, this student recognized some of the power issues involved in how her profession, aviation, interacts with the public: "Airplanes don't usually fly over rich neighborhoods, they fly over low-income areas."

Such an orientation is important to democracy. Higher education and the professions have been criticized as too focused on technical skills (Sullivan, 2000, 2005); with the Certificate in Civic Engagement, we hoped to provide structure for interested students' considerations of how their major degrees prepare them to contribute to their communities. Such an orientation to *civic* and *democratic* is eminently compatible, too, with an "education for practical reasoning" approach, which sees analytic reasoning and knowledge taken in isolation as sterile, and emphasizes instead identity, community, and responsibility in tandem with bodies of knowledge (Sullivan & Rosin, 2008). In other words, why do we know what we know;

how do we use what we know; what is the relationship between what we know and who we are?

Early on, we lacked this articulated definition and theoretical framework. We now realize that having it would have helped us communicate the substance and structure of the certificate more effectively to our colleagues. We examine the consequences of our implicit approach below.

### Intersections: The Absence of Theory and Local Challenges

#### Role of "Democracy"

The consequences of our neglect of theory were embodied in our experience with a postdoctoral fellow we had hired to teach the introductory course and grow the student-development component of the CCEL. She came from a disciplinary and methodological background that made her an expert in participatory democracy as a content area, much more so than anyone already associated with the certificate. We were excited to have a colleague who could help us develop the democratic implications of our program, and she naturally pursued her interests in teaching the introductory class. Yet her content focus was not a good fit for the program. Democracy for us was context and purpose, not content. But because we could not say that, we could not communicate to her that the certificate was not meant to "teach democracy" as such but to help students consider the civic implications of their academic and professional work. Nor did we ask how she anticipated connecting participatory democracy with the various disciplines.

Everyone felt frustrated and disappointed. Few students were drawn to the direct focus on democracy, and for those who were, the lack of explicit linkage to their majors undermined the coherence of the certificate as a whole. When the postdoc funding ended, the fellow moved on to another university. The next instructor we hired did begin to address the civic (and democratic) implications of all disciplines, but was still acting more on intuition than on articulated theory.

The descriptions of other programs in this book suggest that our vision of civic as elaborating on other content is uncommon, though not unique. We consider it a strength that we intended to integrate with other programs by helping students understand the broader implications of their fields. That we conceptualize civic engagement more clearly now is important because we are finalizing new program outcomes and working on a new program structure and new approaches to faculty and student recruitment. We must be able to explain ourselves.

#### Program Outcomes Then and Now

The lack of conceptual clarity was demonstrated also in poor fit between our original program outcomes and our program structure.

Early on, we recognized that our largely nontraditional students[1] (and undergraduates in general) were focused on career preparation; nonetheless, we saw this certificate as an opportunity to reinforce the traditional goals of a liberal education. We used the three domains of student growth documented for service-learning: personal, civic, and academic. Our final list of outcomes was very long and grand, and it did reflect our definition of civic. We included such items as linking professional ethics and civic frameworks, enacting public uses of education, and resolving public problems beyond college. Although we did not succinctly state our approach to the civic arena anywhere in program materials, in the outcomes we emphasized the public, the bigger-than-oneself-and-one's-job implications of students' work and lives.

Despite the program's tie to majors, we were only a 30-credit certificate and had direct control of, at best, half of those credits. As we worked with the first graduates on their program portfolios, it became evident that our initial list of outcomes was an unwieldy framework for documenting students' achievements. This prompted us to reexamine our outcomes. Now that we have communicated what we meant by *civic*, we have reduced the list of outcomes to four:

*Students who earn the Certificate in Civic Engagement will achieve the outcomes of their majors and will be able to*

- demonstrate democratic skills, such as communication, problem solving, and negotiation, necessary for addressing public problems at multiple levels;
- articulate public uses of their education and civic engagement;
- synthesize civic imagination and the abilities and needs of individuals, groups, and communities into a vision for the future;
- compose personal roles and ethical standards for participation in a diverse, global community.

Notably, the first outcome now includes the word *democratic*, and the direct link between the certificate and major degrees is less obvious.[2] However, because these outcomes also guide our program assessment, our focus is on the certificate's intended impact. This list gives us a more manageable frame for examining the work of our graduates. We cannot assess learning in every major from which we hope to attract students, but we can measure the impact of the certificate. This concise list may yet prove too tenuous a link to majors to demonstrate our aspirations; we will see what our future graduates teach us.

## Between the Bookends: The Structure of the Certificate

The certificate was intended to be flexible enough to complement almost any disciplinary major or professional degree program. Several focus-group participants expressed interest in the full certificate, yet found it too difficult to fit it into their major; and many indicated only a hazy understanding of the certificate. Taking these findings and the very low numbers of certificate students together, it seems that our attempt to be flexibile made the certificate opaque rather than helpful. Greater conceptual clarity about our definition of *civic* would have enabled us to operationalize our desire for flexibility—and to respond to challenges and misunderstandings—more effectively.

We believed that prospective certificate students were already taking multiple service-learning courses. We wanted the certificate to provide a coherent structure for those courses, but we thought of coherence as a student-level issue rather than an overall program issue. Thus, we identified criteria for the individual interdisciplinary courses (15 credits) required for the middle of the certificate. Consistent with the Bonner Foundation's "pillars of engagement," and given our vision of students' close relationships with advisors, we said, for example, that one course must have poverty (later, human rights) or sustainability as a substantive focus. Another must have public policy or community building as a focus. Three of the five courses required a community-based learning component. We expected students to choose the courses that would best complement their majors, perhaps ones offered by their majors. Without a specific statement about the civic element of these courses and how they as a group should fit with majors, however, students and advisors had little to guide their choices. To increase flexibility and creativity, we refrained from creating a static list of acceptable courses. Instead, we left students floundering.

Without a firm theoretical foundation, we also were unable to respond well to challenges from other faculty as the certificate was constructed. By having students (with advisors) design their own programs of study, we intended to emphasize the co-creation of knowledge as necessary to academic civic engagement. However, faculty who were unacquainted with the rationale for our approach remained unconvinced and expressed doubt that students could, or even should, be expected to be responsible for their own learning. While the individualized structure was finally approved, key aspects of the program requirements were weaker for the lack of broad understanding of the overall design and rationale.

For example, the criteria for one course were changed quite substantially. The approved certificate required an ethics class. Our original intent was for students to appreciate the complexities of competing demands and finding "better" solutions among choices that were not simply "good" or "bad," so we wanted certificate programs of study to include "some" ethics content. Very intense discussions with faculty from the philosophy department resulted in the requirement of an entire ethics course, generally though not necessarily a philosophy course. This exchange illustrates the political tensions inherent in creating a program that encroaches on the turf of many departments. We appreciate the irony that a program claiming integration as a core principle would be perceived as a threat to territory and expertise.

We also were accused by a member of the curriculum board of limiting the academic freedom of professors by requiring service-learning. In her view, such a mandate interfered with an individual faculty member's choice of pedagogy. Although her criticism was not shared widely enough to prevent approval, a stronger theoretical foundation would have permitted us to explain what the civic aspects of service-learning classes contributed.

A stronger conceptual base would have improved certificate planning and development, but would not have resolved all of the local challenges driving our decisions. In particular, we had a grant to support the creation of the certificate for a limited period, and we wanted the certificate to be finalized before funding expired.

## Building the "Department"

As we described earlier, we have been in a transition period with the certificate, uncertain of what our administrative and staffing structure could or should be. Staffing and funding issues have been a continuing challenge for the certificate, due in part to the hurried nature of the program's development. UAA has never assigned a permanent faculty position to teaching, advising, or chairing the program. The CCEL director was and is the only faculty member at the center, and she has a full-time job. The certificate's development team initially talked about creating a half-time faculty appointment, whereby someone would engage in tripartite work within both the certificate and her or his own discipline. This has not happened. Instead, courses have been assigned and students have been advised on an ad hoc basis. We have been fortunate not to have to rely on contingent faculty whose positions have to be renewed each semester; nonetheless, we have mostly relied on regular faculty, including the director, to take on overloads or shift other obligations—usually diverting funds from other CCEL activities in the process. The third author, for example, launched the introductory course, and the second author has taught it regularly for two years. Both of us have full-time appointments in other departments, and we suffer from the absence of a dedicated chair/advisor and instructors. Meanwhile, the centrality of advising for certificate students has been greatly compromised.

We initially designed the program to rely on thoughtful decisions about courses in multiple disciplines, rather than by one central faculty member. However, that assumed that an advisor in a student's home department was interpreting the certificate requirements in the context of the student's own program. The advisor could help students understand the purposes of the certificate and increase their enthusiasm for it, while helping them navigate the details. The model assumed that many faculty members were knowledgeable about the program and that students knew who they were. In fact, if they did not know one of these "engaged" faculty members, interested students had no obvious person to turn to with questions other than the instructor of the introductory course. Moreover, academic advising is usually a service activity. Faculty who have advising and teaching loads in their home departments have little time or incentive to add advising for the certificate, especially for students in majors other than their own. It might even be detrimental to a faculty member's standing in his or her own department to do so.

A dedicated certificate faculty position could include advising. Still, even if there were a certificate advisor, it is virtually impossible that he or she would be so sufficiently knowledgeable about every major's degree to help all students optimize the major-certificate fit. The certificate needs faculty advocates across the institution who understand it, who can communicate its value to students, and who can advise students on how to make it complement the work they are already doing.

To date, there is no steady funding for the certificate. We continue to seek stable funding for instructors and a designated chair. However, we are unsure of the ideal model for our program. Having provided the certificate collectively up to this point, we are not convinced that a half-time appointment would be optimal. One half-time faculty member could not offer all certificate courses, especially if we continue to offer the introductory course two or more times a year, along with other certificate offerings. And, even if we were somehow to find the funds to support a full-time appointment, no program should rely on one instructor alone, and no faculty member should be that isolated. Yet, an affiliate model leaves us subject to the whim of other programs and administrators. Just as the certificate program has not been a priority for its college, so are certificate classes and service activities unstable if they must compete with units having more control over budgets and faculty time.

Governance also remains a challenge. Without a clearly defined faculty structure, we also had to make ad hoc "departmental" and curricular decisions. Attempts to bring together faculty affiliates to address certificate planning and revisions have been halting, and decisions have often been made by the small group of people who worked together when the CCEL was without a director, or by the CCEL director in consultation with that small group. Until the certificate program has a clearly identified faculty structure or provides some sort of compensation and recognition for faculty affiliates, this will continue to be a challenge.

Creating shared understandings and definitions of the philosophy, goals and structure of the certificate as well as commitment to it among diverse faculty across campus is a challenge we have not yet resolved. We also have yet to determine what this support structure should look like. New programs at any university would never be launched if we waited for all desired funding to be made available. Nonetheless, we are chagrined to realize that our failure to develop a strong theoretical framework for the program and our rush to respond to the initial Bonner Foundation funding opportunity led to our failure to insure that there would be long-term financial and administrative support. We have not even developed a position from which to argue for budget allocations other than: "funding is good." As a result, the certificate has been getting by on CCEL largesse; a great deal of faculty service and volunteer effort by a relatively small number of people; and a few small, temporary windfalls. This is not a tenable position.

Given our articulated definition of civic, we believe the affiliate model, with appropriate codification, would best meet the instructional goals of the program. However, it does not resolve the administrative issues. It seems we need to incorporate the affiliate model into a more stable "semidepartmental" structure that allows us to plan more than just a few months ahead, and that facilitates the creation of a cadre of dedicated, engaged faculty who are involved in a meaningful way and formally recognized and compensated. We encourage others to identify their ideal organizational model ahead of time and to make sure that sustainable administrative, fiscal, and staffing structures flow out of a clear philosophy, vision, and theoretical basis for the program.

## The Importance of Campus Readiness

When we created the Certificate in Civic Engagement, we identified several indicators of UAA's readiness for such a program. We interpreted various events—the creation of CCEL, an increase in the number of service-learning courses being offered, UAA's 2006 designation as a "Community Engaged" institution by the Carnegie Foundation, and the inclusion of community engagement in the university's mission statement—as pointing to a campus that understood civic engagement and engaged learning.

Instead, many faculty, staff, and students have been baffled by an academic program in civic engagement. It will require much more effort than we anticipated at the outset for the program to realize the integration that we have identified as a core value of the certificate. We have learned that not only did we need to articulate our definitions much sooner, we should have actively talked about them with faculty and others beyond our small group. Establishing broad understanding, support, and buy-in could have created the campus culture that we mistakenly believed was nascent but that was in fact embryonic. In hindsight, it seems that if we had perhaps focused on creating the "department," however defined (for us, this crosses all administrative and disciplinary boundaries), it would have facilitated both our programmatic aspirations and broad participation necessary to realize them.

Boyte and Fretz (2010) argue that community-organizing practices can be a means of "building public relationships across lines of difference, creating free spaces for people to work publically with others, and understanding and embracing the messiness of change" (p. 72). Taking a community-organizing approach to drafting and establishing a program can serve to create those networks. If program is to be embraced by the institution, creating a sense of investment and ownership in its formulation is critical.

This community-organizing approach was taken in establishing the CCEL. In following up with the Certificate in Civic Engagement, we could have used the same model of open discussions, broadly representative teams, and regular communication with the university community. We might have asked a broad swath of community members off campus about the vision they had for our institution. Instead, we included community members in our discussions insofar as the CCEL's advisory board included community representatives. As with faculty, we could have been much more inclusive. We should have been much more inclusive. The input would have strengthened our program design, administrative structure, and our outreach to prospective students. Just as importantly, the campus as a whole might have been readier to embrace the finalized certificate and its goals. Of course, when we throw open the door to the community (of the university and otherwise), we have to be ready to listen to and seriously consider what they offer us. *A community-organizing approach most likely would have produced a very different program* from the one we have and the one that we wish to have in the near future.

Because we had only a small grant and limited time to see the program through to final approval, we chose to focus on meeting the grant expectations and the immediate needs of our students. We did successfully launch a new program, but we did not realize our vision.

The certificate's introductory course now serves as our community-building vehicle. It has supporters across the university who are sending us students and is explicitly charged with creating a larger cohort of certificate students at the same time that it helps degree-seeking students across the curriculum fulfill their general education requirements. The introductory course is a microcosm of what we had hoped to establish for the certificate as a whole. The landscape is already shifting. The existence of the certificate itself may have facilitated movement toward embracing civic engagement as an enhancement of other academic programs.

## Concluding Thoughts

### New directions for the Certificate in Civic Engagement

The immediate local challenge is to maintain the integrity and success of the introductory course as a foundation from which the certificate can flourish, and to have coherent, decipherable next steps for students.

We have described our intention to make the design of the certificate very flexible and thus available to almost any baccalaureate student; we have also described how we failed. It has been experienced as neither flexible nor transparent. We continue our outreach to students and advisors and are more thoughtfully developing a team of faculty affiliates to serve as department members and student advisors, and we are creating a predictable group of faculty to teach certificate courses in the future.

We agree that we need to create a sense of cohort/class/community among students so that the relationships fostered in the introductory course do not wither. Especially if advising is likely to be provided by multiple individuals for the foreseeable future, we need something tangible for faculty and another mechanism for students to support each other.

Having revised the program outcomes and having started to adjust to different groups of students in the introductory class, we are now in the process of restructuring the certificate. The bookend experiences are in good shape[3]; now we can concentrate on making the middle more appealing. The working vision, as we write, is that we will remove some of the existing program requirements to create space for a new course, which will build on the introductory course but be tailored to, perhaps even restricted to, students pursuing the full certificate. Here, certificate students will cement their bond as a community of engaged students, and we can offer certificate advising at the group level. This new course will also include work on the program portfolio; this in particular will reinforce for students the need for coherence and integration both within the certificate and in connection with their majors.

We are late in adding a next-step class for students in the introductory course who are interested in the certificate, and we were naive to think that students would think about portfolios in the absence of scaffolding. In our quest to be widely available, we cut ourselves off. But we are still intrigued by the possibilities of a truly interdisciplinary cohort of students, and our all-are-welcome approach is consistent with the values of the faculty and the institution.

## A Shared Vision

As Saltmarsh (2005) points out, even faculty with a shared definition of service-learning do not necessarily share a vision for the civic-learning outcomes thereof. He asks a central question, What is it that we would want a civically educated student to know? For our purposes here, the central question might be, What is it that we would want a civically engaged student to know and do? We have recounted how we have been hindered in our ability to communicate our purpose and vision to students and fellow faculty, as well as our failure to firmly develop our conceptual and structural frameworks before we launched the program.

We did not set out to create the Certificate in Civic Engagement to transform UAA but assumed some transformation had already occurred. We believed the institution was ready, if not waiting, for such a program to serve as a home for students and faculty already dedicated to service-learning. We thought a faculty position was imminent, that the programmatic "middle" thrived, and that our colleagues perceived how the certificate fit into undergraduate education. Instead, we find that these are the areas in which we have most had to muster our efforts since the certificate was approved. We are now undertaking this work, which may or may not truly be asking for transformation. Had we started the process with a broader discussion, an open, campus and community wide conversation, we would likely face very different circumstances.

However, we must ask ourselves, are we better positioned to encourage students to take service-learning courses and to encourage faculty to teach them? Does having an academic program—despite the lack of funding or logical home or faculty lines, or anything else we might lament the lack of—give faculty expanded tools for influencing the direction of the institution? Butin (2010b) argues that service-learning must become "disciplined" to mature and flourish in the face of the economic and social pressures facing higher education. We did not envision service-learning as a discipline, but we created our certificate to enhance the civic implications of an undergraduate education and to encourage students to think about the civic applications of their home disciplines. We see our program as a value-added component of undergraduate education, tightly linked to other areas. Despite myriad pitfalls, we remain committed to this central purpose of the certificate and the definition of *civic* that we have finally articulated.

## Notes

1. The University of Alaska Anchorage main campus serves a largely nontraditional population, although the number of traditional students is increasing steadily. The average age is 25; almost 16% of students are ages 30–39, and 17% are over 40. Of some 16,000 students attending UAA, just over 40% are enrolled full-time. UAA is an open-enrollment, comprehensive university with a community-college mission as well as a baccalaureate and graduate mandate. (Graduate students apply for admission.) Fifty percent of students seek a four-year degree; 14%, a two-year degree. Six and a half percent are graduate students, and 28% are non-degree seeking, a figure that includes students who are seeking a degree but are not formally enrolled in a major. While almost 70% of the students self-identify as white, almost 14% are indigenous (Alaska Native, American Indian, and Native Hawaiian) (Rice et al., 2011).

2. One note regarding our revised program outcomes: the term *social justice* is absent (as it was absent from the original outcomes). Service-learning has been criticized as apolitical, and there have been calls to make service-learning and/or civic engagement more explicit strategies for social justice (e.g. Welch, 2009; cf. Butin, 2007). We could have chosen to highlight social justice within our program; we did not. Partly this reflects prudence given the political climate of our university, our state, and our time. More substantively, it reinforces our inclusive aspirations. We suspect that UAA faculty involved with the certificate to date share a vision of the kind of socially-just world we would like to see, and probably we will appeal most strongly to students who more-or-less share that vision as well. But as we seek to bring in students from all degree programs, we also wish to welcome students who have alternate visions of what social justice is. Perhaps those students will come to agree with us, or perhaps they will convince us; at least, if we are successful, we will all be more thoughtful about the civic implications of our visions.

3. Although we have not discussed our internship or capstone courses here, suffice to say we are so far satisfied with them except that we hope to see higher enrollments.

## References

Boyte, H.C., & Kari, N.N. (2000). Renewing the democratic spirit in American colleges and universities: Higher education as public work. In T. Ehrlich, ed. *Civic Responsibility and Higher Education*. Phoenix, AZ: Oryx Press, pp. 37–59.

Boyte, H.C., & Fretz, E. (2010). Civic professionalism. *Journal of Higher Education Outreach and Engagement 14*(2): 67–90.

Burke, T.K. (2011). Educating citizens as well as professionals: Using service-learning to enhance the civic element of social work education. *Advances in Social Work, 12*(1): 21–32.

Burke, T.K., Smith, T.P., Hirshberg, D., & Britt, J.D. (2010). Engaging non-traditional students in a Certificate in Civic Engagement—or not: Assessing barriers and benefits (poster presentation). Association of American Colleges and Universities: Faculty Roles in High-Impact Practices. Philadelphia, PA.

Butin, D.W. (2007). Justice-learning: Service-learning as justice-oriented education. *Equity and Excellence in Education 40*(2): 177–183.

Butin, D. (2010a). "Can I major in service-learning?" An empirical analysis of certificates, minors, and majors. *Journal of College & Character, 11*(2): 1–19.

Butin, D. (2010b). *Service-learning in theory and practice: The future of community engagement in higher education*. New York: Palgrave Macmillan.

Colby, A., Ehrlich, T., Beaumont, E., & Stephens, J. (2003). *Educating citizens: Preparing America's undergraduates for lives of moral and civic responsibility*. San Francisco, CA: Jossey-Bass.

Ehrlich, T. (2000). *Civic responsibility and higher education*. Phoenix, AZ: Oryx Press.

Meisel, W. (2007). Connected cocurricular service with academic inquiry: A movement toward civic engagement. *Liberal Education, 93*(2). Retrieved from http://www.aacu.org/liberaleducation/le-sp07/le-spring07_featurefive.cfm.

Rice, G., Dong, Y., Matthews, C. & Jones, A. (2011). *2011 Fact Book*. Anchorage, AK: University of Alaska Anchorage Office of Institutional Research.

Saltmarsh, J. (2005). The civic promise of service-learning. *Liberal Education, 91*(2): 50–55.

Sullivan, W.M. (2000). Institutional identity and social responsibility in higher education, In T. Ehrlich, (ed.), *Civic Responsibility and Higher Education*. Phoenix, AZ: Oryx Press, pp. 19–36.

Sullivan, W. (2005). *Work and integrity: The crisis and promise of professionalism in America* (2nd ed.). San Francisco, CA: Jossey-Bass.

Sullivan, W.M., & Rosin, M.S. (2008). *A new agenda for higher education: Shaping a life of the mind for practice*. San Francisco, CA: Jossey-Bass.

Welch, M. (2009). Moving from service-learning to civic engagement. In B. Jacoby (ed.), *Civic engagement in higher education: Concepts and practices*. San Francisco, CA: Jossey-Bass, pp. 174–195.

# CHAPTER 2

# Creating the Character, Culture, and Craft of Engagement

*Sandra L. Enos*
Bryant University

Because faculty members and staff create majors and minors in service-learning, public engagement, civic work, and related areas, it is important that they understand community engagement in context, that is, how it works on specific campuses, depending on the organizational culture, norms, mission and, of course, relationships, both within and outside the institution. As Furco and Miller (2009) document, there are multiple measures of the extent to which community engagement has been institutionalized on campuses. Just as important, however, is the way in which community engagement has been implemented and how it is characterized and understood on campus. In this chapter, I report on community engagement at Bryant University, an organization with a long history and strong tradition as a business school. I examine how service-learning was "branded" and conceptualized in our new sociology major, illustrating how we developed the character, culture, and craft of engagement. Finally, I propose some lessons we learned that might provide guidance to other campuses considering developing a service-learning major within a discipline.

Located in Smithfield, Rhode Island, Bryant University is a private four-year nonsectarian institution, founded in 1863 as Bryant-Stratton National Business College, a member of a national chain of private commercial colleges. The university has made significant changes over the past seven years, transforming itself from a college into a university in 2004 and adding colleges of Business and Arts and Sciences to its organizational core. Bryant's curricular design sets it apart from many other institutions. At Bryant, all students either earn a major or a minor in business. If they major in liberal arts, they earn a minor in business; if they major in business, they earn a minor in arts and sciences. Students may earn degrees in typical business majors, such as accounting, finance, marketing, and international business, as well as in liberal arts, where they can earn degrees in sociology, English and cultural studies, communications, applied psychology, biology, law and politics, and other disciplines. However, despite the addition of liberal arts majors over the past five years, the number of students majoring in the arts and sciences remains small. In the class of 2011, 83 percent of graduates earned degrees in business; 17 percent, in liberal arts (Office of Institutional Research and Planning, 2009).

As part of the college's transition to a university in academic year 2005–2006, liberal arts faculty members who had been teaching courses to satisfy general education requirements and fulfill minors were challenged to create bold and innovative new majors. In 2006, the first new arts and sciences major was established in sociology. The new program created two tracks of study (service-learning and social research), a new minor in service-learning (since a sociology minor already existed at the university), and 11 new courses. Key distinctions in pedagogy, content, and experiences characterized each track. The social research track was described as follows:

> The *Sociology and Social Research* [italics in original] major employs the time-honored practices of reading, writing, discussion, and debate coupled with intense individual research under the close supervision of a member of the sociology faculty.... This course of study invites students to discover the excitement of the sociological imagination and the problem-identifying, problem-solving power of its analytic techniques through the traditional combination of exploring ideas in the classroom and discovering linkages through individual, original research (Tenured Sociology Faculty, 2006, p. 138).

Positioned against the traditional pedagogy of social research, the service-learning track employed service projects and experiential learning as well as classroom instruction. It was believed that service-learning would appeal to students who desired hands-on learning in a nonprofit context. The university had several application-oriented liberal arts programs, such as applied psychology and applied mathematics. As envisioned, the service-learning track would connect classroom instruction and experiences in the community through reflection and study. Using "critical reflection, students [would] bring their service experiences back to the classroom to gain deeper insights into the theoretical perspectives that are at the core of that particular sociology course" (Tenured Sociology Faculty, 2006, p. 139). The service-learning track would rely on service experiences to deepen students, as well as develop their leadership skills and a personal philosophy of engagement. Learning would be applied to real-world situations.

The service-learning major at Bryant meets the four criteria Butin (2010a) specified for institutionalization of the service-learning experience, including an introductory course, particular approaches to how engagement is experienced, field-based experiences, and the capstone course. At Bryant, majoring in service-learning means that a student majors in sociology, taking the service-learning path to mastering key lessons and habits of thinking in the discipline. When it was first established in academic year 2006–2007, the Bryant major in sociology and service-learning was one of the few programs in the nation to incorporate service-learning into so many courses within a department, and of course, it also included a minor in business. I was one of 12 new faculty hired in 2006, recruited to implement the service-learning major and minor. I brought to this new position experience with the national office of the Campus Compact, where I served as a director of the Integrating Service with Academic Study Project, and a long history of employment in child welfare, corrections, policy analysis, and nonprofit management in the state. I had multiple existing relationships with community partners and an understanding of the variety of service-learning practices in place at universities and colleges.

In developing majors, minors, and certificates in community engagement, faculty and administrators face several issues. In planning the service-learning major at Bryant, the faculty faced major questions that helped to frame our design of our program. The first set of questions related to the *character* of engagement on campus. What did we want students to do in the community? What did we want them to learn in service-learning? How would we create learning experiences that would enhance students' development as they moved through the program? How would we distinguish service-learning from community service and from other versions of service-learning and experiential learning on campus? The second set of issues revolved around the *culture* of the program and raised such questions as, How could we create a culture of engagement on campus that reached beyond community service? How did we want the program to be known? How could we attract students to service-learning in a university that historically has focused on business and career success? How could service-learning fit within the organizational culture while challenging dominant ideas and offering new approaches to examining our social world?

The final set of issues addressed the *craft* of engagement. With whom and how would we partner with organizations in the community? What could we do together? Could we create design principles that would govern relationship building and project development? What resources did we need to build our program and create engagement projects that were beneficial to all parties? What principles would guide our work in the community?

In developing the new major in sociology and service-learning, faculty members did not have a vision of transforming the university but instead of finding a place within the organization where a distinctive pedagogy and practice could emerge and thrive. The program was developed in recognition of the site of the university, which is located away from the cities that make up the urban core of the state—Providence, Pawtucket, and Central Falls. It was also developed in the context of the organizational traditions and practice. There is no doubt that the development of our program would have been different had we been situated in a large public university with strong schools in nursing, social work, and education or at a small religious school with a social justice agenda. The challenge and opportunity for faculty was to fit community engagement into the university's culture, while also working to change that culture by establishing a strong identification and practice for service-learning and community engagement on campus.

## The Character of Community Engagement

*What should students learn?* Creating a program in community engagement in an existing department or discipline affords the designers the strong history and legacy of that discipline. Embedding community engagement in a discipline neces-sarily extends the focus of the pedagogy, methodology, and content of what will be taught; what will be investigated; how it will be approached; and how learning will be assessed. There are many good arguments for creating a major in service-learning in a department of sociology. In many ways, sociology is an ideal setting for service-learning. Sociology's perspectives lend critical power to what faculty members intend to teach about community and social organization. Key lessons from C. Wright Mills (1959) on the sociological imagination direct individuals to understand the connections between individual lives and larger social forces and how these forces fashioned "the kinds of people they were becoming. They do not possess the quality of mind essential to grasp the interplay of individuals and society, of biography and history, of self and world" (p. 4).

Mills argued that mastery of the sociological imagination would transform pas-sive citizens into active individuals engaged with public issues. Teaching sociological theories about stratification create classroom opportunities to examine the nature of inequality and the ways these processes affects social outcomes. The analysis of the relationship between income and various social measures creates a forceful platform for students to understand the connections among income, social structure, race and class, opportunities, and achievement. Similarly, sociology affords important insights into the creation and "solution" of social problems—all important perspec-tives in how Bryant conceptualized service-learning and community engagement.

The aim of the new major in service-learning was to combine rigorous study in sociology with structured and sustained engagement in the community. The pres-ence of the service-learning major on campus identifies the sociology program as an area where students can locate the projects, courses, and faculty members that can help connect their academic interests to work in the community. In the courses that constitute the major, students are exposed to broad definitions of community engagement and are encouraged to create their own paths to active citizenship.

*How should they learn it?* In designing a high-quality program of study in com-munity engagement, faculty must develop a well-articulated plan for how students will move through their programs of study. This can be thought of as creating a scaffolding experience for students —the skills, knowledge, and perspectives gained in each subsequent course build upon earlier lessons as they make their way through the major, from the introductory course through the capstone experience.

Although it may seem like an obvious first step in creating a program of study, attention needs to be paid to laying out the landscape for community engagement. In implementing the major, we aimed to create a broadly defined territory for service and engagement.

At Bryant, this definitional work begins with Service-Learning and Community Engagement, the gateway course, which extends the term *service* to incorporate a broader definition of service-learning than is typically employed. As part of the effort to create scaffolding experiences for students and to define the landscape of engagement, we were deliberate in the design of the first course in the major. In this course, we problematize service and engagement, presenting readings and other materials that challenge students' beliefs that good intentions are equivalent to good outcomes. This approach continues as students move through their studies, facing more complexity in their reading assignments and service projects, more responsibility for their learning, and greater focus on understanding the complications of trying to make a contribution to the greater good. The readings, class exercises, discussions, course assignments, and service opportunities are intended to engage students in a broad examination of doing "good," including disrupting conventional thinking about service, investigating unanticipated consequences of service and philanthropy, examining what works in addressing social problems, and exploring positionality in the ways in which we examine who benefits from service. Among the key questions posed in the course are, Can we shop our way to goodness? Is charity ever bad? What are the appropriate roles for government, nonprofit organizations, and corporations in addressing social problems like hunger and food insecurity? What paradoxes exist in volunteerism and philanthropy?

In the first half of semester, we focus on the social institution of education as a means of understanding the roles of social structure, culture, and institutions in determining educational opportunities and disadvantages for children. We start out with a key question and follow it throughout the semester: among the factors of individual motivation, the quality of a school, and parents' income, which one best predicts academic success? We explore this through multiple approaches. Students tutor in local schools and after-school programs and reflect on their experiences in writing and in class discussions. Using data-analysis techniques, we examine the relationship between household incomes and the New England Common Assessment Program test scores in cities and towns. Finally, students complete structural analyses, comparing the schools they attended to those in which they are tutoring and to the high school profiled in *A Hope in the Unseen* (Suskind, 1998), a key text for this course.

Through exercises and readings related to their service experiences, students begin to comprehend the wide variety of "educations" afforded to children in our nation's schools. In the gateway course, students typically tutor children in low-income schools or serve as helpers in after-school programs, like the Learning Community in nearby Central Falls, where the child poverty rate is estimated at 40 percent. In class reflections, students write that they are surprised that their students work so hard on their school work, have so much curiosity, and have dreams of attending college. These experiences then become the topic of class discussions about how to make education better for more children. Class readings focus on school reform and various strategies to improve schools through testing, assessment, better pay for teachers, longer school days, school vouchers, and other approaches. Connecting student experiences with "big" questions about improving education grounds sociology and service-learning in issues that become important to students, as reflected in their final class essays.

There are challenges in teaching sociology to first-year students, who make up a sizable portion of the students in this course. In teaching the introductory course in community engagement and sociology, faculty members faced the twin challenges of getting the community engagement experience right (more about that later in the chapter) and battling the well-reported difficulty of teaching students who embrace the myth of individualism (Callero, 2009). Beginning sociology students typically reject out of hand a key sociological perspective, that is, that structural factors, not individual characteristics, predict social outcomes. These students also typically discount information that contradicts their personal experiences. As Strand (1999) cautioned, students engaged in community service work may rely on their personal observations at a service site to reinforce, for example, their ideas that homelessness is caused by mental illness, a poor work ethic, or alcoholism. As Seider, Gillmor, and Rabinowitz (2011) reported, business students are particularly resistant to the sort of critical thinking encouraged in courses that explore the growing inequality and opportunity gaps found in American society. These challenges make it imperative that course design supports multiple ways of addressing these issues.

It should also be noted that few students at Bryant come from the communities we serve in the urban core. Most come from suburban, predominately white communities and have had a good education, obtained in either high-quality public schools or in private schools. Orienting students to work in low-income communities is important, and we increasingly rely on community partners for classroom training and for preparation before the students begin their service assignments. Class discussions and assignment about service experiences connected with assigned readings provide opportunities for frequent check-ins about how students are "reading" their service projects and interpreting what they observe.

Finally, because over 80 percent of our students major in business, and because liberal arts majors are also enrolled in business courses, all students are exposed to business thinking. Courses in sociology and service-learning, along with other courses in the liberal arts curriculum, may serve as an effective counterweight to the dominant instruction in courses taken by most of the students at a business-oriented campus like Bryant. As discussed later in this chapter when we take up what students learn in service-learning, we can see that students themselves position their sociology classes against the business courses they take in in two ways—in the content of what is addressed in class and in the wider and more critical perspective in sociology of questioning the taken-for-granted nature of social interactions and social relations.

As students in the major advance to 300-level courses, we can expect them to move beyond direct service and become engaged with community partners in project development and design. Several courses, including Sociology of Work; Sociology of Sport; Urban Sociology; Gender, Health and Illness; Social Problems/Social Solutions; and Globalization and Childhood offer service-learning opportunities at this level. Creating service-learning projects in these courses has in some instances been challenging. Matching student abilities and interests with community-partner needs and goals and aligning these with faculty objectives in teaching the course is key to addressing the multiple goals in play. In the 300-level courses, we expect students to take a leadership role in organizing and designing projects. Students have designed and managed programs, developed materials for agency use and dissemination, worked with partners on feasibility studies to extend the reach and scope of agency operations, and other projects.

In designing majors, it is important to consider how the major may impact other practices in the university. In other words, creating these opportunities for students also creates opportunities for institutional change. An apt illustration of this has been in international service-learning at Bryant. Like many campuses, Bryant champions the idea of study and travel abroad. In addition to the typical junior study abroad semester, the campus also offers the Sophomore International Experience in which students accompany faculty and staff on 10–12 day trips, learning about other cultures and how businesses operate in other nations.

In crafting an international service-learning experience, we aimed to problematize international service work while affording students the opportunity to learn about life in a small village in the Dominican Republic. This project, three years in development, has morphed from a community service project into a course-embedded service-learning experience. Early on, our goal was to bring students to Guayacanes, a seaside village on the southern coast of the Dominican Republic, for a week-long experience in learning and serving in a small community. With each successive trip to this community, our focus for learning and serving has changed. In the spring 2011 semester, a special-topics course, The Impact of Globalization on the Dominican Republic: A Service-Learning Case Study, examined the impact of all-inclusive tourism on a small community and a "batey," a former sugar plantation. In this course, students critically examined the promise of tourism for the economic development of nations by interviewing residents of the batey and teaching at the batey's community school. In responding to the question about the costs and benefits of all-inclusive tourism, students were challenged to create plans for alternative models of tourism that could support local interests and local communities. Once again, the emphasis here was on deepening students' understanding of engagement, reaching beyond direct service to considering how patterns and practices of consumption, in this case tourism, have important impacts on poor communities. Courses and experiences like this one more carefully articulate the intentionality with which the service-learning major defines and enacts engagement at the university.

In designing a new program of community engagement, one could begin at the end—what students should have learned during their college experience—and work backwards. The capstone experience should serve to showcase what students have learned in the classroom and beyond and how well they have demonstrated the integration of academics and real-world experiences. Requirements for the capstone include (1) a specification of a research question about a social problem they would like to address; (2) the creation of a reading list that includes literature that both describes the problem and identifies the multiple approaches that can be taken to address it; (3) a description of the context of the social setting; (4) a detailed report presenting the project that was implemented; and (5) an evaluation of the project outcome on multiple measures. As discussed below, assessing learning requires a continual process of defining and refining the goals, objectives, and methods of the major.

*What do students learn in sociology service-learning?* One of the major thrusts in creating service-learning opportunities is the belief that service-learning teaches material, perspectives, skills, and dispositions that cannot be taught in traditional classrooms. In designing their courses, faculty members may emphasize technical mastery of the discipline, multicultural understanding, community empowerment, building civic skills, or other outcomes (Butin, 2010b; Brownell & Swaner, 2010).

Challenges remain for our program and for the field at large in making clear connections between the intentions of service-learning pedagogy and the desired outcomes. The role of assessment is significant here. Successful service-learning course design should account for anticipated changes in learning as well as those that may not be expected. In our experience, students learned unintended but powerful lessons. Providing an array of ways in which to harvest learning creates a great opportunity for faculty to understand what students have learned. In many of sociology's service-learning courses, students complete reflective essays examining how their thinking about social responsibility—what have I learned?—and their role as informed citizens has changed over the course of the semester.

In a brief review of five years' worth of these essays from the Community Engagement and Service Learning (SOC250) course, several themes emerged: Students position their learning in the course against their lived experiences and against what they learn in other courses at the university. The course's deliberate focus on expanding the idea and conceptualization of service pushes students to consider a more holistic perspective on what it means to be an engaged citizen on the multiple levels of social responsibility and awareness.

The following excerpt from one student's reflective essay illustrates the broad conceptualization of service and community engagement that we hope our students will grasp. The program's aim is for students to understand the complex nature of the globalized world and to consider that every act they take may have implications—positive and negative—for others whose fates appear to be far removed from their own.

> Any struggling person deserves to have a privileged person hear their story. Because my privilege might be what touches them, not through money or time spent with them, but through my actions such as my career, future companies I invest my personal assets in, the things I buy, the people I influence, and the example of the life I live.

This student suggested that the course be required for every undergraduate, to both educate them about outstanding social problems they could be creating and to build skills and the disposition to address those social problems.

Students also typically expressed their new understanding that social problems are hard to fix, that their root causes are more difficult, and more important, to address than simply doing service.

At the end of their academic program, students complete an exit essay in their capstone course, tracing their intellectual journeys as sociologists and service learners. Service-learning and sociology, according to the students, provide them with a place and platform for examining and experiencing social issues, of which other students are unaware. Students see themselves changed in comparison to both earlier versions of themselves and to students majoring in other fields. It should be noted again that sociology students, like other liberal arts students on campus, often view themselves as pioneers, going against the dominant culture and traditions of the university. In these essays, sociology majors observe that their perspectives are broader than those of students in other disciplines, that they have become more critical thinkers, and that their curriculum allows them freedom to explore topics that other students do not examine in business courses.

A lot of my friends and peers in the sociology department also appear to have this sociological perspective, which allows us to analyze and discuss many aspects of life that other students find to be common sense and truth. . . . The best gift anyone can give is [to] set your mind free to see an aspect of the world in a whole new light.

This student observed that while students in other disciplines were critical thinkers in their majors, the sociology majors were critical of the "very systems that we live by." Typically, students remark that they see that the world is more complex than they had imagined, see that social problems have multiple causes, and understand that changing the world for the better is itself a contested idea.

A formal in-house assessment of the sociology major using 10 reflective essays from a semester's capstone course observed that students connected their sociological training to deep and engaged learning. The assessment revealed that the sociology major had a "distinct, positive impact upon participants' intellectual and personal development." Students pointed to "service-learning activities in which classroom theory could be applied in a real world setting." Interestingly, this was the case for students in the social research major, as well as for those in the service-learning major (Fraleigh, Ciliberto & Enos, 2009).

## The Culture of Engagement

In creating a culture of engagement, service-learning programs can model distinct practices and philosophies of community work for other forms of service-learning on campus. Because we are rooted in sociology and embedded in an institution with such a long-standing business and management orientation, we wanted to carefully consider how to "brand" service. We wanted to extend our definitions beyond valuable work, such as one-on-one tutoring and mentoring, serving in a soup kitchen, and other forms of direct service. Because there were no pre-professional programs in education, nursing, or social work on campus, we had no direct service or casework tracks students could pursue in their majors. Also, since we were developing a major, we wanted to create a series of experiences and opportunities for students to understand various aspects of community work. Accordingly, our definitions of service included direct service (e.g., tutoring, mentoring, providing support for caseworkers); indirect service and organizational support (e.g., creating organizational plans, supporting fund-raising activities in organizations, developing marketing plans for nonprofits); research and data collection (supporting the investigation of broad-based questions); and developing innovative approaches to social problems (working with and as social entrepreneurs).

As the service-learning courses and placements are being organized for the coming semester, faculty members in sociology meet with community partners to develop projects that meet mutual needs and interests. Often, these are projects that neither party had considered before the meeting but are the result of relationship building and refining the partnerships over several years. So, branding our major is a continuous process, where we understand and learn from campus and community partners and seek to develop opportunities for student engagement. For example, new opportunities emerge as we consider leadership of a new program in social entrepreneurship. What does that mean for service-learning and for the work students do in the community? Similarly, the greater interest of our students in international work may lead to new programs designed and led by faculty in arts and sciences and connected to service-learning and engagement.

At the same time the new major in sociology was introduced on campus, a new course, Management Principles and Practices, was introduced in the Department of Management. This course, taken with few exceptions by all undergraduates, was designed to introduce students to the discipline of management by partnering them with nonprofit organizations in semester-long service-learning projects. Over the course of a semester, more than 350 students, working in teams of four to six students, partner with nonprofit organizations to design and execute projects. For the most part, these service projects can be characterized as indirect service or organizational development. In this course, students have created web pages, developed marketing campaigns, organized events, supported fund-raising efforts, and similar activities. The focus of this course is on the design, management, and execution of the project rather than on the role of the nonprofit in addressing social issues or on understanding the social problems or conditions that led to the founding, development, and problem-solving approach of the nonprofit organization. As central as the service-learning experience is to this course, there is no mention of service-learning in the catalogue listing; nor do students taking the course earn any service-learning credit. It is also the only service-learning experience that the majority of business and liberal arts encounter during their studies.

By contrast, service-learning in sociology examines the nature of social problems and social organization. Sociology students are more likely to be engaged in direct service and to establish relationships with the clients in agencies and with students in local schools. In reflective essays, they are more likely to write about the role of social class in determining social standing and less likely to examine how to manage an effective team project.

To create a "brand" or an identity for service-learning on campus, we focused on some key issues areas and showcased student work through frequent placement of articles on the campus webpage. In the sociology program, students work as tutors, mentors, and program designers. Student service occurs within the context of a broad understanding of social issues. While the focus in a typical sociology course may be on teaching students about the structural underpinnings of social inequality, the service-learning course helps students see the manifestations of inequality in local social institutions and guides them to design, develop, and test "solutions" to these issues. Because we have no schools of education, social work, or health professions on campus, sociology can claim these fields as areas of interests for our students. Our aim is for students to consider the multiple ways they can work with nonprofit partners and the larger community in their undergraduate careers and beyond. As a de facto home for community engagement, the sociology major supports students from multiple majors and minors in special projects, honors capstones, independent studies, and other academic courses.

## The Craft of Engagement

*Partners and relationships with the community.* In creating programs to support community engagement, defining the "community" landscape is a project in constant development. Because most of the community service projects do not occur in Bryant's neighborhood, there is little institutional identity associated with this work. There is no overall strategy or planning on campus for community engagement. Most community partners work directly with faculty and students and do not feel the impact of institutional policies or identity on their neighborhoods, schools, or other institutions. Bryant's suburban location isolates it from many of the challenges encountered by urban institutions. These include a history of contested campus-community issues, such as campus expansion and neighborhood displacement, and a series of unfulfilled promises and missed opportunities for better and more equitable relations (Cone & Payne, 2001). On the other hand, our distance from our partners also leaves community engagement a matter of individual preference, choice and discretion, rather than institutional engagement, planning, and consideration. Community engagement at Bryant is rooted in the work of individual faculty members and students; it is not deeply integrated into the university's overall strategic planning or mission.

In a typical semester, the service-learning in sociology program supports approximately 70 students in the community, doing work that ranges from after-school tutoring in a local charter school in the gateway course to the development of a two-semester college advising seminar, designed, and implemented by an honors student for a senior capstone project at a local high school. As discussed below, we are focusing on key partners, working with them to develop a series of projects, to define our craft of engagement

University-wide, we estimate that more than 100 community organizations work with campus partners over the course of the academic year. This includes agencies connected to student-led service and fraternal organizations, as well as those linked to academic courses in the department of management, sociology, and English and cultural studies. It is important to note that we do not attempt to integrate our various excursions into the community or to articulate our philosophy of community engagement across departments, disciplines, or faculty. Similarly, there is no central office of community service or service-learning on campus, although as discussed in the next section, a proposal to create such a center was submitted for review to the administration.

*Resources for community engagement.* There is little question that engaging with the larger community requires resources, including time, energy, and attention paid by faculty, staff, students, and community partners, to create service opportunities and develop relationships. Sustained engagement requires a greater commitment from the university and its partners. As noted earlier, locating the service-learning major in sociology has made sociology the de facto home for community engagement on campus, but there are strong arguments for extending this work beyond sociology.

To support the major and to build and deepen community engagement across campus, in 2007 we proposed that the university establish a Center for Character and Civic Engagement. We developed the proposal in conversations with a local community foundation and community partners as well as with faculty, staff, and students on campus. The center would be located in the Academic Affairs division, reporting directly to its vice-president, and would serve as a coordinating and planning body linking the campus to the community for projects that would be broadly defined. The center's mission would be to integrate and embed the work of community engagement throughout the campus. Staffed by a master's-level professional, and supervised by an advisory council made up of staff, faculty, and community partners, the center would assume leadership in all matters related to engagement with the larger community. Unfortunately, the administration did not support the proposal. Accordingly, at Bryant there is no staff or center dedicated to community service or service-learning on campus. Community engagement exists as a discipline-level or faculty-initiated practice rather than as a university-level program or priority.

As on other campuses, at Bryant a lot of work is done under the broad umbrella of community service and service-learning. However, it can be assumed that the level and quality of community engagement varies widely on campus. The deeper lessons of service-learning are in some important ways "threatened" by the torrent of community service projects and efforts promoted by student groups and the sororities and fraternities on campus. During a semester, community organizations, especially those well-known to students, are often contacted by multiple student groups "looking for a community service project." Much of this is unquestioned good work, uncoordinated service, and undigested activity (Marullo, Moayedi & Cooke, 2009). Without a center to identify and coordinate service projects, faculty, students, and organizations receive little help in managing and creating opportunities in the community. For organizations wishing to work with faculty and students, there is no front door or central point of contact. Nonprofits that contact the university looking for an appropriate and potential partner are often passed from one office to another.

This is not to say that a center would take the place of the close, direct relationships that sociology faculty have with community partners. It does suggest our sense that projects and relationships could be deepened and better focused with a well-designed and managed center. For community partners, it would be helpful for the university to clearly articulate what they can expect from Bryant partnerships. Without professional staff to connect with agencies, it falls on faculty members to be responsible for identifying, organizing, managing, monitoring, and evaluating community partnerships. This becomes especially challenging when faculty members are teaching multiple sections of service-learning courses, as they do in sociology and management.

For several years, we supported an AmeriCorpsVISTA member to help coordinate placements and serve as a link between academic and student affairs. Though the volunteer did manage some tracking and paperwork, as a recent college graduate, she was not prepared to create the sorts of systems and opportunities that would support engaged community work. And as a VISTA volunteer, no sooner had she become oriented to the campus and the larger community, than she completed her year of service and left the position.

During the first five years our major has existed on campus, we have defined a program of study, created a space on campus for community engagement, and narrowed our partner base while expanding our ideas about what is means to serve and to be engaged. The major in service-learning has provided students with practice-based opportunities to learn how to make a contribution to the larger community. As outlined below, much work remains to be done, if we are to further institutionalize and expand community engagement across campus and deepen it within the sociology program.

### Final points and challenges ahead

The framework of the character, culture, and craft of engagement has provided an organizational lens through which we have created a program of study that fits within the institutional context at Bryant while also challenging and changing that institutional culture. As we have discussed, creating a service-learning major within a department opens up an alternative path for students to major in a discipline while engaging in set of community-based learning opportunities. Linking community engagement to sociology and other liberal arts disciplines can bring to students the idea that liberal arts have application to real-world issues though the asking of important and "big questions." This can be achieved with deeper intentionality in what our aims are in community engagement, both within the sociology program and across campus.

*Curriculum development.* At the end of the first five years with a major in sociology, it is an appropriate time for program review. When we established our new major, we needed to attract students to both the research track and the service-learning track. This remains a priority. As we did in our first five years, we should continue to broaden and deepen our definitions and practices around community engagement. Since establishing the major, we have added a number of new courses and built a new concentration in social entrepreneurship, which we see as directly connected to our service-learning major. The Concentration in Social Entrepreneurship will critically examine the art and science of problem solving in complex settings. Typically, minors or concentrations in social entrepreneurship are located in schools of business. At Bryant, we have strategically located social entrepreneurship in the school of Arts and Sciences, with three courses in sociology, one in legal studies, and two in the business curriculum from finance, marketing, and management. Like the major in service-learning, this concentration is structured with an introductory course, scaffolded learning experiences, and a capstone seminar. This concentration will allow us to connect with faculty members who have not historically been involved in service-learning on campus and to expand our community engagement work to micro-finance, organizational founding, the creation of income–generating enterprises for local nonprofits, and other fields under the social entrepreneurship banner.

### Partners, neighbors, and casual friends: Relationships with community partners

Like many programs in service-learning, the sociology major started out with many partners, and has now narrowed its involvement to key partners and sustained relationships. On a campus lacking staff to supervise, set up, and assess placements, fewer partnerships work better than many. After several years of working with multiple partners, our choice was to limit our number of partners so that we could understand their needs and better focus our teaching and programming. From among the many partners with whom we have worked, these emerged as the ones that share interests. We have mutual understandings in terms of what students are able to do and a clear understanding that working with college students demands flexibility on the part of both parties. Finally, we share with these partners strong agreements about social change theories and strategies (Morton & Enos, 2002).

Our work in the future will focus on creating shared resources with our partners. In the past year, we have partnered with two schools and one after-school program for most of our service-learning placements. These partnerships accommodate students from several of our courses, from the introductory level through the capstone course. Working with fewer partners, we create appropriate placements and challenges for the students, supporting our curricular design of scaffolding learning opportunities for our majors. To further develop these ideas, Bryant will share an AmeriCorpsVISTA with a local charter high school. VISTA will be working with both parties to understand how we can extend our work more deeply into each other's organization.

Our goal in sharing with VISTA is to develop a pilot program to learn how we can develop service-learning projects in sociology courses and other departments that would respond to the needs at our partner school to enhance readiness for college, respond to student interests in subjects not offered by the high school, and to support the college search and application process for these students. This partner school affords our students and faculty the opportunity to understand the challenges facing first generation students in accessing and succeeding in college, to examine the operations of a charter school, and to problem-solve around issues of resource scarcity.

*The future of community engagement.* I would argue that a center for community engagement, as originally proposed, still makes sense. At Bryant, there is increasing emphasis on student engagement and active learning, and members of the campus increasingly look to service-learning to create opportunities for deeper learning. Perhaps, it is an appropriate time for faculty, staff, and community partners to conduct a self-assessment of where we are in service-learning, within and across departments and colleges. Perhaps, the best place to support the development of community engagement on campus could be linked with our Center on Teaching and Learning. More communication among faculty members about intentionality of including service-learning in courses would improve the teaching and learning experiences of students and enhance our community work, as well.

Within the past year, Bryant has hired a full-time director of Faculty Development. Under the leadership of that office, we are moving toward a deeper examination of the scholarship of teaching and engagement. Connecting service-learning to this office and making the argument that the campus focus on engaged learning is congruent with the service-learning model embraced by the sociology program should make service-learning, community engagement, and social entrepreneurship more attractive to more faculty.

In fall 2011, we launched a faculty discussion group on service-learning and community engagement that has attracted faculty from management, English and cultural studies, modern languages, marketing, and sociology. Perhaps the most useful project this group can accomplish would be to develop a plan for community engagement—an articulation by interested faculty of what they would like to accomplish in service-learning, how they would get there, and what resources are necessary for community engagement to be sustained at the university. On a practical level, this discussion group will afford faculty members a forum to exchange ideas and best practices, as well as create cross-disciplinary projects. A useful model for this sort of assessment has been developed by Chadwick and Powloski (2007), as an important exercise in sense making and program building and development. The need for faculty support is important here. As documented by many researchers, faculty members can become overwhelmed and exhausted by the demands of service-learning pedagogy. Faculty members across campus can benefit from understanding what each other have learned in service-learning pedagogy. For example, in the Management 200 course, faculty has created a series of materials that help students who are designing projects to organize their work and enhance their service projects. These materials may be very helpful to faculty members in other departments who work on complex projects with student teams. Similarly, materials from courses in sociology could help orient students in the management course to the role of the nonprofit sector in solving social problems, as well as create the context for social problems addressed by these organizations.

*Deepen institutionalization.* As discussed above, key elements of the service-learning major suggest that it is institutionalized as a practice on campus. However, the program can be strengthened by a stronger demonstration of our distinct work in the community and by extending service-learning to other departments on campus. The new concentration in social entrepreneurship should allow us to further articulate our definitions about community engagement by more broadly defining our partners and our work. Institutionalization can also be deepened by connecting the service-learning major with new initiatives developed in the strategic plan, such as a focus on experiential and active learning, and a Masters of Arts in Teaching, recently approved by the Board of Trustees.

To further extend institutionalization, deeper partnerships can be extended to the community of arts, historical and cultural organizations, involving more faculty and programs in community engagement. Examples of this work are already in place in English and cultural studies projects. Finally, the service-learning track in sociology should develop closer connections with both Career Services and Enrollment Management to better articulate our perspectives and "stories" about what we teach and what students experience in their service-learning studies at the university.

*Assessment and evaluation.* Courses in sociology and service-learning typically receive above-average scores in students' course evaluations. Additional insights about the service-learning program can be gained by reviewing the reflective essays we have collected on how students believe they have changed as a result of their service-learning experiences. Involving students as coders would support the development and refinement of new learning objectives and create the framework for an enhanced system of assessment and learning measures.

## Summary

It is important to note here that our major in service-learning is just five years old and was launched when a new College of Arts and Science had only recently been established. In retrospect, the aims of the founders of the major were bold—to create an academically rigorous new major in sociology, with a unique cache for students and a distinct identity on campus. Creating the major within a department has provided students with a clear path to community engagement through a standard discipline. It can also be said here that the major in service-learning has raised the visibility and viability of community engagement on campus. The challenge to define and re-define our place at the university and to connect to developments on campus and in the field remain if we are to promote our vision of what it means to be engaged faculty, students, and community members. The broad vision of engagement we have employed at Bryant connects us to many important conversations about how we work, serve, consume, communicate, and participate in a complex world. Finally, the major adds a critical look at engagement and community service onto the curriculum, examining the role of power, of institutions, and the place of the university in addressing the challenges, needs and opportunities facing our communities.

## References

Brownell, J. E., & Swaner, L. E. (2010). *Five high-impact practices: Research on learning outcomes, completion, and quality.* Washington, D.C.: Association of American Colleges and Universities.

Butin, D. W. (2010a). "Can I major in service learning?" An empirical analysis of certificates, minors, and majors. *Journal of College & Character, 11,* 1–19.

Butin, D. W. (2010b). *Service-learning in theory and practice: The future of community engagement in higher education.* New York: Palgrave MacMillan.

Callero, P. L. (2009). *The Myth of individualism: How social forces shape our lives.* Lanham, MD: Rowman and Littlefield.

Chadwick, S. A. & Pawlowski, D. R. (2007). Assessing institutional support for service-learning: A case study of organizational sense-making. *Michigan Journal of Community Service Learning, 13,* 31–39.

Cone, D., & Payne, P. (2001). When campus and community collide: Campus- community partnerships from a community perspective. *The Journal of Public Affairs, 6,* 203–218.

Fraleigh, M., Ciliberto, D., & Enos, S. (2009). *Sociology program self-assessment.* Smithfield, RI: Bryant University Sociology Program.

Furco, A., & Miller, W. (2009). Issues in benchmarking and assessing institutional engagement. *New Directions in Higher Education, 147,* 47–54.

Marullo, S., Moayedi, R., & Cooke, D. (2009). C. Wright Mills's friendly critique of service learning and an innovative response: Cross-institutional collaborations for community-based research. *Teaching Sociology, 37,* 61–75.

Mills, C. W. (1959). *The sociological imagination.* New York: Oxford University Press.

Morton, K., & Enos, S. (2002). Building deeper civic relationships and new and improved citizens. *Journal of Public Affairs, 6,* 83–102.

Office of Institutional Planning and Research. (n.d.). *Bryant University.* Retrieved from Common Data Set 2009–2010: http://www.byant.edu/~opir/cds/fall2009.pdf.

Seider, S. C., Gillmor, S. C., & Rabinowitz, S. A. (2011). The impact of community service learning upon the worldviews of business majors versus non-business majors at an American university. *Journal of Business Ethics, 93,* 458–504.

Strand, K. J. (1999). Sociology and service-learning: A critical look. In J. Ostrow, G. Hesser, & Enos S. (Eds.), *Cultivating the sociological imagination: Concepts and models for service-learning in sociology* (pp. 29–38). Washington, D.C.: American Association of Higher Education.

Suskind, R. (1998). *A hope in the unseen: An American odyssey from the inner city to the Ivy League.* New York: Broadway Books.

Tenured Sociology Faculty. (2006, January 16). *Proposal for a Bachelor of Arts in Sociology.* Submitted to the Curriculum Committee, Bryant University . Smithfield, RI.

CHAPTER 3

# Negotiating the Boundary between the Academy and the Community

*Hollyce (Sherry) Giles*
Guildford College

Over the past 30 years, the landscape of higher education has undergone dramatic changes, many of which have led to a more permeable boundary between the academy and the world around it. Colleges and universities have been called to collaborate with their broader communities to address societal issues and needs (Boyer, 1990; Campus Compact, n.d.; Carnegie, 2006; Weerts & Sandmann, 2010) and, at the same time, to participate more fully in the free-market economy (Nussbaum, 2010; Slaughter & Rhoades, 2004). As the boundary around the norms and practices of their work in the academy has shifted, this changed land-scape has evoked uncertainty and raised questions about faculty's professional role identity. These questions include, What happens to the academic norms of neutrality and disinterested inquiry when faculty members collaborate with community orga-nizations, public institutions, or corporations with particular perspectives and inter-ests? In what ways might academic freedom be threatened when faculty's engaged teaching or scholarship challenges the interests of powerful individuals, institutions, or corporations? And, the overarching question, how can faculty maintain both legit-imacy in the academy and the integrity of their work with community partners?

These questions and the turbulent higher education environment form the con-text for the emergence of a growing number of undergraduate majors whose mis-sion is to integrate scholarship with community engagement (Butin, 2010). Situated squarely on the boundary between the academy and the larger community, these academic programs experience in a particularly intense way the opportunities and challenges of the overlapping but partially contradictory missions, roles, and values of these two social systems.

This chapter looks at one such program, the Community and Justice Studies major at Guilford College in Greensboro, North Carolina, to examine the organizational dynamics and issues involved in an undergraduate major integrating the missions, roles, and values of the academy with those of partner organizations in the broader community. The location of the major on the boundary between the academy, with its traditional emphasis on theory and disinterested inquiry, and the community, with its priority for action and engagement, and both situated within the contemporary market-driven, neoliberal political economy, has evoked issues and dynamics creating challenges for the major and significant role binds for program faculty.

Three key issues related to the major's dual commitments and identities surfaced in the study. First, many college faculty perceive the major as being "practical," and not sufficiently theoretical or academic, particularly when compared with traditional liberal arts majors. Second, tensions exist around the major as a justice-focused program within a neoliberal institutional context. This is a context that many faculty already experience as placing unwelcome demands that threaten the status of the college as a "place to think" apart from the fray. Third, the program's union of ideas with action, reflected in its collaboration with local community organizations having particular political perspectives on social issues, raises complex and difficult questions about teaching, research, and academic freedom.

The chapter considers the social-emotional and structural aspects of faculty members' efforts to create and sustain the major in the context of these issues, efforts that receive strong support from some colleagues, including high-level administrators, and significant resistance from others. The study on which the chapter is based shows that it is critically important that faculty create new boundaries around their professional roles and their academic programs to locate the major "in the world, but not of it." These include engagement with the community that is close enough and deep enough to allow for Weber's notion of *verstehen*, that is, an insider's understanding of the issues and concerns at hand (Roth, 1971) and, at the same time, provide the critical distance offered by practices informed by the core values of higher education, "intellectual pluralism, rational discourse, intellectual autonomy, open-mindedness, and civility" (Colby, Beaumont, Ehrlich & Corngold, 2007, p. 21). The study also concludes that it is crucial for the success of community engagement majors for high-level administrators to support both academic freedom and the college's role in public life, and to develop "holding environments" at the college that enable faculty to address the issues evoked by shifting roles and organizational identities.

The author, an associate professor and coordinator of the Community and Justice Studies major, used the method of action research (Stringer, 2007) to conduct the case study on which the chapter is based, drawing on her interviews with faculty colleagues, staff, and administrators; her participant observation in the major, department, and college; and broader community and archival documents relevant to the major as data. Group relations theory (Gillette & McCollum, 1997; Neumann, 2010; Miller & Rice, 1967) and boundary theory (Beck & Young, 2005; Gieryn, 1983; Lam, 2010) from the author's home discipline of psychology are used to illuminate the dynamics and issues that surfaced in the formation and development of the major, and to identify possible resolutions of the issues that may be useful to faculty and administrators involved with community engagement majors.

### Group Relations Theory: A Systems Perspective on Faculty's Responses to Shifting Organizational Boundaries

Group relations theory (McCollum, 1995) conceives of groups and organizations, such as the Community and Justice Studies major, as bounded systems that sustain their vitality by importing the materials they need to conduct their primary task across the boundary with the environment. The boundaries of a group must be sufficiently permeable to allow in people, ideas, and other materials necessary to its task, but not so permeable that it cannot keep out people, ideas, and materials detrimental to its task. Groups and organizations are conceptualized as interdependent subunits, with smaller systems embedded in several larger ones (Alderfer, 1987; McCollum, 1995). For example, the Community and Justice Studies major is embedded within the Justice and Policy Studies department, which is contained within the Guilford College system, which is a part of the American higher education system—and all are located within American society. Other subsystems relevant to the major would be local nonprofit organizations with which the major collaborates to do community-based teaching and learning. The interconnectedness of these subsystems means that events and dynamics in one part of the system affect the entire system to a greater or lesser extent.

Another key component of group relations theory is that it gives attention "to sources of energy and motivational forces being experienced within individuals, small groups, their leaders, and the linkages between them" (Neuman and Hirschhorn, 1999, p. 685). One common motivational force experienced by individuals in organizations is anxiety, evoked by work tasks and organizational changes over which they feel they have little or no control. Group relations theory posits that when individuals in groups do not have sufficient opportunities to discuss and work through their concerns and anxieties, they engage in regressive defenses against anxiety, such as splitting (seeing individuals and groups as having either all positive or all negative qualities), projection, scapegoating, and denial. Gould et al. (1999) offer a succinct description of this phenomenon at the group level:

> Groups come to share collective, unconscious assumptions about other relevant groups that constitute their social/organizational environment. These assumptions are manifested in both conscious and unconscious processes, including projections, attributions, and stereotyping which shape the ensuing quality and character of their intergroup relationships. (p. 700)

When these "social defenses" against anxiety and other unsettling emotions are adopted systemwide, they can be woven into the structures and processes of a workplace. These structures may help to manage anxiety, but they avoid addressing its causes and often ultimately interfere with the group's ability to accomplish its primary task (Gould et al.,1999; Kets de Vries, 2004; Menzies, 1975). In their analysis of urban education, Powell and Barber (2004) note that responses to anxiety in organizational systems may take several forms, including "fear of innovation, workaholism, political paralysis, turf wars, etc." (p. 315). To help organizations to dismantle such social defense systems, it is important to develop organizational processes and structures in which individuals feel safe enough to address conflicts, debate issues, clarify assumptions, and take risks in order to grow and learn. In group relations theory, such spaces are known as "holding environments."

## Boundary Theory: Understanding Faculty Responses to "Fuzzy" Boundaries between the Academy and the World

A related body of scholarship from sociology on "boundary work" examines academic scientists' efforts to manage their professional role identities in response to changing work boundaries (Beck & Young, 2005; Gieryn, 1983; Lam, 2010), specifically, closer university-industry ties. This literature proposes that academics create and recreate "the boundaries of their work to defend their autonomy and secure resources in pursuit of professional goals" (Gieryn, 1983). Alice Lam's (2010) study of academic scientists in "fuzzy university-industry boundaries" (p. 307) is particularly relevant to the present case study in which faculty face shifting boundaries between their colleges and their communities. In a study of 734 academic scientists from universities in the United Kingdom, Lam identified four faculty orientations actively shaping the boundary between academic science and industry and their own professional role identities.

*Type I Traditionalists*, are characterized by "a strong belief that academia and industry should be distinct, and they pursue success primarily in the academic arena" (p. 317). They see the university as a place for "disinterested basic research" (p. 319) and believe applied work should be conducted in industrial settings. They respond to the incursion of industry into the academy by avoiding working with business or actively contesting the legitimacy of the pursuits of faculty who do work with industry.

At the other extreme, *Type IV Entrepreneurial* faculty "see the boundary between academic and industry as highly permeable, and they believe in the fundamental importance of science-business collaboration for knowledge application and commercial exploitation" (p. 317). They do everything possible to bring "applied people" into the university. The boundary work of Type IV professors is fraught with conflict and tension; they criticize and dismiss the traditional norms of academic science, which "risks jeopardizing their acceptance by academic colleagues" (p. 331).

Lam characterizes faculty who fall between the two extreme orientations as "hybrids," combining characteristics of both the Type I Traditionalists and the Type IV Entrepreneurs. Type II academics, which Lam calls *Traditional Hybrids*, believe that the boundary between the academy and industry should be distinct, but also see the benefits of collaboration between academics and business in the generation of new scientific knowledge. They are willing to test the academy-industry boundary and experiment with new work practices, and at the same time, they are committed to maintaining "established scientific norms and their dominant academic role identity" (p. 322).

Type III faculty, *Entrepreneurial Hybrids*, combine an entrepreneurial orientation with a belief in the core values and norms of the academy. They see the university-industry boundary as permeable, and as providing "an open space within which knowledge production and application can be effectively combined" (p. 323). They understand this boundary as "an overlapping space where bargaining and negotiation take place" (p. 324). And they tend to draw on academic frames to resolve tensions between university and industry norms. Lam notes that this group of faculty accomplishes a "paradoxical combination of the logics of science and business in their work" and uses "seemingly conflicting frames to legitimate their boundary crossing activities" (p. 333).

Lam's four orientations offer a particularly apt heuristic framework for this case study of the Community and Justice Studies major, given the similarity in the dimensions of organizational boundary work by undergraduate faculty at the "college-community" boundary, and that of academic scientists at the boundary between the university and industry. Both groups of academics must negotiate their work boundaries and role identities as the ivory tower opens its gates to the outside world and alters traditional norms of disinterested inquiry and the generation of knowledge with and for fellow scholars. As the case study shows, the different attitudes and behaviors of faculty at Guilford College regarding the academy-community boundary fit well within Lam's orientations.

To adapt the language of Lam's schema to faculty's relations with the community as opposed to industry, the term "community partner" is used in place of "entrepreneur" for the orientations in the analysis in this chapter. Type III is thus labeled *Community Partner Hybrid*; and Type IV is *Community Partner*. A more in-depth revision of Lam's orientations for faculty's relations with community is beyond the scope of this chapter; however, the change in terminology is helpful for the heuristic use of the schema in the present analysis.

## The Community and Justice Studies Major

A brief description of the Community and Justice Studies major provides a platform for the unfolding story of the dynamics and issues intertwined with the program. The mission of the major is:

> To support students as they integrate scholarship from the body of Social Theory with community engagement to develop knowledge and skills relevant to citizens organizing in communities and institutions, the roles of public service organizations, and the larger institutional structures of society, understood as operating systematically to generate unjust inequality. Students also acquire problem solving skills, an understanding of their own values, others' diverse values, and the values reflected in public policies.[1] (Community and Justice Studies, 2011)

The major currently has two-and-a-half full-time faculty and an enrollment of 101 students, which places it among the larger majors at Guilford, which has approximately 2,800 students, and 38 majors (Guilford College, *Guilford at a Glance*, n.d.). About a fourth of the students in the major are traditional-age students, and three-fourths are adults over the age of 23, known as CCE (Center for Continuing Education) students. Over the past five years, the major's enrollment of traditional-age students has shown a dramatic 300 percent increase from 6 to 25 students, and the numbers of CCE students have continued a pattern of steady growth, with an increase of 27 percent.

The major's curriculum consists of 32 credits, eight 4-credit courses, with five required core courses: Community Problem-Solving, Restorative Justice, Public Management and Organizational Theory, Research Methods, and a capstone course, along with a choice of three elective courses from within the Justice and Policy Studies department. The most popular elective courses include Community Building, Conflict Resolution, Understanding Oppressive Systems, Trust and Violence, Race and Criminal Justice, and Juvenile Justice.

Most of the courses take students into the local community for projects and field trips, and invite guest speakers to class sessions; however, three courses have concentrated community engagement components: the introductory course, Community Problem-Solving, includes a 30-hour community-learning requirement; the Research Methods course requires that the entire class complete a Participatory Action Research project, collaborating with a local community organization; and an elective, Reclaiming Democracy: Dialogue, Decision-Making, and Community Action, brings together students and faculty from six area campuses with the broader community to study local democracy, culminating with a public conference presenting students' group projects investigating local community issues. The major also offers an elective internship.

The Community and Justice Studies major shares its home department, Justice and Policy Studies, with the Criminal Justice major. Though each major has its own core requirements, students from both majors frequently choose their elective courses from offerings within the other program.

## History and Organizational Context of the Major: Guilford College

The history and mission of Guilford College suggests that it would be hospitable to the efforts of faculty in Community and Justice Studies to engage the college with its local community. The college was founded in 1837 as the New Gardens Boarding School by Quakers seeking to provide their children with an educational experience grounded in their normative testimonies of integrity, simplicity, equality, peace, and direct access to God/Truth. The storied woods that form part of the campus were the site of a stop on the Underground Railroad during the antebellum period, a fact that features prominently in the college's self-portrayal, and reflects an association with efforts toward justice and equality in the community that is integral to Guilford's institutional DNA (Guilford College, *History*, n.d.; Stoesen, 1987). Reflecting similar priorities, the college's mission is "to provide a transformative, practical and excellent liberal arts education for every student," and the core values, grounded in Quaker testimonies, are "community, diversity, equality, excellence, integrity, justice, and stewardship" (Guilford College, *Mission and Core Values*, n.d.).

There is ample evidence of institutional support for community engagement at Guilford. Since the early 1990s, community engagement units have been located within academic affairs, as opposed to student affairs, indicating the importance of these efforts to the academic mission of the college. Two major program centers offer support to faculty and students involved in community engagement—the Bonner Center for Community Learning, founded in 1991, and the Center for Principled Problem Solving, launched in 2007. The review process for faculty tenure and promotion of the values of engaged teaching and scholarship have, along with high-level administrators, affirmed the importance of integrating study in the liberal arts and sciences with education in practical skills, including those gained through community-based teaching and research.[2]

Despite these origins, guiding principles, and strong institutional support, faculty's involvement with community engagement, particularly as it relates to the academic program, has been somewhat uneven. Some key issues emerged in the study which offer hypotheses for this apparent reluctance of many Guilford faculty to cross the college-community boundary in their teaching. These issues will be discussed in full, following a description of the history and development of the Community and Justice Studies major.

## The History and Development of the Community and Justice Studies Major

At Guilford, the story of the formation and development of the Community and Justice Studies major over its 12 years of existence is one of faculty attempting to open up the boundary between the college and community, and the consequent intellectual, emotional, and organizational turbulence their efforts caused in the Justice and Policy Studies department. To create this new major, the more community-oriented faculty (Type IV Community Partner orientation), moved away from the Criminal Justice major, with its aspiration to greater academic legitimacy and adherence to traditional academic norms (Type I Traditional orientation). In addition, the new program was grounded in a bottom-up, grass-roots liberal perspective on justice, whereas the Criminal Justice major had a more conservative perspective and study of the formal, institutionalized dimensions of justice. This section offers an account of the dynamics and issues in the still-unfolding story of this uneasy collaboration.

In the late 1990s, two Criminal Justice faculty members, from the disciplines of sociology and social work, realized that they were "moving themselves away from the field of criminal justice," and so decided to create a new major in the context of a collegewide curriculum revision. They were soon joined by faculty colleague from the field of education. An excerpt from an early document formulating the major gives a sense of its philosophy and scope.

The Community and Justice Studies major offers a profoundly hopeful vision of what our lives with each other can be. This vision differs fundamentally from the social reality we live with each day, in which massive structures not only systematically exclude and create growing inequality among those on the margins, but also exercise power over and demand conformity from largely isolated individuals inside the structures.

As students inquire into what are just communities, they also examine strategies for working on real problems in local neighborhood communities. They struggle with solving problems in ways that strengthen justice and equality in communities. A central principle is that the people most affected by problems are those who lead in defining and working on them. Experience reveals that ignoring this principle leads to an "us serving them" orientation, which in the long run reinforces existing power inequalities.

Students also learn strategies for both surviving in and transforming formal institutions such as schools, businesses, and non-profits. (Community and Justice Studies, 2001)

Moreover, the creators of the new major viewed it as grounded in a democratic thesis, "people coming together and trying to govern ourselves, rather than be governed by others." They crafted a curriculum and pedagogy intended to serve as "prerequisites for fundamental social change," educational experiences in which students could change from being "isolated, individualism-oriented people...to relate well enough to form a strong collective to create social change." (Community and Justice Studies, 2001)

To create courses, the founders drew heavily on their own experience and their commitments in the local community. Two of the faculty members were involved in M. Scott Peck's Foundation for Community Encouragement and similar local initiatives, and they brought that experience to the development of the Community Building course. One of the founders, who had taught at Guilford since 1980, also brought his knowledge and experience with several other community initiatives to the creation of courses, including the creation of a local organization providing mediation and conflict resolution services and alternative sentencing; helping to start a residential self-help organization for substance abusers, ex-convicts, and homeless people; working with an organization offering antiracism training; co-chairing citizens' commissions on reducing crime and violence; and initiating a police review board in Greensboro. These experiences informed the content of several of the courses in the new major.

This infusion of knowledge, experience, and priorities from the broader community into the curriculum of the new program opened up the boundary between the college and community in significant ways. Indeed, the founders of the major intended to break down the wall between the academy and communities, seeing that wall as a manifestation of an undemocratic and oppressive hierarchy.

Their colleagues in the Criminal Justice major objected to both the content of the new major and the process by which it had been created. Some felt excluded from decision making about the shape the major would take, and felt that the curriculum lacked coherence and rigor and that it was "indoctrinating and not educating" students into a "politically correct" perspective on issues. Community and Justice Studies faculty viewed the Criminal Justice faculty as politically conservative and closely identified with the status quo in both the criminal justice system and the larger society.

Given these sharp criticisms, the Community and Justice Studies faculty soon did not trust the Criminal Justice faculty to have a hand in curricular decisions, and the boundary between the two majors became less and less permeable. Criminal Justice faculty resented being excluded from curriculum decisions, and levels of trust and communication sank quite low. However, both majors managed, largely separately, to develop and sustain successful academic programs, as indicated by their strong enrollments.

Changes in the department's faculty composition in recent years have led to some shifts in this dynamic. Over the past five years, the founder of the major with the longest tenure in the department retired, and three new faculty members were hired. Two of the new faculty members bring knowledge and experience relevant to both Criminal Justice and Community and Justice Studies, which has facilitated communication between the majors. The author, who also was among the new faculty hired, drew on a fellowship to clarify and strengthen the conceptual foundations of the program's curriculum; to initiate retreats for faculty from the Criminal Justice and Community and Justice Studies majors to find ways to work together more openly and productively; and to conduct the present case study to better understand the issues and dynamics affecting the functioning of the major. These efforts have resulted in more open communication and collaboration between the majors on curricula and teaching, and a renewed resolve to work through the long-standing conflicts and tensions.

## *Three Key Issues Evoked by the Major's Boundary Location*

Three central issues emerged in the study which shed light on the tensions and struggles surrounding faculty's efforts to create and sustain the Community and Justice Studies major. All three issues reflect the influence of broader college and societal dynamics and tensions, and affect faculty's autonomy and resources relevant to sustaining the major.

### Perception of the Major as Not "Academic"

The first issue was the perception by some faculty colleagues that the major was undertheorized and not sufficiently academic. Though the major is a close fit with the mission, core values, and academic principles of the Quaker-founded college in its embodiment of the 'practical liberal arts,' and though it enjoys the support of high-level administrators and some faculty, other faculty see the curriculum insufficiently rigorous, ideological, and "activist." As noted earlier, some of the strongest criticisms of the major come from colleagues in the other academic program located in the same department, Criminal Justice.

A dynamic among the broader college faculty offers important context for some of the strong feelings evoked by the major's engagement with the community: long-standing tensions between faculty in traditional liberal arts majors—such as English, History, Philosophy, and Political Science—and those in what have been called the "preprofessional" majors—such as Business Management, Education Studies, Sports Studies, Criminal Justice, and Community and Justice Studies. In what may be viewed as an example of the social defense of "splitting," liberal arts academic programs have contained positive projections of being rigorous, intellectual, theoretical, and of a generally higher status than the preprofessional majors, which hold negative projections of being easy, lacking rigor, and being practical. Tensions and anxieties around this split run high on both sides. The threat posed by declining enrollments and perceived diminished value in the job market of the traditional liberal arts, both at Guilford and nationwide (Nussbaum, 2010) has created serious concerns among liberal arts faculty. Indeed, in response to those concerns about Guilford's status as a liberal arts college, a high-level administrator presented data at a fall 2011 meeting reassuring faculty that enrollment in liberal arts majors continues to be significantly higher than in the preprofessional majors, and that the ratio had held steady for the past several years.

Faculty members in the preprofessional majors tend to be insecure about the perceived academic legitimacy of their programs. Reasons for that insecurity can be found in the efforts to close Criminal Justice in the 1980s and early 1990s. As one interviewee reported, "There was a prejudice against Criminal Justice because it was a new field in academia, and was a long way from being 'pure,' but instead was very practical." Aware of the negative connotations and marginalization inherent in the preprofessional label, faculty members in affected majors have fought against its use in college parlance. The relevance of this dynamic for the Community and Justice Studies major is that faculty in preprofessional majors aspiring to greater academic legitimacy for their programs may feel threatened by, and therefore, particularly averse to majors like the Community and Justice Studies major that integrate community priorities and values and "doing" with traditional academic norms. To address this issue of being perceived as insufficiently theoretical and academic, faculty in the Community and Justice Studies major have worked on two fronts: to strengthen the theoretical foundation of the program, while preserving the practice component, and at the same time, to engage in concerted efforts of "impression management" (Goffman, 1959) with colleagues, intended to replace negative projections with information about the program's integration of theory with practice.

## A Justice-Focused Program in a Neoliberal Institutional Context: One More Threat to Faculty Autonomy and Academic Freedom?

Another key theme that emerged in the study concerns the perceptions of some faculty that the Community and Justice Studies major represents yet another incursion of external demands on the curriculum, alongside those stemming from the growing influence of the marketplace and neoliberal economic policy on the college. Though the ethics of equality animating the justice-oriented major differ significantly from the ethics of individualism, market efficiency, and profit underlying the pressures on the college from the broader political economy, both are viewed by some faculty as transgressing the boundary that has protected the college as a sanctuary for thinking apart from the interests and demands of the world.

Two recent examples illustrate the market-based demands that many faculty perceived to have diminished faculty autonomy. In 2009, Guilford accepted a grant from the Branch Banking and Trust (BB&T) Foundation, which stipulated that the college would offer a new course, "The Moral Foundations of Capitalism," requiring Ayn Rand's *Atlas Shrugged* as one of the readings, once a year for ten years, and also distribute the book to all juniors majoring in Business, and in Economics, as well as to the two to three Ethics of Capitalism scholars selected during this ten year period (Zweigenhaft, 2010). The college's decision to accept the grant generated significant controversy among faculty. Critics were troubled both by the lack of review of the grant by the Educational Policy committee and the collective faculty, and their sense that the college was "selling a piece of the curriculum," with disturbing implications for faculty autonomy and academic freedom. Other professors and administrators defended the decision, as offering needed funding, and argued that the grant's conditions did not pose any real threat to faculty autonomy or academic freedom.

The second example of the intrusion of norms and practices from the corporate sector into the life of the college took place during 2010–11 when Guilford completed an academic prioritization process that placed every major in a top, middle, or bottom tier, based on a set of criteria weighted toward the contribution of the major to the college's bottom line. Tier placement will be used to determine the future allocation of resources to the majors. This process evoked a barrage of criticism from faculty, and significant anxiety and concern about its impact on the survival of majors in the lowest tier, several of which are known for teaching excellence, academic rigor, and a close congruence with the college's core values. Many faculty members experienced the process as another major step in a shift toward the market and corporate needs shaping the college curriculum and priorities, and a diminishment of faculty autonomy and authority.

As faculty members experience these pulls toward a more permeable boundary around the academy, both from community and corporate sectors, concerns about their autonomy, academic freedom, and traditional norms of neutrality and disinterested inquiry, may elicit a response of "circling the wagons" ever more tightly, to defend against these changes. Such a response is likely to work against faculty support for majors with strong community engagement components such as Community and Justice Studies, even from faculty with a similar justice-oriented philosophy and ethics.

### The Consequences of Connecting Ideas with Action for Teaching, Research, and Academic Freedom

In the traditional notion of the academy, imbued by liberal values of ideas being distant from action, the conflicting ideologies and ethics underlying different majors may well spark a lively debate among the majors' faculty. However, when radically different and contradictory ethics are acted upon by majors in partnerships with various local institutions and community organizations, controversy is likely, along with complex and thorny questions related to teaching, research, and academic freedom. This constellation of issues emerged as a key third theme in the case study.

A description of a course offered by the author in fall 2010 and events related to it, illustrates these issues. The course, a section of Research Methods intended primarily for Community and Justice Studies majors, involved the entire class working as a research team to study an issue identified by a local community organization, the Beloved Community Center of Greensboro (BCC) (Beloved Community Center, n.d.). Using the method of participatory action research (Stringer, 2007), the class collaborated with BCC to research the question, *What are Greensboro residents' perceptions of the city's police department, and their thoughts about a citizens review board with subpoena power to evaluate police conduct?* BCC's interest in this area of inquiry grew out of its efforts to increase police accountability and professionalism in Greensboro. Their focus on this issue was grounded in a history of concern about police responses to members of the African American community and several recent incidents involving the police, including 39 lawsuits for discrimination filed against the police department by African American and Latino officers, and controversial terminations of several officers of color.

Under the guidance of the author and her teaching assistant, students interviewed 97 diverse Greensboro residents about their perceptions of the police and their thoughts about BCC's proposal for a citizens review board with subpoena power. The class then analyzed and presented the themes from the data at a community meeting open to the public in December 2010. Participants at the meeting, consisting mostly of people associated with the Beloved Community Center, interpreted the findings and discussed their significance for the initiative on police accountability and professionalism.

During the the research, two issues had emerged related to teaching and research on the boundary of the academy and the community: the first is the question of the neutrality of research when it is conducted in collaboration with a community partner with a particular, "interested" perspective on the issue under study; the second, related issue concerns the choice of controversial community partners that may adversely impact the interests of one's college or university, which in turn may jeopardize academic freedom.

The issue of neutrality surfaced in students' discussions about the topic and method of the study. Students expressed a broad range of views about the police, from quite favorable to deeply critical. Some students who felt positively about the police raised concerns that the study would be biased, given the critical stance of BCC toward the police department. In response to these concerns, the author acknowledged the "nonneutral" perspective of the community partner, and at the same time, emphasized that the research itself would be unbiased, valid, and reliable— that BCC needed an accurate sense of the community's views in order to develop effective plans for the initiative. The author and teaching assistant also devoted significant class time to discussions scrutinizing the research question, interview questions, and method for any signs of bias. Finally, to clarify their relationship with the community partner, the author identified the stance of the research team as that of a "critical supporter." They were bringing a critical perspective and research tools to assist the organization with the project, and part of this collaboration involved questioning BCC's interest in the topic, as well as its strategies for addressing it. Indeed, in response to students' question of why BCC had not initially included police officers in the sample of groups to be interviewed, BCC agreed to include the police.

While these explanations and strategies helped to assuage students' concerns about bias, a small number of students with close associations with the police were still not happy to be supporting BCC's police accountability initiative. They did not see themselves as any kind of "supporter" of BCC, critical or otherwise. Two criminal justice majors opted to drop the course for this reason. To address this issue of students' reluctance to work with a particular community partner, in future semesters, students will have the option to take another section of the course if they have objections to the partner.

The second issue, concerning the choice of community partners, emerged midway through the research methods course, when the author learned that a high-level police official had contacted a top administrator at the college to criticize the project and ask that it be stopped. The police official challenged the validity of the project's method and also observed that a citizens review board would "ignite" police officers and be "unpopular" with them. The administrator responded to the police official by affirming the college's long history of educating area police officers and its desire to continue that collaboration, noting however, both the importance of research to improve the functioning of public institutions and that the college does not censor faculty's academic work. The administrator assured the police official that the project would be reviewed to ensure that the method was well-designed and included diverse perspectives. Once it was clear that the project was valid, it was suggested that the author send the final results of the study to the police official, which she did.

This administrator's support of faculty and defense of academic freedom in the face of a direct challenge from a powerful public official exemplifies both the risks inherent in community engagement and the possibility of a deft response, affirming both the college's independence *and* its role in the public life of the community. This administrative stance is akin to the "being in the world, not of it" position advocated for community engagement academic programs.

Some faculty in the Criminal Justice major expressed concern that the police department would retaliate against the college by refusing to hire Guilford graduates and exclude their students from internships. Fortunately, these fears have proved to be unfounded.

The three central issues described in this section reveal the challenges involved in the efforts of Community and Justice Studies faculty to negotiate the academy-community boundary as they developed their major. Understanding these issues sheds light on the motivations and considerations involved in Criminal Justice and Community and Justice Studies and facultys' various and at times conflicting orientations to the boundary (Lam, 2010), evident in their struggles around the contested development of the major. The discussion that follows draws on an academic frame to offer further analysis of the case and to consider possible resolutions of the issues and dynamics that have been articulated.

## Discussion

The impetus for this study grew out of the author's interest in understanding the complex and, at times, intensely emotional responses the Community and Justice Studies major evoked in colleagues, and the need to find ways to more fully and fruitfully collaborate with colleagues to educate the students under their care. The discussion begins with a summary of the author's insights around *process* issues, that is, the social, emotional, and structural issues related to the formation and functioning of the major, and suggestions from group relations literature of approaches to address these issues. Consideration is then given to several *content* issues, specifically, neutrality in community-based teaching and research; choice of partners that may adversely impact the interests of the college; and implications of these issues for the curricula and pedagogy of community engagement academic programs.

A summary of the dynamics of the major through the lenses of boundary-work theory and group relations theory sets the stage for recommendations for resolution of some of the process issues faced by the major. To begin with, the social system in which the major is embedded, Guilford College, is experiencing the incursion of corporate and community sectors across its boundary into the academic space of the college, as well as tensions between the liberal arts and practical arts. Both dynamics reflect struggles over the mission and identity of higher education, as manifested at Guilford. To what extent will the college be a "space apart" for thinking, distant from the interests and demands of the world, and to what extent and in what ways will it engage with social and community issues, and/or become imbued with corporate values and practices?

Within this somewhat turbulent college context, the curriculum and pedagogy of the Community and Justice Studies major has served to shift this contested and unstable academic-community boundary. Extrapolating from Lam's (2010) schema, the program's founders, with their Type IV Community Partner orientations, moved the major toward the community, aiming to build bridges or even to break down the boundary between the two social systems, challenging traditional academic norms as they did so. The move troubled colleagues in the Criminal Justice major with Type I Traditional orientations, who were strongly motivated to be identified as a major with traditional academic norms, steeped in theory, and distant from the practical. These colleagues leveled extensive criticism against the Community and Justice Studies major, questioning its academic legitimacy. To protect the major and preserve its integrity, its faculty created a fairly impermeable boundary between it and Criminal Justice, allowing a minimal exchange of ideas and information between the two programs. This dynamic of splitting contributed to a breakdown in trust and communication among faculty in the majors, and functions as an impediment to the department's primary task of educating its students.

Group relations theory literature suggests that to resolve this kind of adversity between organizational units, the primary task of these "inter-organizational domains" is to convene the groups to discuss and discern their areas of interdependence, identifying each group's self-interest and discovering their collective interest (Trist, 1983). A related, promising approach consists of "naming and selecting 'collaborative routines in action' that need to be improved together" (Neumann, 2010, p. 320), and "repeatedly enact[ing] this cross-boundary collaboration" (p. 317). As applied to the majors in the Justice and Policy Studies department, such collaborative routines could include activities ranging from curriculum development to co-hosting public panels on issues relevant to both majors, such as prison reform. It is important in these cross-boundary collaborations that leaders create a "holding environment" in which participants feel safe enough to directly address contentious issues.

Drawing on a cognitive strategy similar to that advocated for the boundary work between the academy and community, it also may be helpful for faculty to step back and take a more "academic" perspective on the tensions between the majors. This metacognitive move would entail reflecting on their thinking about the dynamic they are caught in and the factors contributing to their situation. Such a move would draw on the core values of "higher education, intellectual pluralism, rational discourse, intellectual autonomy, open-mindedness, and civility" (Colby, et al., 2007, p. 21) to work through the dilemmas they face. This discussion might even lead them to consider how they may be working through issues on behalf of the college as a whole.

Stepping into the middle of intense conflict between colleagues with Type I Traditional and Type IV Community Partner orientations, the author demonstrated a Type III Community Partner Hybrid orientation, creating a space in which she had to negotiate conflicts in values, norms, and practices between the college and the community. At the same time that she was working to open up the boundary between the Community and Justice Studies and Criminal Justice majors, she was testing the college-community boundary through her research methods course project on police accountability. The traditional academic norm of neutrality in teaching and research became a clear point of contention in the project. William Friedland (2008), the sociologist who led in the creation of the Community Studies department at the University of California at Santa Cruz in the late 1960s, offers an analysis that is helpful in addressing the neutrality issue. Noting that Max Weber, considered the "patron saint of value-neutrality," emphasized neutrality in the research process, but that this did not imply "general political nonpartisanship" (Roth, 1971, cited in Friedland, 2008, p. 16), Friedland observes that "researchers can do their best research when they hold their values as neutrally as possible while conducting research despite sympathizing with the general orientations of a movement" (p. 16). He proposes a new role for academics in relation to social movements, that of being "critically supportive" of them, "engaging in critical analysis which movement participants might not consider 'loyal'" (p. 16).

Adapting Friedland's analysis for community-based teaching and research, professors would offer a critically supportive perspective on the work of community partners, and create expectations for students to do the same, both in research and classroom discussions. In the example of the police accountability project, students supportive of the police as well as students supportive of BCC would be expected to take a critical perspective, identifying strengths and weaknesses of each organization.

The related issue of choosing controversial community partners for research and teaching also arose in the police-accountability project. Though the police department has not retaliated by withholding employment and internships from Guilford students and graduates, such a response is within the realm of the possible. Given this risk, what criteria should guide community engagement majors in their choice of partners for community learning and research? Should academic programs avoid partners that might harm the interests of their colleges? Insights relevant to these questions can be found in the emerging literature on law school clinics' representation of clients that threaten the interests of the clinics' academic institutions

(Babich, 2011). The catalyst for this scholarship was the threats in 2010 by state legislatures in Maryland and Louisiana to cut funding for law school clinics at the University of Maryland and Tulane University for representing clients who might negatively affect the financial interests of powerful businesses in their states (Blum, 2010; Fahrenthold, 2010). Babich (2011) frames the issue quite powerfully.

> [S]hould universities sacrifice educational and public service goals and design their curriculums to tiptoe around issues that might annoy people with influence? Or should academic institutions maintain independence from their constituents' points of views? (p. 507)

Babich concludes that while it may be difficult to go against the preferences of financial supporters, academic institutions value their independence too much to succumb to the influence of such supporters. He argues that professors should make decisions about whether to take on clients without the involvement of administrators, and that in situations when a potential client is likely to be "genuinely toxic to the university," clinic professors should balance "(1) their concerns about consequences to the university, (2) the potential client's need, and (3) the damage to the clinic's principles from turning down the case" (p. 511).

These principles may be usefully applied to community engagement professors' decisions about potentially controversial partners, both in community-based teaching and research. Academic programs typically choose community partners based on their missions and educational goals, that is, the knowledge and skills they hope their students will gain through the experience of working with them, as well as the positive impact they aspire to have on community issues. In the case of a partner that might threaten the interests of their academic institution, balancing concerns for the consequences for the college and the importance of the community issue or need with the damage to the principles of academic freedom and the college's contribution to social change if they reject the partner offers a promising approach, rich in learning opportunities.

Babich (2011) also makes an important pedagogical point in his analysis, an insight shared by community engagement scholars Swords and Kiely (2010) that crucial learning resides in the complex interactions, and often difficult decisions made in the context of teaching and learning in communities. Babich encourages educators to make decisions about ethical dilemmas like choosing clients transparent to students, as teachable moments that will help to prepare them for the dilemmas that they are likely to face in their professional lives. In the same vein, Kiely's research highlights the importance of students' critical reflections on their community learning experiences, including the ways in which "context, ideology, hegemony, history, institutions, and policies affect how people perceive and approach social problems and campus-community relationships" (2002, cited in Swords & Kiely, 2010, p. 152). Creating the conditions and expectations for this kind of complicated and sometimes troubling thinking can be deeply motivating and empowering for students, and as professors, models the engaged citizenship that community engagement academic programs claim is central to their missions.

## Conclusion

Drawing on a case study of a community engagement major as an exemplar, this chapter considers the organizational dynamics and issues that can be evoked when academic programs attempt to bring together the norms, values, and practices of the academy with those of the broader community. The analysis rests on the assumption that the boundary between higher education and the world has become porous and thin. That is, with its increasing involvement with the corporate and community sectors, the academy is certainly in the world; the question is *how* will it be in the world? The chapter suggests that faculty have markedly different responses to this question, grounded in their diverse orientations to the academy-community boundary, and that it behooves campus leaders to create forums, safe-enough spaces, for faculty to consider together how they will collectively negotiate this boundary. An unappealing alternative is that faculty will defend against their anxieties about shifting role and organizational identities, through turf battles, splitting, and other unproductive behaviors, to the detriment of their shared educational mission. The chapter also lifts up the importance of college leaders supporting both the college's independence and its academic freedom, *and* its role in the public life of its community.

The resolution offered in this chapter to the dilemmas of the turbulent new terrain in which community engagement faculty members find themselves is to be "in the world, not of it"; that is, to engage deeply enough in the life of the Mission and Core Values to have an insider's understanding, and remain distant enough to bring the insights of a critical supporter, informed by the core values of higher education. This location is far enough inside the academy to be perceived as legitimate by colleagues, and close enough to the world to offer a useful vantage point for offering a critical perspective and instigating change in communities and in higher education, and in the relationship between the two worlds. The learning in these efforts can be profound, for faculty, students, and the broader community.

## Acknowledgment

The author wishes to thank her colleagues at Guilford College for participating in the interviews for the case study presented in this chapter and the Center for Principled Problem Solving at Guilford for the faculty fellowship that funded the research for the study.

## Notes

1. The Community Studies minor, also founded in 1998, is not included in the case study, given that it is not as significant as the major in the organizational dynamics of the college. The minor requires four courses, worth four credits each: Community Problem Solving, Community Building, Understanding Oppressive Systems, and the choice of an elective course from a list of options within and outside the Justice and Policy Studies department.

2. In 2010, Guilford College joined the Campus Action Network (CAN) of colleges and universities supporting Liberal Education and America's Promise (LEAP), an initiative of the Association of American Colleges and Universities to promote practical liberal arts education.

## References

Alderfer, C. (1987). An intergroup perspective on group dynamics. In J. Wl. Lorsch (ed.), *Handbook of organization behavior.* Englewood Cliffs, NJ: Prentice Hall.

Babich, A. (2011). Controversy, conflicts, and law school clinics. *Clinical Law Review 17,* 469–513.

Beck, J & Young, M. (2005). The assault on the professions and the restructuring of academic and professional identities: A Bernsteinian Analysis, *British Journal of Sociology of Education 26*(2), 183–197.

Beloved Community Center of Greensboro (n.d.). *About us.* Retrieved June 30, 2011, from http://www.belovedcommunitycenter.org/about-us.html.

Blum, J. (2010, May 14). Industry targets law clinics. *Baton Rouge Advocate.*

Boyer, E. (1990). *Scholarship reconsidered: Priorities of the professoriate.* San Francisco, CA: Jossey-Bass.

Butin, D. (2010). *Service learning in theory and practice: The future of community engagement in higher education.* New York: Palgrave-McMillan.

Campus Compact (n.d.). *Campus compact: Who we are.* Retrieved June 22, 2011 from http://www.compact.org/about/history-mission-vision/.

Carnegie Foundation for the Advancement of Teaching (2006). *Classification descriptions.* Retrieved June 22, 2011 from http://classifications.carnegiefoundation.org/descriptions/community_engagement.php.

Colby, A., Beaumont, E., Ehrlich, T., & Corngold, J. (2007). *Educating for democracy: Preparing undergraduates for responsible political engagement.* San Francisco, CA: Jossey-Bass.

Community and Justice Studies (2001). *Draft formulations of the major in Community and Justice Studies.* Greensboro, NC: Guilford College.

Community and Justice Studies (2011). *Annual assessment report, 2011–2012.* Greensboro, NC: Guilford College.

Fahrenthold, D. (2010, March 28). Maryland legislature scrutinizing law clinic over chicken farm suit, *Washington Post.* Retrieved June 20, 2011 from www.washingtonpost.com/wp-dyn/content/article/2010/03/27/AR2010032702380.html.

Friedland, W. (2008). *New ways of working and organization: Alternative agrifood movements and agrifood researchers.* Paper presented at the Miniconferences on "Agrifoodies for Action Research" at the Agriculture and Human Values Society in Austin, TX, and the Rural Sociological Society in Santa Clara, CA.

Gieryn, T. (1983). Boundary work and the demarcation of science from non-science: Strains and interests in professional ideologies of scientists. *American Sociological Review 48*(6), 781–95.

Gillette, J. & McCollom, M. Eds. (1985). *Groups in context: A new perspective on group dynamics.* Lanham, MD: University Press of America.

Gould, L. Ebers, R., & Clinchy, R. (1999). The systems psychodynamics of a joint venture: Anxiety, social defenses, and the management of mutual dependence. *Human Relations 52*(6), 697–722.

Goffman, E. (1959). *The presentation of self in everyday life.* New York: Doubleday.

Guilford College (n.d.). *Academic program: The five academic principles.* Retrieved June 23, 2011 from http://www.guilford.edu/academics/academic-programs/.

———. (n.d.). *Guilford at a glance.* Retrieved June 23, 2011 from http://www.guilford.edu/about-guilford/guilford-at-a-glance/.

———. (n.d.). *Mission, values, and strategic plan.* Retrieved June 23, 2011 from http://www.guilford.edu/about-guilford/values-vision-strategic-plan/.

Kets de Vries, M. (2004). Organizations on the couch: A clinical perspective on organizational dynamics. *European Management Journal, 22*(2), 183–200.

Lam, A. (2010). From 'ivory tower traditionalists' to 'entrepreneurial scientists'? Academic scientists in 'fuzzy' university-industry boundaries. *Social Studies of Science, 40*(2), 307–40.

McCollom, M. (1995). Group formation: Boundaries, leadership, and culture. In J. Gillette & M. McCollom (eds.), *Groups in context: A new perspective on group dynamics* (pp. 34–48). Lanham, MD: University Press of America.

Menzies, I. (1975). A case study in the functioning of social systems as a defense against anxiety. In A. D. Colman & W.H. Becton (eds.), *Group Relations Reader 1* (pp. 281–312). Washington, DC: A.K. Rice Institute.

Miller, E. & Rice. A. (1967). *Systems of organization: The control of task and sentient boundaries.* London: Tavistock.

Neumann, J. (2010). How integrating organizational theory with systems psychodynamics can matter in practice: A commentary on critical challenges and dynamics in multiparty collaboration. *The Journal of Applied Behavioral Science, 46,* 313–21.

Neumann, J. & Hirschhorn, L. (1999). The challenge of integrating psychodynamic and organizational theory. *Human Relations, 52*(6), 683–95.

Nussbaum, M. (2010). *Not for profit: Why democracy needs the humanities.* Princeton, NJ: Princeton University Press.

Powell, L. & M. Barber (2004). Savage inequalities indeed: Irrationality and urban school reform. pp. 303–20. In S. Cytrynbaum & D. Noumair (eds.), *Group dynamics, organizational irrationality, and social complexity: Group relations reader 3.* Jupiter, FL: A.K. Rice Institute.

Roth, G. (1971). "Value neutrality" in Germany and the United States. In R. Bendix & G. Roth, *Scholarship and partisanship: Essays on Max Weber* (pp. 34–54). Berkeley: University of California Press.

Sandmann, L. & Weerts, D. (2006). Engagement in higher education: Building a federation for action. Report of the proceedings for a Wingspread Conference establishing the Higher Education Network for Community Engagement (HENCE). http://www.henceonline.org/hence.pdf . Accessed June, 21, 2011.

Slaughter, S. & Rhodes, G. (2004). *Academic capitalism and the new economy: Markets, state, and higher education.* Baltimore, MD: Johns Hopkins University Press.

Stoesen, A. (1997). *Guilford College on the strength of 150 years.* Greensboro, NC: Guilford College Board of Trustees.

Stringer, E. (2007). *Action research.* Thousand Oaks, CA: Sage Publications.

Swords, A. & Kiely, R. (2010). Beyond pedagogy: Service learning as movement building in higher education. *Journal of Community Practice, 18,* 148–70.

Trist E. (1983). Referent organizations and the development of inter-organizational domains. *Human Relations 36*(3), 269–84.

Weerts, D. & Sandmann, L. (2010). Community engagement and boundary-spanning roles at research universities. *Journal of Higher Education 81*(6), 633–57.

Zweigenhaft, R. (2010). Is this curriculum for sale? *Academe.* Washington, DC: American Association of University Professors. http://www.aaup.org/AAUP/pubsres/academe/2010/JA/feat/zwei.htm. Accessed June 24, 2011.

# CHAPTER 4

# Contending with Political and Cultural Campus Challenges

*Arthur S. Keene and John Reiff*
University of Massachusetts Amherst

## Introduction

This chapter chronicles our efforts to establish a certificate (i.e., an interdisciplinary minor) in public service and civic engagement at the University of Massachusetts Amherst. The proposal, which we submitted in 2009, initially met with considerable resistance from some members of our Faculty Senate. After more than a year of negotiations, modifications, and compromises, we arrived at a much stronger proposal, which was endorsed by the Faculty Senate and implemented in fall 2011. We describe the certificate and its academic rationale, recount the objections of our colleagues, and offer an anthropological analysis of their resistance. From this experience we are able to offer some advice to colleagues hoping to undertake a similar endeavor, including a mapping tool that can help them organize to get their own programs approved.

## Background

Community Service Learning (CSL) at UMass Amherst has a long history going back at least to the 1960s, when individual faculty began to design ways for their students to work in community settings as part of their academic course work. In 1994, the campus established the Provost's Committee on Community Service Learning (PCSL) to promote and oversee service-learning across the campus and to advise the provost on these matters. In 1999, the decision was made to make CSL a core value of the new Commonwealth Honors College and to create an Office of Community Service Learning (OCSL) to support community engagement in the honors curriculum and serve as a campuswide system of CSL support. In 2008, the Carnegie Foundation designated UMass Amherst as a Community Engaged University, with over 100 CSL courses enrolling over 3000 students annually. Beginning in the late 1990s, OCSL developed and ran two UMass flagship CSL programs within the Honors College and provided support to two others. IMPACT!, a first-year Residential Academic Program, built a year-long CSL learning community around courses that explored diversity, social justice, and civic leadership (www.honors. umass.edu/impact). The Citizen Scholars Program (CSP), a two-year CSL leadership-development program, offered a five-course curriculum (www.honors.umass. edu/csp; Colby, Beaumont, Ehrlich, & Corngold, 2007; Mitchell, Visconti, Keene, & Battistoni, 2011). OCSL also supported the UMass Alliance for Community Transformation (UACT), an organization that sponsors a set of courses centered on student-facilitated curricular alternative spring breaks (Addes & Keene, 2004; www.umass.edu/uact), and Student Bridges, a student-initiated, student-funded, and student-run program that aims to increase college access and success for students from underrepresented groups by providing tutoring and mentoring in area middle schools and high schools and by advocating for policy changes that increase support for these students (www.studentbridges.org). The students in these programs were the primary, but hardly the exclusive, constituents of the proposed certificate in civic engagement.

Throughout this period of CSL development, faculty and staff involved with OCSL worked to align CSL courses and programs with the work of social justice and social change. This led us to focus more intensely on preparing students for service, interrogating the difference between charity and justice (Morton, 1995, 1997). We also interrogated their personal beliefs, assumptions, and behaviors relating to the power and privilege that might be associated with their own social identities as they prepared to enter communities to work with people whose social identities might differ significantly from theirs. It also led us to encourage students to look at the social, political, cultural, and economic roots of the social problems they encountered during their service.

Two other concepts emerged as central to OCSL's approach. We moved from seeing our community relationships as placements to seeing them as partnerships. We also became more deeply committed to providing as many students as possible with broad civic preparation as part of a general liberal studies approach, to prepare them for a life of active citizenship in a diverse democracy—an idea that is relevant across all majors and disciplines.

## The Certificate

The aims of the UMass certificate are the following:

1. Meet an established need to organize and credential the work of students who actively combine civic engagement with their academic course work. For years, students had been asking us to create a framework to bring coherence to CSL classes and activities elected outside of the major, connect them to work inside the major, and offer recognition for such substantial involvement. A credential accomplishes all three goals.

2. Effect specific learning outcomes, including the following:
   - Prepare UMass students for a life of active and engaged citizenship. The certificate insures that students develop the knowledge and skills needed to promote this goal and is consistent with the overall general education objectives at UMass Amherst.
   - Provide specific preparation that enables students to connect the work in their major to lifework in the public or civic sphere. This not only enhances the major but also meets the market demand from students for more classes that connect academic work to practical work outside the university.
   - Provide specific preparation for those interested in employment in the civic sphere or in the nonprofit sector or who aim to work in the field of politics. The certificate promotes a body of knowledge and skills that are widely considered to be useful, perhaps necessary, preparation for such work. The certificate is not a substitute for majors that provide such preparation, but it does provide a substantial baseline preparation for students from any major.

We decided to push for the certificate in order to claim ground for CSL during a period of administrative budget cuts that were eliminating key parts of the infrastructure that supported CSL. Because we were operating in a budget-cutting environment, we designed the program to use existing courses and resources, requiring no new budget commitments and aiming to create further justification for continuing the remaining CSL infrastructure.

In the following section, we describe the certificate in the form that was approved by the Faculty Senate. We then describe the resistance to the original proposal we encountered, and in so doing, reveal some of the elements that were absent from the earlier incarnations of the curriculum.

## The Curriculum

The curriculum consists of a minimum of six courses of at least three credits each, at least one from each of five core content areas: social justice, civics and/or political theory, public policy, community/political organizing, and diverse publics. In addition, students must fulfill a praxis requirement of at least three CSL courses—many of which can be found in the five content areas. Students complete a praxis gateway course that provides an introduction to service-learning and a praxis capstone course that pulls together the core areas of learning. Here, we describe each content area, explaining why it is important and how together the five areas form a coherent whole to achieve the CSL objectives.

1. *Social Justice.* Courses that offer an introduction to the bases for different kinds of oppression or injustice in contemporary society; the theories that explain that oppression; and the theories and practices associated with creating a just society.
2. *Civics and Political Theory.* Courses that explore the meaning and the practice of citizenship in a democratic society or offer foundational knowledge in

political theory that enables students to understand the workings of democracy and their position within a democratic society; the theoretical foundations for understanding the dynamics of power and governance.

3. *Public Policy.* Courses that provide an understanding of the legislative process, how policy gets made, how it affects our lives, and how citizens can impact the creation of policy.

4. *Community/Political Organizing.* Courses that introduce students to the ways citizens can mobilize to use their collective power and bring about change.

5. *Diverse Publics.* Courses that help students complexify their understanding of the term "public" by offering in-depth exploration of different constituencies within American society.

6. *Praxis.* Hands-on work with a substantial civic engagement orientation in CSL classes or through guided internships. The aim is to afford the student the opportunity to connect classroom theory with life in the outside world and to direct action.

For each of the five content areas, students can choose from a list of 10–15 courses that have been vetted by the PCSL. The CSL courses that count toward the praxis requirement are scattered throughout the five content areas; additional praxis options are contained in a separate list. There are five gateway CSL courses, including the first course in each of the four flagship CSL programs and a fifth general introduction to the practice of CSL. Students enrolled in any of the four flagship programs find it relatively easy to complete the certificate by adding a few courses to those program requirements; students not in those programs can still complete the certificate within two years by choosing one or two designated courses each semester.

The five content areas reflect the model of civic education that evolved in the CSP over its 12-year history (see Polin & Keene, 2010, pp. 35–37). Students begin the program by asking how society should be organized if it is to be truly good, and they inform their exploration of this question by examining the different ways human beings in a variety of cultures have organized their societies to try to fulfill basic human needs. As they articulate their visions of a good society, students explore structures of power and privilege in our own society that act as barriers to more just relationships, and they learn how individuals can engage each other as allies across the boundaries of social identity. They take a course in social or political theory to gain the tools for analyzing power relationships; a course on public policy to explore how a government can be directed by its citizens to create public good; and a course on organizing to learn some of the strategies and tactics behind the power of combining to create organizations, networks, and movements that work for structural change. Because four of the courses are CSL courses, students continually bring together their classroom learning and their learning in their service sites, and each informs the other. Although the knowledge, skills, and vision/values/attitudes students develop in this set of courses does not include everything we would like them to know and be able to do, we believe that it is a substantial preparation for a lifetime of engagement as a democratic citizen. We believe that in mapping this structure onto the certificate program, we have set up students to access the tools for democratic change in whatever pathways they create through the five content areas and the praxis requirement.

### The Process

All new programs at UMass Amherst must be approved by the Faculty Senate. Proposals are typically brought forward by departments or, in the case of interdisciplinary programs, by coalitions of faculty with the backing of their departments. Our proposal was unique and destined to encounter opposition, partly because it was not based in an academic department but was the creation of a faculty committee working directly under the aegis of the provost. The job of vetting the proposal primarily fell to the Academic Matters Council (AMC) of the Faculty Senate. The AMC was charged with assessing whether there was a need for a CSL certificate program on the campus, whether the program demonstrated academic rigor, what benefits would accrue to the campus and to specific students if it were adopted, whether it duplicated existing efforts on the campus, whether it had reasonable support among other faculty or academic departments, and whether it had sufficient resources to deliver on its promise (i.e., sufficient course offerings and staffing to support students who elected the program). The AMC was also charged with evaluating objections to the program by members of the campus at large. Researching these questions fell to a subcommittee of the AMC—the Program Subcommittee (PSC). Although the approval process can be held up at any juncture in the chain of evaluation, from subcommittee to the final Faculty Senate vote, most of the evaluation, negotiation, and revision typically takes place in the subcommittees of the University Councils. Indeed, we spent a year and a half engaged in negotiations with members of the PSC. The negotiation process was educational both for us and the PSC and resulted in a stronger and more academically rigorous and coherent proposal than the one we originally submitted. Nonetheless, knowing what we know now, we believe that we could have anticipated many of the objections we encountered and thus considerably shortened the time between submission and approval.

At the same time, we also encountered objections to the proposal that were grounded in matters of educational philosophy and epistemology, and these were much more difficult to transcend. Indeed, it was only near the conclusion of that process that we were able to name philosophical and epistemological differences as contributors to our impasse. As we show later, this recognition helped us to move the process forward, but we did not feel that it fully assuaged our adversaries' discomfort, because the subtext of our discussion was really about what it means to be educated, how we educate effectively, and what the role of the faculty ought to be within a university that is increasingly governed by neoliberal sensibilities.

We have been on both sides of the table when it comes to program approval. We believe that the approval process is a good one and that having a system of checks and balances helps to insure the academic integrity and rigor of new programs, avoid faddishness, and protect the interests of the multiple stakeholders that may be impacted by the addition of a new program. But the process is inherently fraught—especially in an environment in which units are encouraged to compete with each other for resources and students and where an idiom of monetization and a trend toward devaluing the liberal arts increasingly prevail (Giroux, 2011). The challenge is even greater for interdisciplinary programs that promote intellectual border crossing. Hence, the proposer of any new program in service-learning or civic engagement ought to expect multiple queries, concerns, and objections that originate in thoughtful but also rather parochial understandings of the proposal's content. In what follows, we do not review all the concerns that were raised but instead focus on a few of the major objections and our responses to them, including our adoption of two substantial compromises. The objections fell into two categories: academic and administrative.

## Academic Objections

Early in the evaluation the PSC raised two prominent objections to the academic content of the proposal that persisted throughout most of our negotiations.

1. The field of community service learning lacks a canon or an intellectual core.
2. The proposed program lacks intellectual coherence and offers students too much choice.

Let us consider each one in turn.

### Core Body of Knowledge

The PSC expressed concern that the certificate did not offer a coherent set of courses representing a core body of knowledge and skills. They argued that there was no agreed-upon canon for community service learning or civic engagement and that this had been affirmed for them by our menu-driven curriculum that allowed students far too many choices/pathways for completing the program (a point we explore more fully later). We acknowledged that some experts in our field agree that we lacked a canon (Butin, 2010a; Butin, 2010b) but countered that in our own disciplines (anthropology and American studies), there was hardly an agreed-upon canon, much less a standard curriculum across campuses. We pointed out that at UMass Amherst, the anthropology major offers a greater menu of choices than our proposed certificate and that there were only two required courses that every anthropology major, without exception, elects. The committee acknowledged this but argued that fields like anthropology enjoy a disciplinary authority—that being part of a widely recognized academic discipline confers credibility that CSL lacked. This struck us as a tautology as well as a paradox. If the standard for legitimating a core body of knowledge is the discipline, and if the discipline is still forming (see Butin 2010a; 2010b)—as we pointed out was the situation only a short time ago in such recently recognized disciplines as women's studies or environmental studies, to name a few—then, we asked, by what measure is it possible to demonstrate a coherent core body of knowledge prior to the formal establishment of a discipline, and how can a discipline be established without a core body of knowledge? We maintained that while civic engagement is often discussed under a number of rubrics (e.g., community service, community service learning, community-based learning, public service), it clearly represents an academic body of knowledge with an intellectual core. And we asserted that the core curriculum in our certificate represented precisely the knowledge and competencies that are at the heart of this emerging field. Although there is considerable debate within the field of civic engagement about what constitutes that core, we argued that civic engagement, service-learning, or public service was associated with all the commonly agreed-on indicators of an academic field. That is, we have a recognized body of scholarship; specialized journals and professional meetings; colleges, departments, and academic centers; faculty appointments; and minors and majors. In Massachusetts alone there are two prominent schools of public service that are well grounded in our approach to civic engagement: the School of Public and Community Service at UMass Boston and Tisch College of Citizenship and Public Service at Tufts. We also noted that while majors and minors in civic engagement and public service were not numerous, they were growing rapidly, and we cited the more than 50 such programs nationally that Butin and his colleagues had documented. Finally, we noted that the development of an intellectual core in civic engagement and public service was supported by the work of the 26-year-old national organization Campus Compact (http://www.compact.org/), a membership organization of college and university presidents, of which UMass is a member, dedicated to the promotion of precisely the kind of work that the certificate supported.

We argued that the core competencies we had selected made sense to us as active and long-time practioners in the field and also to other advanced practitioners. We pointed out that we had shared our proposal widely and discussed it at national roundtables sponsored by the Association of American Colleges and Universities (AAC&U) and The Research University Civic Engagement Network (TRUCEN), and at the First National Conference on the Future of Civic Engagement. Moreover, the curriculum had been thoughtfully developed over several years, based on our experiences in one of our flagship service leadership programs. We had made a conscious effort to seek feedback from prominent people in the field. The feedback we received and the letters of support that these professionals volunteered to provide suggested strongly that our proposal made sense to the people who do this work. In response to this objection we solicited a dozen letters from prominent colleagues in the field, supporting the certificate and the proposed curriculum and attesting to both its intellectual coherence and to the intellectual coherence of the field of civic engagement. These letters proved invaluable. Prior to submission we had solicited six internal letters of support, from two deans, two department chairs, and two program directors, including the chair of the certificate in public policy (who might have seen us a competitor for the same students); the director of the Bachelor's Degree with Individual Concentration (BDIC), who volunteered staff resources to help manage our certificate; and the chairs of the anthropology and political science departments, whose courses made up a significant portion of the CSL offerings. In retrospect, we think we should have solicited the external letters from the outset. We believe that these letters assuaged concerns of most members of the PSC about the intellectual integrity of the field and the coherence of the proposal, by showing that that those objections were in conflict with expert testimony.

Finally, we asserted our belief that our five areas of competency were those that collectively best addressed the outcomes we hoped to produce. One might reasonably ask, why not seek different outcomes? Why not prepare people for specific jobs in human or government service? Why not require a course in economics or constitutional law? These might be reasonable aspirations, but they were not in our judgment the most direct route to fulfilling the goals that we established for *our* program. Our goal was to provide multiple routes to fulfillment so that all students, be they anthropologists or zoologists, could acquire the knowledge, skills, and experience they would need to embark on a lifetime of engaged citizenship. We argued that the options we provided offered optimal opportunities given the resources we had at our disposal.

### Too Many Choices

The second substantial complaint—and the one that was hardest to get past—was the objection that we offered students too many choices. Initially, the PSC told us that they would be more comfortable with the proposal if, instead of being given many choices in each category, all students would be required to take the same courses. It took us some time to realize what the committee was getting at.

We noted on multiple occasions that we expected that students would come to the study of civic engagement from a variety of experiences and majors, with a variety of motivations, and at different times during their tenure at UMass. We said that we approached the challenge of educating college students to be citizens from the perspective that everyone benefits from this kind of education and that scientists, financiers, teachers, and artists ought to be citizens too. We argued that core courses insured that students would come out of the program with a common core of knowledge and competencies (though not necessarily precisely the same knowledge or experience); yet, they had room within that structure to customize their curriculum to meet their specific needs (e.g., their exposure to public policy might be from the perspective of environmental science, urban planning, political science, or social justice, based on their backgrounds and interests). We noted that other UMass certificates, for example, the Certificate in International Agricultural Studies or the Public Policy and Administration Certificate, were also menu-driven and not tied to a a rigid curriculum (though all, except for the Certificate in Culture, Health and Science, do appear to have a required core of courses that everyone must take). And while public service majors and minors were (and still are) not common around the country, menu-driven minors, certificates, and majors were found in other public service programs. We emphasized that what we were proposing was neither radical nor outside of the range of existing examples and provided a list of existing programs with core competencies that very much resembled ours.

Unfortunately, the PSC was not persuaded by this rebuttal. They returned to the intellectual coherence argument, saying that there was no way that (to use their examples) courses in theraputic horseback riding, community journalism, and community theater could present the same material and hence fulfill the same requirement. They argued that there could be no equivalence among such widely disparate courses, suggesting that the requirements themselves had little integrity. We responded that all these courses fulfilled our praxis requirement and that, despite their disparate content, they shared (1) an introduction to the method and theory of civic engagement; (2) the experience of bringing theory to practice by applying classroom learning in a community setting to address a specific community need; and (3) the development of a regular practice of reflection connecting thought and action and requiring students to think about how their work fit into the larger society.

The concern over too many choices also stemmed from a concern about consistency and quality control and a fear that students' taking "a random set of courses" might not end up making much sense. We argued that there was no chance of this happening within our proposed framework because our categories offered considerable structure and coherence. In addition, a PCSL subcommittee had been designated to serve as a body of advisors to support certificate students and help them make informed choices. The PCSL had also agreed to assume responsibility for the academic oversight of the certificate and to review and revise the list of approved courses every other year. Hence, there would be a continuous process of quality control by a body representing all sectors of the campus.

Two additional objections did not take up as much of our time but still merit mention.

## Social Justice

We understand that the social justice requirement has been a point of contention on other campuses, but we ran into only minimal opposition to it at UMass Amherst. The objection, which was couched in euphemism, went like this: social justice is only of interest to "certain kinds" of students. It's a narrow and highly politicized topic that doesn't have the academic standing of, say, civics. It can be an alienating topic, one that makes "other kinds" of students uncomfortable, so it doesn't seem reasonable to make it a requirement. And social justice politicizes work in a way that may push students into activism for causes that they do not believe in. Hence, a social justice requirement is unnecessarily coercive and should be abandoned, or at least made optional. Objectors also noted that our campus had recently been singled out by David Horowitz (2011) as one of the most intolerant environments for conservative students in the country and suggested that a program that foregrounded social justice might invite further national opprobrium.

During our creation of both the certificate and a major track in civic engagement (see www.umass.edu/bdic/civx), we purposefully and forthrightly engaged colleagues who raised the concerns noted above. Those objecting were mostly politically conservative colleagues who eventually acknowledged that they feared we were setting up a space to advance a liberal agenda, from which conservative students would be excluded or within which they would be marginalized or disenfranchised. Other colleagues, largely positivists, subscribed to a notion of intellectual neutrality and objected to any enterprise that would undermine the objectivity of scholarly inquiry by injecting a political orientation. Some of these arguments followed the lines of Stanley Fish's complaint (2008) that it is not the job of students and their teachers to save the world, and that they should solve the world's problems on their own time.

Our approach to these objections fell into three broad areas and can be summarized as follows:

1. We noted that part of the objection to the inclusion of social justice was epistemological. We acknowledged colleagues' concerns but also noted that what was being contested were beliefs about how knowledge is constructed, what constitutes an education, and the purpose of the university. We argued that while epistemological debates have always been part of the university and of disciplinary practice, it was inappropriate for the committee to try to force us to embrace an epistemological position at odds with how we had always done our work and with our understandings of how knowledge is created and what it means to be educated. That is, we argued that there are matters on which we must agree to disagree.

2. We acknowledged our stated goal of trying to prepare our students to live a life of engagement in a vibrant and diverse democracy. We underscored the current timeliness of such a goal given the diminishing civic understanding among the current generation of college students. We underscored our intention to serve students from all political orientations, and to provide them with the knowledge, skills, and experience that would enable them to be active in their communities, embrace their own agency, and work on issues they cared about. We offered examples of conservative students who had gone through our flagship programs and had positive experiences.

3. At the same time, we were unapologetic in arguing that we live in a world in which there is considerable human suffering and in which our well-being is interdeterminate. We explained our position that it is in the interest of every citizen to understand the sources of prejudice, oppression, and injustice and the things people can do to address these sources of human misery. While this may reflect a progressive disposition, we do not see it as a form of liberal indoctrination but rather something at the core of liberal arts education. Knowledge of justice and of people unlike ourselves (diverse publics) engages core questions of what it means to be human, what kind of world we wish to live in, and how our lives and actions are tied to consequences. We argued that formal exposure to social justice ought to be part of everyone's education. And we noted that although UMass has a long-established two-course diversity requirement, the university does not require a specific course in social justice.

In the end, the concerns of our colleagues were assauged, although they were perhaps still suspicious. Nonetheless they passed the proposal, asking only that we change the title of the requirement from "Social Justice" to "Issues in Social Justice."

## Confidence

We want to mention one final objection, not because it was particularly substantial but because it was so intractable. Citing all the objections we reviewed above, the adminstration's representative on the committee argued that it was hard for him to have confidence that we could actually deliver what we were promising to the students. That is, we had specified some desirable outcomes. But why, he asked, should he believe that the program as proposed could deliver those outcomes? We asked him what might instill that confidence. He responded that answering that question was our job, not his, and that we had yet to offer any information or argument that was compelling. Fortunately, in this instance we had concrete supportive data because the program curriculum, as we noted above, was derived from the curriculum of the CSP, which was then in its twelfth year. Although the CSP does not offer the same range of choices as the certificate, the categories of competencies are identical, and the CSP has a long record of assessment (Polin & Keene, 2010; Mitchell et al., 2011), is the subject of an ongoing longitudinal study (Visconti, Mitchell, Battistoni, Reiff & Keene, 2010), and has specified 17 explicit desired outcomes (Polin & Keene, 2010, pp. 35–37) that it succeeds in fulfilling for its graduates. The CSP, we said, offered us substantial reasons to believe that the curriculum was well designed to produce the civic outcomes we seek. And our track record of ongoing assessment and evaluation supported our commitment to the ongoing evaluation of our students and their work in reference to our desired outcomes. Hence, previous work in the CSP offered substantive reasons for having confidence in the program.

## The Compromises

After considerable engagement, we were presented with a series of requests for specific compromises. We found two of these requests to be reasonable or sympathetic to the professed goals of our program, and these were adopted in whole or in part. However, two others did violence to the intent of the program, and we firmly rejected them, explainining why they were not consistent with or supportive of our goals. Following our embrace of two of the four requested compromises, we revised and resubmitted the proposal, and within 30 days it sailed through the PSC, the AMC, and the Faculty Senate without further objection. We briefly summarize below the two compromises that we adopted.

*Foundations course.* The first compromise request was to add a foundations course to the program. It was framed as a desire to ameliorate the PSC's concern that there was no common foundation of knowledge that all students completing the curriculum would share. The PSC reasoned that if there was an intellectual core for CSL or civic engagement, then all students seeking the certificate should begin the quest with a common introduction. We had long desired to offer a general introduction to CSL/CE on the UMass campus but lacked the resources to offer it beyond a few small sections within the Honors College. So we were immediately sympathetic to the request but had not pursued the idea because we saw it as beyond our means. We countered with a compromise. We noted that many of the students seeking this certificate would come from our four flagship service-leadership programs, each of which had its own gateway course. We noted that while the curricula in each of these programs was not identical, there was substantial overlap in the knowledge, skills, and attitudes that were promoted in these four gateway courses. We embraced the idea of a gateway course with the following objectives:

- Connecting topical course content to out-of-classroom experiences
- Promoting skills and knowledge necessary to engage in effective service, including preparation to work in a community that is not one's own
- Understanding differences between charity-based service and justice-based service
- Exploring modes of critical reflection
- Developing skills of interpersonal and inter-group dialogue
- Debating the role that service can or ought to play in addressing social problems
- Introducing work in social identity and positionality
- Providing a preliminary introduction of social justice and systems of power, privilege, and oppression as a basis for exploring difference in American society
- Developing the skills necessary to work in a community unlike one's own

Because each of our campus's four service-based leadership programs has its own comprehensive foundation course, we proposed that any one of the four courses should suffice to fulfill the foundation requirement. In addition, we pointed out that the Commonwealth Honors College offers a general foundations course in community service learning (Engaging with the Community) for students not enrolled in any of the aforementioned programs, and we proposed that this course should fulfill the requirement as well. We noted our desire to offer additional foundational courses when resources become available. We proposed that in the meantime students from the general population who, after taking a couple of CSL courses, found that they wanted to pursue the certificate and who could clearly demonstrate that they had accumulated the equivalent of the foundation knowledge in their other CSL experiences could petition the PCSL to have other course work accepted retroactively in lieu of the foundation course.

*Capstone course:* The PSC also requested that every person seeking the certificate be required to complete a capstone course. Although this is not a requirement for any of the existing interdisciplinary certificates at UMass, all UMass students must complete an upper–level integrative-experience course that ties together their general education courses. We thus saw the capstone request as consistent with general curricular trends at UMass. The idea of a culminating experience that requires the student to make the connections among the disparate threads of their learning made sense to us. The CSP (on which the certificate curriculum is based) already required a demanding, year-long capstone course combining policy research and community organizing in service to an established community partnership. We readily embraced the capstone concept, but noted that we did not have the resources to create new capstone experiences for everyone electing the certificate. We therefore designated seven existing service-based capstone courses (four in honors and three in anthropology) to fulfill the certificate. We also specified an individualized option, allowing students to fulfill the capstone requirement by planning and completing an approved internship with a community-based organization including both an advisor-approved project and a considerable reflective component, or by completing an independent-study capstone course approved by the PCSL. We also committed to seeking additional courses to fulfill the capstone in the coming years.

## Administrative and Procedural Objections

One aim of the approval process is to expose unforeseen administrative and procedural shortcomings. All proposals for new programs must demonstrate the availability of sufficient resources to support the program. In our case this would require, among other things, demonstration of our capacity to staff our courses, our advising, and our program administration. Any new program must demonstrate that the program can be fulfilled in a reasonable amount of time (we suggested four semesters) and without requiring extraordinary measures. We offered multiple models of how students could accomplish this with regular course offerings. Throughout the process we were challenged on a number of procedural and administrative matters, many of which we had anticipated in advance. These concerns were mostly routine and not especially interesting, and it was easy enough to address them. Because of space limitations, we will not explore them any further in this paper.

## An Analysis of The Objections

In the appendix to this chapter, we offer a mapping tool, "Tool for New Program Creation," to help map out the process of approving a new program. The tool illustrates the kinds of things that proposers ought to take into consideration and poses questions that will help proposers get the information they need to move forward and to anticipate and effectively navigate the bumps in the road, regardless of the unique features of their campus cultures. In the previous section we outlined some of the prominent bumps in our own road. But we have not yet considered why we encountered those particular objections and what they meant to the objectors and to us. As social scientists, we can't help but ask, Why do people take the positions that they do and what kinds of meanings do they assign to their own actions and to ours? Part of the frustration of this process was that when we asked our interlocutors to clarify their meanings or intentions, they were often perplexed by the request. As we note below, we believe that they were not always clear with themselves about what bothered them or about the unstated assumptions governing their assessments. We might say that whereas we saw our debates as a struggle over meanings and purposes, they possibly saw what we were doing as a struggle over procedures and prerogatives. We can't be sure because we were unable to produce much engagement in these terms. It is something we hope to explore further with some of the primary actors now that the approval process is behind us. We briefly review some of our thoughts about underlying meanings and motivations below.

*Disciplinarity.* Much of our effort to advance the proposal was tied up with our gatekeepers' perception that CSL/CE is not a scholarly field but a pedagogy, and that it lacks a recognized canon or intellectual core. We have offered some narrative and tactics that can be used to rebut this argument, but it is useful to consider where the argument comes from. We believe it emanates from the hegemony of disciplinarity. For our adversaries at least, the legitimacy of what we do in, for example, anthropology stems from our standing as a recognized discipline as much as from our body of scholarship. And of course it is for this reason that Butin (2010a; Butin, 2010b) has called for formalizing CSL or CE as an academic discipline. Our certificate proposal challenges the conventional thinking that disciplines are the only way to organize intellectual or educational labor or to constitute an education or to vet preparation for the contemporary world. Our proposal elided boundaries that are quite actively defended in the academy and are part of its common sense. It emphasized collaboration, border crossing, complementarity, collaborative relationships, applied work, and the search for common cause in praxis, and this grates against conventional conceptions of how a university ought to work (including the very real consequences and benefits of departmental territoriality). It strikes us that our adversaries were constantly pushing to make the certificate more closely resemble a conventional, discipline-based major or minor. Some of the resistance to our vision, it seems to us, stemmed from the PSC's inability or unwillingness to embrace the clearly stated objectives of the program, which are foremost to prepare students across the campus for a life of active citizenship and civic engagement and to give them meaningful experiences that allow them to connect the work in their major(s) to their lives as citizens. This is not simply interdisciplinary work; it is also metadisciplinary work. Remarkably, some of our strongest allies in promoting the certificate, the department chairs in anthropology, political science and public policy, might have seen what we were doing as encroachment on their turf. But they did not. We met with each of them early in the process and emphasized our common interest in preparing students for a life of active citizenship. We highlighted the essential contributions that each department could make to that end, and they supported the proposal.

*Standardization, Epistemology, and Neoliberalism.* We believe that the PSC's concerted effort to force us to adopt a standard curriculum raises fundamental questions about what we are vetting when we give a credential and to whom we are being responsible. In retrospect, we believe that the example offered by our adversaries—that students taking courses in community journalism, therapeutic horseback riding, and community theater would have totally different experiences—is telling. Their fear was that the curriculum did not produce a standard (and we believe they meant a measurable) outcome. And how could the credential have any credibility or value if it could not produce standard, replicable results? We think they believed that these three courses could not legitimately fulfill the same requirement since the students would be learning different things. As we noted, the thread that links those courses and, indeed, all of our praxis courses is praxis—a combination of method and theory and civic engagement. The courses produce an overlapping set of skills but not identical skills or knowledge sets. In retrospect, we believe that the impasse over a fixed versus a menu-driven curriculum, and the concern over too many choices, reflects fundamental differences about what we think needs to happen in the classroom. We believe in retrospect that the principal objection here was that our program would not yield a standard result in the sense that one could, in the neoliberal sense of testing and standards (Ravitch, 2010), determine whether everyone had come out mastering the same knowledge base. We cannot produce, nor would we desire to do so, an end product that resembles a final exam in say, Physics. And we suspect that this was the itch that continued to trouble the PSC. This was never clearly stated to us, but it does strike us as a likely subtext of our debates. We of course argued persistently that our students would all come out with a broad set of skills and sufficient knowledge to facilitate a lifetime of engagement, and that this would likely look somewhat different for a rocket scientist and a studio artist. This reasoning never sat well with our opposition, and we believe it is because they brought with them the epistemological frame of testing and standards that is central to the current educational reform movement and to the explosive neoliberalization of education (Giroux, 2011). We now think that this impasse was fundamentally about epistemology and the philosophy of education, but because we never really identified the objections as such during the negotiations, we only obliquely spoke about education and philosophy. These differences (as we hinted above in our discussion of social justice) may be irreconcilable, but it certainly helps to be clear about what one is debating. If what is really being contested is epistemology or what it means to be educated, it helps to say so. At least we can be clear about what it is about which we do not agree.

### Lessons Learned and Advice To Colleagues

Our advice is pretty simple and perhaps intuitively obvious to CSL faculty and staff who are already engaged in a practice of service and partnership building and organizing. Our advice is to bring those same skills of engagement to promoting your proposal.

1. *Know your campus culture, and use it.* We took our desired outcomes and framed them in the language of campus strategic mandates. For example, we could demonstrate a substantial student demand for the credential, and hence we addressed an administrative concern about marketing (without pandering) to student desires. We noted that CSL/CE were increasingly becoming part of the UMass brand (we are the only multicampus system in the country at which every campus has received the Carnegie Community Engaged classification), and our unique programs could draw out-of-state students (addressing mandates to enhance national recognition and to increase out-of-state enrollments and therefore revenues). For us, adopting strategic objectives and language does not subvert our aim of educating for citizenship in a democracy. Rather, by also using language that is consistent with current administrative mandates, we are able to show how our work is allied with addressing some of the university's most pressing strategic needs. That is, we

are able to demonstrate that there is considerable breadth to the benefits that will accrue from this program.

2. *Know the process of approval.* The process of adoption will vary by campus, and each will have its own peculiar politics. Know the steps, gatekeepers, actors, expectations, and experiences of those who came before you. (We were heartened by the story of a colleague who proposed a minor in Information Technology; it was held up for two years by the same subcommittee, and then, after clearing the subcommittee, moved rapidly through the rest of the process. Its approval by the Faculty Senate received a standing ovation.)

3. *Approach the initiative as a problem in community organizing.* Think strategically about your end goal, and design tactics to reach the goal. Prepare by using the mapping tool that we provide in the Appendix (which we used more or less intuitively and then wrote up at the end of our process). Know who the gatekeepers are at various stages of the process and what their interests are. Identify and enlist allies and work purposefully to win over potential adversaries. Seek common ground. Anticipate bumps in the road.

4. *Organize external support proactively.* Bring in as much expert testimony and scholarly documentation as you can. We did this, but we could have done more. And the external letters from nationally prominent experts in CSL seemed to make a difference and to disarm many of the arguments about intellectual integrity.

5. *Provide lots of rationale for what you are doing.* Our campus process requires concision in the formal proposal, but being concise subjected us to multiple rounds of questions and concerns that we could have and should have anticipated. When we pre-emptively provided too much information or background and anticipated objections, we had smoother sailing, even if people grumbled about the volume of our documentation.

6. *Curriculum development is central, and it takes time.* Know what you want to accomplish and why. Be clear in your own thinking about the rationale for your curriculum. Our program was many years in the making. We had explored and developed the curriculum over a decade within the Citizen Scholars Program. We had spent nearly two decades rehearsing the arguments about social justice and the legitimacy of bringing social and political analysis and action into our classrooms and our service. We sought feedback from other advanced practitioners. We had a strong understanding of what we were doing and why, and this not only allowed us to stand firm on issues when we needed to but also enabled us to recognize fruitful compromises when they presented themselves. But because we had a strong sense of what we wanted to accomplish and what we needed to do to get there, and because it was grounded in a lot of thoughtful previous work, we were able to avoid being forced into compromises that threatened the integrity of the project. Because we had laid the groundwork for addressing what is a controversial issue on many campuses well in advance of submitting our proposal, it was pretty much a nonissue for us. But on campuses where proposers can expect harsh critiques, for example, those that demand neutrality, it makes sense to develop well-reasoned strategic arguments in advance. It is our position that

you can't very well prepare students for a life of engaged citizenship without the skills to understand political and economic systems, without a strong foundation in theories of justice, and without exposure to how a wide range of communities experience life in this country. And so we take a stand on that, even though some colleagues might see such a stance as straying from some imagined ideal of neutrality.

7. *Getting approval is just the beginning.* Now we need to attend to promotion, advising, and sustaining the program. Don't forget about this when planning a program.

8. *Emphasize the benefits of your program to specific constituencies.* Deans tend to ask: how does this help my unit? We claimed that it enhanced the experience of their students, allowed students to connect work in their own majors to their lives as citizens, and produced transformative experiences that increased student satisfaction and positive identification with the major, college, or campus. And we could do this without diminishing enrollments or costing the deans any money. Hence, there was good reason to get on board.

The mapping tool follows below in the chapter appendix. We recommend that proposing a new program be viewed as a campaign. Planning the campaign requires being able to answer all of the questions in the tool. We probably could not have answered half at the start of our own process, so if we had made this tool at the beginning, our story might be much shorter. We encourage our readers to take a look and see how well they can do.

## References

Addes, D. & Keene, A. (2006). Grassroots community development at UMass-Amherst: The professorless classroom. In E. Zlotkowski, N. Longo, & J. Williams (eds.), *Students as colleagues: Expanding the circle of service-learning leadership* (pp. 227–40). Boston: Campus Compact.

Butin, D. (2010a). *Service learning in theory and practice: The future of community engagement in higher education.* New York: Palgrave McMillan.

———. (2010b). "Can I major in service-learning?" An empirical analysis of certificates, minors, and majors. *Journal of College & Character, 11*(2).

Colby, A., Beaumont, E., Ehrlich, T. & Corngold, J. (2007) *Educating for democracy: Preparing undergraduates for responsible political engagement.* San Francisco: Jossey-Bass/ Carnegie Foundation for the Advancement of Teaching.

Fish, S. (2008). *Save the world on your own time.* New York: Oxford University Press.

Giroux, H. (2011). Neoliberal politics as failed sociality: Youth and the crisis of higher education. *Logos #2.* http://logosjournal.com/2011/neoliberal-politics-as-failed-sociality-youth-and-the-crisis-of-higher-education.

Horowitz, D. (2011). How bad is the indoctrination at our colleges? *Frontpagemag.com.* http://frontpagemag.com/2010/03/02/indoctrination-in-american-colleges/.

Mitchell, T., Visconti, V., Keene, A., & Battistoni, R. (2011). Educating for democratic leadership at Stanford, UMass and Providence College. In C. Gibson & N. Longo (eds.), *From command to community: A new approach to leadership education in colleges and universities* (pp.115–48). Medford, MA: Tufts University Press.

Morton, K. (1995, Fall). The irony of service: Charity, project and social change in service learning. *Michigan Journal of Community Service Learning, 2(1),* 119–32.

———. (1997). Campus and community at Providence College. In *Expanding the boundaries: Building civic responsibility within higher education. Volume 2,* (pp. 8–12). Providence, RI: Campus Compact.

Polin, D. & Keene, A. (2010). Bringing an ethnographic sensibility to service learning assessment. *Michigan Journal of Community Service Learning, Spring,* 22–37.

Ravitch, D. (2010). *The death and life of the great American school system: How testing and choice are undermining rducation.* New York: Basic Books.

Visconti, V., Mitchell, T., Battistoni, R., Reiff, J., & Keene, A. (2010, October). *Civic identity in the real world: How multi-term undergraduate civic engagement programs impact civic action after college.* Panel presented at the Annual Conference of the International Association for Research on Service-Learning and Civic Engagement. Indianapolis, IN.

## Appendix

## Tool for New Program Creation Institute
## June 26, 2011

### Part I: Curriculum Design

1. What are the GOALS of the curriculum?
2. What are the components of the curriculum necessary to achieve these goals?
3. How does the curriculum represent intellectual coherence?
4. How does each element contribute to a desired outcome?
5. Administrative management systems
   A. Who does the advising for the program?
   B. Who vets the curriculum and the addition or subtraction of courses to the curriculum?
   C. Who oversees/decides on exceptions/transfers/waivers or equivalencies?
   D. Who tracks student progress through the program?
   E. Who ultimately evaluates each student's progress and grants the credential?
   F. Who promotes and advertises the program and takes responsibility for recruitment?

### PART II: Institutional Analysis

1. CONSTITUENCIES OR STAKEHOLDERS
   A. Who are potential allies to this program? What are their interests?
      i. Faculty allies
      ii. Administrative allies
      iii. Community allies
      iv. Student allies
      v. Expert witnesses
   B. Who are the gatekeepers that govern the process of approval? What are their interests?

    C. Who are potential adversaries and what are their interests?

    D. Who are known adversaries and what are their interests?

2. INSTITUTIONAL CULTURE
   A. What is your campus mission and how does service learning (SL) or civic engagement (CE) align with that mission?
   B. How does SL or CE align with/enhance other campus-wide initiatives that have administrative support?
   C. What is the state of knowledge about SL/CE on your campus? How much education about the field is necessary? What is the attitude about experiential learning and academic credit (e.g., is there a tradition of granting credit only for work that happens in a classroom)?
   D. What are the steps in the process of getting a new program approved?
      i. What is the sequence of steps?
      ii. Which bodies need to weigh in for approval, and who on those bodies are likely to be allies or adversaries?
      iii. What paperwork is necessary? Can you review recent examples of successful proposals?
      iv. What kind of narrative is expected (how much explanation is enough and how much is too much)?
      v. Where does the critical decision really happen?
      vi. What objections can be anticipated and from whom?
         1) Administrative/technical
         2) Intellectual (including epistemological)
         3) Resources/turf
      vii. What responses can you prepare in anticipation of the objections listed above?
   E. History – how have similar proposals fared in the past? What can be learned from those experiences?

3. What RESOURCES are necessary to implement this curriculum effectively?
   A. What resources would you ideally want to have?
   B. What's possible given the current realities of your institution?
   C. Do you have access to new resources not currently in play?
   D. Are sufficient seats/classes available so that a student can complete the curriculum in a reasonable amount of time?
   E. Provide one or more models of a pathway to completion for students situated in different majors and/or colleges.

4. What is the CONSTITUENCY for your program (among students, prospective students, faculty, administrators, and community members)? (Research the anticipated market demand for this program and support with data.)

5. Are there places where your proposal will BREAK NEW GROUND? (For each precedent-setting aspect of your proposal, a detailed rationale should be provided, objections should be anticipated and a preemptive strong case should be made for that particular aspect of the proposal.)

6. VALUE ADDED. How does adding this new program enhance the mission, image, standing, or brand of the campus? If an interdisciplinary program, how does it add value to specific majors? How does it enhance or complement existing programs?

## PART III: Notes on Strategy

1. Set the table.
   i. Do the institutional analysis in Part II and use it to design your strategy.
   ii. Identify successful models from other campuses—especially those that represent the kind of institution your campus aspires to be. Also acquaint yourself with the scholarship on such programs and on SL/CE in general.
   iii. Outreach to allies to line up support. Collect letters of endorsement (both internal and external). Make a case for how your program benefits other constituencies across campus.
   iv. Outreach to potential adversaries to preemptively address concerns. Your aim is to enlist them as allies or at least get them to commit to remaining neutral.
   v. Precirculate a draft of proposal to key players to gauge their reactions.
   vi. Collect stories of SL/CE student successes and use them to support the proposal.
2. If you hit active opposition, evaluate whether compromise is possible or whether it threatens the integrity of the proposed program.
3. Be persistent. If you hit obstacles, create a response and come back. Again and again...

# CHAPTER 5

# Process, Content, and Community Building

*Keith Morton*
Providence College

## *Overview*

In 1993 Providence College (a Catholic, undergraduate liberal arts college operated by the Dominican Friars, located in Providence, Rhode Island) piloted concept courses for a new major and minor in public and community service studies (PSP) under the administrative umbrella of its just-founded Feinstein Institute for Public Service (FIPS). This chapter provides a brief overview of the major, focusing on the conceptual framework it embodies; describes how ongoing reflection based on the experiences of alumni and community partners allow for coherence and diversity in the curriculum; and discusses the ongoing "interpretation" of community partnerships that is central to its work. The chapter closes by describing how an understanding of community as relationship is leading to an understanding of service-learning as an integrated system of learning processes shared by campus and community, an understanding that is gradually replacing a view of service-learning as a collaboration across separate systems of campus and community systems.

## *Introduction*

The founding of the Feinstein Institute for Public Service and the major in Public and Community Service Studies (FIPS/PSP) has been well documented by William Hudson and Robert Trudeau (1995), and the design of the PSP curriculum by Rick Battistoni (1998). Focused on the "problems" of community, service, and democracy, and supported by a $5 million grant from Rhode Island philanthropist Alan Shawn Feinstein, PSP and FIPS were intentionally organized as academically situated service-learning initiatives, framed by higher education's growing interest in service and civic engagement. A research team composed of eight faculty and three students, advised by four community partners, developed the curriculum from the ground up as an interdisciplinary, developmental, experientially grounded, liberal arts major. The college approved the PSP curriculum in 1995, the first minors graduated in 1996, and the first majors in 1997. Through 2011, 144 majors and 138 minors have graduated from Providence College with a degree in Public and Community Service Studies (Registrar, 2011).

At the time they were writing about the founding of FIPS/PSP, Hudson and Trudeau were full professors of political science and members of the original research and planning team; Hudson had also served as FIPS's acting director during its 1993–4 pilot year. They predicted Providence College's institutional embrace of service-learning and deep community engagement. "Institutions that define themselves in terms of a distinct tradition, whether based on religion or a particular historical experience," they wrote, "might provide the most fertile ground for service-learning" (Hudson and Trudeau, 1995, p. 157). This appeared true, as service and citizenship were values reflected in the college's mission statement, but Providence College's "distinct tradition" as the only college in the United States operated by Catholic, Dominican Friars, also placed the major in tension with institutionalized understandings of academic rigor, service as "selfless" charity, and diversity.

### Process and Content: Major, Minor, and Pedagogy

While some of the more ambitious programmatic ideas of FIPS advanced very slowly through 2005 because of tensions with the executive leadership of the college, the faculty, students, and community partners designing the PSP curriculum were conscious from the outset that it was arguably the "first" degree-granting academic program of its kind. The major they conceived was new in its combination of student leadership development; ethics, values clarification, and reflection; community service experiences (in courses, practicum, internship, capstone); and its focus on "problematizing" practices of community, service, and citizenship. All these elements were organized into a major of 14 courses and a minor of six courses.

The fundamental puzzle the committee grappled with in establishing the new curriculum was differentiating process and content: arguably, service-learning is a process integrating action and reflection, described in what were established and rapidly growing literatures on experiential learning, popular education and organizational leadership (Kendall, 1990; Schön, 1983; Kolb, 1984; Chickering & Reiser, 1993; Kupiec, 1993; Horton, Kohl & Kohl, 1997; Freire, 1970). That is, it is a process for inserting a purpose into any course by using the knowledge base of the course to positively impact a community problem and a process of learning from experience (based on the skills of observation, interpretation, and action, as well as the life histories and interests of participants) to achieve that purpose. From this perspective, service-learning is a meaning-making process grounded in shared experience. If service-learning is a process, the committee asked, then what content will support each course and a curriculum? And if public and community service is a field of study, what should its students know?

The committee located their answers in the broader arguments regarding civic engagement that were coalescing into a movement. Inspired by Frank Newman's

(1985) Carnegie-supported *Higher Education and the American Resurgence*; Robert Bellah and colleagues' (1985) *Habits of the Heart*; Robert Coles' (1994) *Call of Service*; de Tocqueville's (1835/1840) *Democracy in America*; the National Society for Experiential Education's (Kendall, 1990) *Combining Service and Learning;* and Campus Compact's (Kupiec,1993) *Rethinking Tradition: Integrating Service with Academic Study on College Campuses*, the committee argued that "[t]he Major is a systematic and rigorous study, in the liberal arts tradition, of four major conceptual themes: 1) community 2) service 3) change (or: social change) 4) leadership" (Research Committee, May 1994, p.1). Early syllabi from the program's introductory course (Morton, 1998) reflect the committee's ongoing efforts to answer these questions: "How are you a citizen? What is higher education's role in 'preparing citizens' for participation in local, national and global democratic culture? What does community service have to do, if anything, with being a citizen?"

The tension between process and content remained, however, emerging with sharper definition over time. Service and citizenship are actions, framed by choices, themselves framed by values. Over time the content of the major and minor focused increasingly on experience and reflection, with reflection understood as a way of sorting out values, meaning, and action—the ingredients of personal practices of citizenship and the bridge into effective public work.

Even though they were becoming more comfortable emphasizing process, the experiences faculty and students were having resisted fitting neatly into the narrower framework of citizenship. In the "Irony of Service" (Morton, 1995) I attempted to describe an alternative typology to "politicizing" students through service-learning (often articulated as "moving them from charity to justice"), arguing that people tend to hold differing values and commitments that lead them to serve other individuals, local communities, or more abstract "publics" in different ways (charity, project, change), with lesser or greater depth and integrity. The major point, however, was that any narrow construction or interpretation of service, or any attempt to limit it to the frame of citizenship, was likely to contain the seeds of its own contradiction.

Another partial response to the tension between process and content emerged in the description of "service as text" (Morton, 1996), which I crafted as a strong metaphor intended to collapse the tension by arguing that experiences minimally meeting criteria described in John Dewey's (1938) *Experience and Education*—were content: messier, co-created, nearly simultaneous with interpretation, but content nonetheless.

As our group of practitioners began to focus on integrating intention and action, reimagined experience as content, and viewed learning as the product of reflecting on experience, we changed our curriculum in subtle ways. Our approaches to teaching were increasingly deliberate and faithful to a shared process, and more differentiated by how each of us was making sense of the experiential "ground" of service. The content of courses—the context, texts, and assignments—began to reflect the types of experiences and questions that interested individual faculty, even as the courses shared a consistent process. Multiple sections of the introductory course, for example, would choose very different service sites and questions as their point of departure. Each section of PSP 101 would require an average of 30 hours of service at one of 3–4 sites; each would require 4–8 written reflections of 3–5 pages; each would require student presentations. The classrooms were arranged in circles, emphasizing discussion. One section would "read" a neighborhood adjacent to the campus. Another would investigate urban public schools. A third would explore poverty. A fourth would concentrate on cross-cultural dialogue and the ethical and moral dilemmas that surface in biography and autobiography.

One product of the growing emphasis on experience and reflection was a tool that helped to unify the curriculum, an exercise that came to be called the "philosophy of service." This was a deceptively simple exercise, devised early on for senior PSP majors. Capstone students were asked to write their own "philosophy of service" and to formally share this with faculty, staff, other students, community partners, and other meaningful people in their lives. Typically, it would be a brief statement of core values followed by a longer, often autobiographical, commentary. This assignment was repeated regardless of who was teaching the Capstone seminar with the expectation that it was a useful, if somewhat crude, indicator of what students had learned.

By 1998, we had agreed to also make the philosophy of service an assignment in PSP 101, the introductory course. We collected the philosophies from all students taking PSP 101 and returned them to PSP majors in Capstone. Students near graduation would typically find that their fundamental beliefs and interests in service had not changed much at their root. They would, however, have called those values and interests into consciousness, deliberately chosen them, and been able to use them in building the relationships that were central to their service and the pursuits they intended after college. They would also tend to see their past "self" as naïve. Whereas at the outset they tended to believe in the inherent and obvious "rightness" of their intentions, now they understood that their perspective was one of many available, that advancing what they saw as a positive agenda could be contentious and often unpredictable. Jessica Cigna (Capstone Seminar, 2001) opened the essay accompanying her philosophy of service by saying, "As a young and naïve high school graduate, I was resting on my laurels entering the Feinstein Institute as a Public Service major....It is interesting to look back [four years] to my old reflections, to see my progression. I often wrote about communication and relationships, but I feel that I always missed the point, somehow." Brooke Huminski (Capstone Seminar, 2007) wrote: "As I progressed in my years at Providence College, I changed locations and settings in my volunteer placements, but the question was still the same, why do people suffer? I wondered, 'What is so universal about suffering, in its different forms and degrees?'"

### Diversity and Unity in the Curriculum

Even as our decision-making process has remained very collegial, democratic, and consensual in FIPS and PSP, and as we have articulated a shared process, individual faculty bring to their engagement a multiplicity of core values, disciplinary backgrounds, and life experiences that lead them to diverse perspectives and so to different ways of "being in the problem." One perspective has focused increasingly on student ownership of the learning process, treating the classroom as a community and as a hub for personal reflection and action; another explores what I would characterize as a more "therapeutic" perspective for linking self and community, with a particular interest in persons who are excluded from participation; a third frames the situation in terms of practical problems that attend "doing good," emphasizing the institutional realities (especially the resources and organizational structures) of the nonprofit sector and how to negotiate them; and a final perspective is increasingly committed to an exploration of alternative, deliberately countercultural experiments in community building, shaped in part by interests in ecology, nonviolence, and cultural change.

## Student-centered

This approach is perhaps the most explicitly theorized within PSP, framed by faculty members Rick Battisoni and Nick Longo (2011) who write: "When we talk about building student civic agency through the practice of democracy, it means including students in the planning, development, and implementation of civic engagement opportunities" (p. 205). Emphasizing voice and listening as core competencies, the student-centered approach is interested in the nature of relationships between faculty and student, student and student, and with community partners. It is significantly influenced by the democratic and liberatory pedagogies of Jane Addams, Myles Horton, Paulo Freire, and many others (Longo, 2007), with a goal of making education a process for personal and communal development and freedom. From this perspective, education is a process that helps people discover their voices and, to use Nell Morton's phrase, "hear others into speech" (Morton, N., 1985, p.128). It is one powerful way that people discover their self-interest and their vision of the future, and so is itself a profoundly democratic and civic practice. It starts from the idea that the challenge of realizing ourselves as full human beings begins with being able to self-consciously tell our own stories and make meaning in our lives. This challenge is also faced by people in the broader community, and community partnerships are designed to "co-create" meaning. And there is a grace note in the student-centered approach of a more formally critical pedagogy—influenced by semiotics—that calls attention to the provisional nature of meaning and challenges the hegemonic dimensions of institutional systems that lead us away from authenticity.

## Therapeutic

What I call the therapeutic approach is influenced most heavily by the realities and demands of the "helping professions," particularly social work, with an emphasis on being present to people experiencing a given problem, understanding how that problem is manifest, and searching for practical ways to provide relief or resolution. The emphasis is on helping and on the development of robust, specialized knowledge and skills that make helping real and minimize unintended side effects. It emphasizes a more technical approach, a combination of "systems knowledge" of problems and the ability to respond to individuals experiencing those problems. Most often, the emphasis is on helping particular persons: mitigating harm and restoring wholeness. The therapeutic approach is also concerned with the ethics of role definition between served and servant, paying particular attention to imbalances of power and dependence and independence in helping relationships. While conscious of and adaptive to structural inequalities or violence, such as poverty or racism, a therapeutic approach asks, What can be done here and now to mitigate suffering and create opportunity? It seems to me to take as given the "modern" condition of communal disintegration and alienation described by Alan Wolfe (1989) and to concentrate on providing assistance within this context, most often by working within nonprofit, human service institutions. In particular, within our program, the question becomes one of relationship: whereas a student-centered approach emphasizes co-creation, the therapeutic approach accepts that the relationship between caregiver and client, or server and served, will adhere to formal boundaries intended to protect the privacy and autonomy of each. In other words, the initial emphasis is on responding to the problems caused by the crisis of community, rather than building community over time. For students and faculty, this means using community engagement and the classroom to develop technical skills, discover and try on professional roles, and articulate and work within "logic models" that describe problems or needs, interventions, and measurable ways of assessing impact.

### Doing good and servant leadership

The perspective of servant leadership describes as a starting point our collective responsibility for one another and explores how to successfully embody that responsibility in a variety of arenas—including philanthropy—often articulated in terms of "servant leadership" (Greenleaf, 1970). It describes the institutional systems of voluntarism, philanthropy, and the helping professions, and emphasizes increasing the capacity of "good" persons, organizations, and institutions to lead through their work. It accepts as given that social problems are caused by human decisions, and it assumes that the goal is to recognize and resist decisions that cause harm and to direct resources toward repairing the harm that is done. For example, the breakdown of community is evidenced in part by a struggle between winner-take-all individualism and our collective responsibility for one another. This model emphasizes the role of the individual—developing her or his capacities and integrity—as an actor in relationship to other persons and organizations. The focus for individuals and organizations is on creativity, capacity building, and creating opportunity and momentum through a combination of visioning and practical accomplishment. Relationships and leadership from this perspective tend to emphasize mentoring and capacity building, and share with the student-centered approach an interest in increasing the capacity of persons to be their best selves. It argues more precisely, however, that the goal of being a full human being—the exercise of authentic power—is achieved through service; service is a way of being in the world that is the fullest expression of our selves. It negotiates the dilemma of relationship somewhat differently than do the student-centered or therapeutic models by placing engagement within a more explicitly teleological or spiritual framework: being of service is a way of being in the world. It is not opposed to, but does not valorize, civic life or democratic practice, asking instead whether or not and how the persons and community grow as a result of the caring energy that has been contributed. And it emphasizes, I think, an existential choice each of us has about our relationship to the larger society: alienation is the result of our decision not to serve, and community results from our choice to serve, from deliberately "stepping into" our relationships with institutions.

## Alternatives and Community Building

This perspective is concerned fundamentally with illuminating the cultural and structural contradictions that surface in community-based work and partnerships, and joining with community partners who are experimenting with alternative ways of doing and being. As one community partner who teaches regularly with PSP explains (Morton, 2011), "The focus [in my teaching] is on how to surface for all of us [students, faculty, community members] the system dynamics that produce the dilemma [evidenced by poverty, racism, hunger, inequality, violence, ecological degradation] and frustrate efforts to change things…so the focus is on the efficacy and meaning of our work. And the enlivening question is, how do we ease the transition to more sustainable and happier ways of living?" This perspective might begin by arguing that the practices of capitalism and democracy are in profound tension with one another, and that our broader economic and political systems are what produce much of the structural violence affecting human relationships and ecological degradation. It argues as a starting point the proposition that current systems are nearing collapse and asks what an alternative future, based on values of community, might look like. The emphasis here might be on experiments like that described in Alan Weisman's (1998) *Gaviotas: a Village to Reinvent the World*, or Helena Norberg-Hodge's (1992) *Ancient Futures: Learning from Ladakh* or *The Economics of Happiness* (2011); in alternative philosophies or lifeways, such as nonviolence (Chodron, 1994; Gandhi, 1993; King, 1990), or simple or communal living (Berry, 1987; Day, 1952; Elgin,1998); in efforts to build alternative systems such as local economies or food systems (Wheatley and Frieze, 2011; McKibben, 2007); and in partnerships that flip or erase traditional boundaries of service-based relationships. This emphasis on alternatives asks questions about systems and cultural change, and looks at the processes by which experimental alternatives aimed at building community can be developed, such as urban agriculture, local economies, co-housing, re-neighboring, intentional communities, learning about survival from the experiences of marginalized people, or the practice of nonviolence.

Our various approaches do not so much represent different theoretical positions, as they argue for placing different types of experience at the center: the student-centered approach begins by considering that the primary situation is one framed by the experiences of students. That is, it assumes that students have had too few opportunities to discover, act on, reflect on, and organize around their own interests. The problem is the paucity of certain kinds of experience, and the need to design learning situations that will spark the civic imagination of students and community partners.

The therapeutic focus places emphasis on the day-to-day challenges faced by people who are suffering in various ways and for various reasons, and offers as the central experience the challenges of understanding these situations, and enacting a plan that will mitigate the problem in the short and long runs. It assumes that much of the complexity that slows positive change comes from human-created systems, and concentrates on figuring out the political and communications problems that will allow positive steps to be taken.

Servant leadership suggests that a primary focus should be on developing the perspectives, knowledge, and skills necessary to being an effective leader grounded in an ethic of serving others. The immediate questions are those of ethics: how do you figure out a right course of action? And so in this approach, service is an opportunity to find yourself in a situation that poses an ethical dilemma—with the knowledge that the choices made will be consequential. Additionally, this perspective is likely to focus on other characteristics of leadership, such as moral courage, and the ability to recognize, organize and use power appropriately.

And the alternatives perspective starts with a different sense of what constitutes the situation. It makes a systems argument: poverty, growing inequality, violence, and environmental degradation are related phenomena, and together constitute evidence that our current human systems are not working well. Add to this observation the discourse on "limits to growth," and it becomes evident that the core question is how to imagine and enact alternative systems that have the potential to achieve better outcomes (increased happiness and sustainability, decreased suffering and degradation). The experiential ground becomes twofold: learning to see current systems for what they are, and enacting alternatives that expand understanding and possibility.

As different as they are from one another, in practice these approaches tend to overlap and reinforce each other more than they diverge. Together, they model a range of possible responses to the problems of community and service, and reflect the degree and type of experimentation encouraged in our department and institute. Our common practice has been influenced by the work of Parker Palmer (2007), especially his idea that good teaching begins with the integrity of teacher. Our goal is to support one another in such a way that each of us is more successful over time in integrating our service, scholarship, and teaching. Much as we have written personal practices such as authenticity and the practice of diversity into the core competencies we expect for our students, we look for ways that each of us can better integrate how we are with how we know and how we teach.

We are also united, I think, by a shared belief in the integrity of the individual, human person, reinforced by Catholic social teaching (US Catholic Bishops, 1986), the United Nations Declaration of Human Rights (United Nations, 1948), the liberatory pedagogy of Paulo Freire (Freire, 1970), and the compassion-based imagining of the future represented by Margaret Wheatley (Wheatley, 2002; Wheately and Frieze 2011). This emphasis on the integrity of the person leads in several directions, including a sense that one of life's purposes is helping one another discover and steward this integrity, and a focus on connectivity—seeking ways to connect people, ideas, and institutions as a fundamental, learnable attitude and process. And the animating idea, across the varied approaches, is that learning to build personal, organizational, and institutional relationships is the common starting point for resolving the historic and existential problem of community.

A final observation I draw from these four approaches is that they suggest that we approach the "civic" in civic engagement not as a specific, discrete, definable body of knowledge or behaviors, but as something that is in fact created in a context and involves meaning making; relationships with other persons and the world; and the expression of self-interest, agency, and power. That is, "civic" does not exist apart from experience, but emerges from certain types of situations. And each of these four approaches offers and argues for placing people in very different situations in which they make meaning, explore and develop relationships, and look for ways to act.

If the field of civic engagement is to emerge with sharper definition or evolve into a discipline, we would do well to imagine process as content—an experientially grounded way of learning that encourages a pluralistic and multivocal conversation in which civic agency is the term used to describe people acting in the world in such a way that they are participating in meaning making, developing and extending their relationships, and finding ways to participate as ethical actors in the world.

### The Problem of Community

A more general shift in our curriculum has been that the "problem of community" has moved to the foreground, a product of our reflections on the tension between process and content. Jim Tull was one of the original community advisors to the research committee and in 1995 piloted with us the first faculty/community partner co-teaching of a PSP course. At the time, he was finishing a 13-year stint co-leading Amos House, a shelter and food kitchen in South Providence. Modeled loosely after the Catholic Worker's houses of hospitality, Amos House was in transition to a more formal intervention and human services program model. Jim was stepping aside in the transition— and bringing with him growing insights about the origins, purposes, and meaning of "service." "Service is a poor substitute for community," he argued, "...service is our culture's way of compensating for the dissolution of communities...and all our community partners are in the thick of struggling with this compensation" (Morton, 2011). Tull's critique and framing echoed a literature used in many of our courses: Ivan Illich's (1990) "To Hell with Good Intentions," John McKnight's (1995) *The Careless Society: Community and its Counterfeits*, and Wendell Berry's (1987) "Does Community Have a Value?" We noticed, as well, that a similar critique appeared as a constant theme in the works of the "grandparents" of service-learning, including Jane Addams, John Dewey and Dorothy Day (Morton and Saltmarsh, 1997). Increasingly understanding ourselves as a community of practitioners—students, staff, faculty, community partners—we began to see as our task the challenges of learning to "build community" in modern contexts, and over time we placed the idea and practice of relationship, expressed in a variety of forms, at the center of community building (Enos & Morton, 2003).

It is my sense that we make community building and relationship building central concepts and skills in our curriculum, and understand "citizenship" as one way we express this, drawing on Dewey's (1927) concept of public life as something created through social imagination and action. We approach community and relationship in multiple ways, and each is treated more as question and process than as content: What is authentic community and how do we experience it? How does place matter? How does globalization change the meaning of community? How do we help build, or rebuild, community and place? What relationships can we see? Which are we likely to miss? How do we enter into relationships with the "other" in such a way that the potential for building community is increased? What is an "authentic" relationship? How do we deal with the difficulties posed by cultural fragmentation and conflict? How do we create and sustain projects that connect people to people and people to place?

This shift in approach is reflected with remarkable consistency in the philosophies of service presented by graduating PSP majors. Stephanie Blank (Capstone Seminar, 2000), who now works as a counselor and educator combating domestic violence: "Most of the ills of the world I see as a lack of reciprocal relationships, where people or organizations do not understand one another and thus fear one another; people become marginalized and oppressed. These relationships need to be worked on. That need is service." Brock Leiendecker (Capstone Seminar, 2010), now working with high-risk, gang-affiliated youth, wrote: "Great acts of humanity and compassion are developed through the relationships and learning communities of which a person is a part." Brock's emphasis is shared by his classmates. Elena Piperno (Capstone Seminar, 2010), now coordinator of after-school and summer programs for a consortium of Catholic schools, writes, "[I have become] someone who believes in the fundamental connection between all people....In *Ulysses* Tennyson wrote, 'I am a part of all I have met.' This one sentence is the basis of my whole story....[T]he beauty of the Public and Community Service major can be summed up through one word: interconnectedness." And Amy Baker (Capstone Seminar, 2007), a development director for an antipoverty social change organization, writes, "Focusing on the importance of personal relationships, community development and problem-solving, I began to view my role in society with a larger purpose: we are called to serve one another."

### *Action, Reflection and Curriculum*

The vehicle through which we investigate questions of community, democracy, and service is our curriculum (Hudson and Trudeau,1995; Battistoni,1998; www.providence.edu/fips). It is composed of three "building blocks": foundation courses, leadership courses, and content courses. The six foundation courses introduce various conceptual frameworks for thinking about community-based work (what is "good" service; how do nonprofit organizations function; what is community organizing; what are the philosophical and spiritual dimensions of "helping"?) The five leadership courses—two semesters of practicum, internship, and two semesters of capstone—place students in situations where they are expected to organize and participate in work they help create. The three content courses, selected individually by each student, are intended to give them familiarity with a topical subject or issue, such as hunger, organizing, youth development, or community economics.

The experiential components of the major and minor make clear how central our community partnerships are to the learning process, and describe how the process of reflection is woven into the curriculum. The curriculum is designed so that each major spends a minimum of 550 hours in community-based work. Quite often, the students also complete a study abroad experience that includes community work—averaging 30 additional hours; volunteer with a project outside the curriculum—another 200 or more hours over four years; and, if eligible, use off-campus work-study, adding up to approximately 800 more hours over four years.

As it has developed in practice, "reflection" has come to mean some combination of dialogue, journaling, focused essays, small group discussion, group presentations, and reacting to a "literature" from others interested in similar situations. Students (and faculty and community partners) practice learning from "situations"—Dewey's (1938) phrase for a focused experience—in this case the community relationships and service the students undertake. The idea has been to use these reflection tools to individually and collectively "make meaning" from and illuminate experience and only occasionally to master a particular skill or content. This process of making meaning is used for developing understanding and "knowledge" that can be used to direct future action. The public dimension of this process—linking service to civic engagement—emerges as divergent interpretations surface, are negotiated and lead toward a common plan about what to do next. This public dimension becomes more apparent as the reflection circle is widened from the classroom to the community, and into the institutions that frame any given "situation."

We are also conscious of the importance of cognitive dissonance and values clarification in our reflection process ( Hutchings and Wutzdorff, 1988 ; Delve and Mintz, 1990; Colby and Damon, 1992; Kohlberg, 1984; Chickering, 1993; Astin and Astin, 1996; Astin, Vogelgesang, Ikeda & Yee, 2000; Parks, 1999; Daloz, Keen, Keen & Parks, 1996). While these are important for the personal growth of students, we are also convinced that experiencing cognitive dissonance and practicing values-clarification are essential building blocks for relationship building, crossing cultural boundaries, and community organizing. It is this aspect of the curriculum—reflection and values clarification—that alumni recall as most significant in their own development (Grove, 2006). Community partners recognize this aspect of our work as our strongest contribution, to the extent that we have offered since 2009 a semester-long seminar on "Reflective Practice" that attracts an average of 15 people working full-time in various community settings.

In 2006, inspired by Maggie Grove's study of our alumni/ae, the faculty, students, staff and community advisors of PSP reviewed the learning outcomes in which we were interested. We drafted the following description of eight competencies:

Eloquent listening
Systems thinking and organizational effectiveness, including specific technical skills
    such as budgeting, development, or power mapping
Group process
Crossing cultural boundaries
Personal practices such as authenticity, values clarification and reflection
Writing and public speaking
Familiarity with the content knowledge of a specific issue

We have looked for these competencies in the portfolios and philosophies of service prepared by Capstone students. Co-teaching the 2010–11 Capstone seminar with Jessica Cigna, Rick (Battistoni, 2010) developed a pre-course self-assessment survey for students, and conducted patterned exit interviews with all graduating majors and minors (Battistoni, 2011). We are just beginning to use these new tools to evaluate the degree to which our students are developing these competencies.

### Organizing service as relationship and process directed toward community building

*"Herein lies the core learning dilemma that confronts organizations: we learn best from experience but we never directly experience the consequences of many of our most important decisions."* Peter Senge, *The Fifth Discipline* (1990, p.23)

Among the most complex challenges facing service-learning programs in higher education is establishing a system that actually accomplishes what it is intended to accomplish. We have debated where our emphasis should be over the last 17 years. One side of the debate (and dominating the literature of higher education–based service-learning) locates student learning as the primary "emphasis." On the other side of the debate, and much more muted, is community impact. Yet we realize that "[b]y not knowing what service-learning does to the communities it purports to serve," as Randy Stoecker, Elizabeth Tryon, and Amy Hilgendorf argue, "we risk creating unintended side effects that exacerbate, rather than alleviate, the problems those communities suffer from." (Stoecker, Tryon & Hilgendorf, 2009, p.7)

The solution to this debate, we are beginning to understand, is a systems solution: seeing the student learning processes and the community engagement processes as part of one system, and increasing our awareness of the ways that the two "subsystems" of campus and community are interrelated and change one another. In other words, it is an invitation to imagine a service-learning program or major not as being about campus or community, but as a new, unique system with particular potential and challenges.

Peter Senge's *The Fifth Discipline* (1990) was published four years before the Feinstein Institute and the Public and Community Service Studies program were established, and his descriptions of systems thinking and the "learning organization" had a significant influence on the way we organized our resources, reflection processes, and decision making—offering a "mental map" that helped us to understand ourselves. Senge argues that systems are less about specific nodes within a system, and more about the connectivity among the parts: the ways that the constitutive elements of a system are linked to one another so that people in the system can become aware of the consequences of important decisions and learn from these consequences, and adjust their system accordingly. It is relatively complex, for example, to design a class, integrate it with a curriculum, and establish an assessment process that measures whether or not it is achieving its goals. And designing community projects that can produce intended results, do not have unintended consequences, and can be assessed in an appropriate and useful way in real time is very challenging. Putting these together increases the overall complexity geometrically: how then do we design service-learning programs that work well?

The focus, we have come to think, should be less on the parts of the system—campus and community—than on the ways they are linked, the richness and timeliness of the feedback loops across the two systems, and the ability of people involved to accurately interpret the feedback they are receiving. As Senge argues, "Systems thinking is a discipline for seeing wholes. It is a framework for seeing interrelationships rather than things, for seeing patterns of change rather than static 'snapshots.'" (Senge, 1990, p. 68)

Over time, we have begun to realize that we are trying to craft a new system that incorporates elements of both campus and community while emphasizing their interrelationship and the common patterns of change that result. In other words, our service-learning initiative challenges us to recognize it as a new system, rather than the interaction of two systems. It invites us to conceptualize our service-learning program and major as a system distinct from either campus or community, and gives us the opportunity to develop this new system as a "learning organization."

While it will always be a work in progress, several things we have done to integrate these subsystems into a new system are worth noting.

Including community partners in the development and delivery of our curriculum and shaping our community partnerships. Their advice in general has been to work in greater depth with fewer partners, to be clear about the contributions the community partners can make to student learning, and to be clear about the value we add to the partnerships, which they identify as our ability to create opportunities for reflection on their work.

Focusing students working as "community assistants" in our two-semester Practicum course on specific community sites, rather than on courses. This makes the Practicum students one of FIPS/PSP's key systems links to its partners, connecting campus and community. It makes our program dependent upon the students' knowledge, judgment, skill, and energy, while providing our community partners with a ready link to student learning.

Assigning our service-learning coordinator (a full-time staff member who coordinates our community partnerships) to co-teach the Practicum course, and encourage her/him to occasionally co-teach other courses in our curriculum, again helping with systems integration and continuity.

While stopping short of formal categorization, approaching our partners as "core" or "placement." Core partners are organizations with which we develop deep, potentially transformative relationships, and placement partners are those with which we have more narrowly defined relationships, often renewed on a semester-by-semester basis for several years (Morton, 1998; Morton and Callahan 2009). This has the merit of simplifying our overall system by allowing us to concentrate more fully on a smaller number of partners and deliberately integrate them into our organizational development, even as we direct extra attention to the partners in the form, for example, of joining boards, developing research projects, helping with organizational and staff development, and making campus space and resources available.

Inviting community partners to co-teach our courses. Community partners who teach with us are called "community advisors." Each semester between two and eight community partners join in teaching PSP courses, with roles that vary depending on the interests of the professor and the advisor. This encourages faculty/community partner relationships, provides our classes with grounded community perspectives, ensures that a growing number of people in the local community have been or are involved in our reflection process and understand our curriculum, and it gives the partners an opportunity to reflect on their lives and work. The community advisors tend to participate actively in our departmental retreats and planning sessions, and are a consistent source of perspective, insight, and challenge.

### Opportunities and Challenges of Institutionalization

At present, FIPS is undertaking two large-scale projects that have the potential to help us move more fully toward conceptualizing our service-learning initiative as a single system of interrelated parts, rather than as collaboration by two distinct systems. One project, known simply as "the annex," begins with leasing 1,500 square feet of storefront space from a local community development corporation. Influenced by the University of Pennsylvania's work with West Philadelphia Improvement Corporation, Augsburg College's Jane Addams House, and Miami University Ohio's Center for Community Engagement in Over the Rhine, the "annex" is intended to operate as a liminal contemporary settlement house: a space for campus and community members to come together formally and informally for dialogue, shared discovery, popular education, and cooperative action. Community youth and Providence College students share interests in music, dance, photography, and documentaries. Neighborhood residents and the College's students and faculty are interested in local histories, immigration, and community-safety issues. Everyone is interested in housing, economic revitalization, job development, and life planning. People want entertainment, opportunities to learn, access to health and wellness tools, and opportunities to help create positive change. The agenda is to create a safe, hospitable space that will be energized by the continual, shared practice of "border crossing" and result in the annex and its projects operating as a "learning organization" with the potential over time to transform both curriculum and community in a more integrated system.

FIPS is also experimenting with a college-access program called EXPLORE (Expanding Possibilities through Local Relationships), started in 2008 by a PSP minor who graduated in 2011 and who is returning as a VISTA volunteer to help develop the program. Providence College students lead the program, which introduces freshman and sophomores from four urban high schools in the greater Providence area to college life, while several faculty members link their classes to specific high schools and their teams of college and high school students. As Barbara Jentleson writes of a similar project (2011, p. 5), "The case for building robust and positive university partnerships is grounded in the urgency of current social realities." EXPLORE offers everyone involved an opportunity to experience the linked phenomena of urban high schools, college access and community building, and to use their reflections to co-create positive ways forward. Like the annex, EXPLORE introduces a relational and experiential complexity capable of sustaining the unity and diversity in our curriculum, and has potential for helping us transform into a more integrated service-learning system.

As the college's investment in the Feinstein Institute for Public Service continues to increase, and as the political complexity of stakeholder relationships increases, PSP/FIPS's potential for learning and community building will likely increase, but holding onto and developing our understanding of FIPS/PSP as a distinct system will be challenging.

### Lessons

Shortly after FIPS/PSP was established in 1994, Providence College conducted a review and revision of its core curriculum, led by the Faculty Senate. The deliberations were fierce, and those resistant to change used FIPS/PSP as a straw man representing diminished academic rigor and cultural relativism to polarize the discussion. The revision stalled until 2010, when a new core curriculum passed by a vote of 29 to 1 (Faculty Senate, 2010). Among the changes are required "proficiencies" of diversity and civic engagement. In its "General Rationale" the Faculty Senate bill (2010) argues that, "the College must provide opportunities for students to be engaged in their learning and to engage what they learn in what matters to them." Experiencing diversity, civic engagement, and engaged learning are now mainstream values of the college.

Over the years one key to FIPS/PSP's growth despite institutional ambivalence has been practicing the reflective processes it teaches: constant interpretation by its faculty, students, and staff of what they are experiencing, leading to strategies and action steps. The practice and sensibility of shared process is maintained through constant, deliberate conversations among faculty, students, staff, and community partners. Community partners co-teach courses with faculty, deepening our campus/community partnerships and expanding our circle of dialogue and reflection, and participate in spring and winter retreats each year; we "mentor in" faculty who are teaching PSP courses for the first time by having them co-teach; and we encourage faculty teaching sections of the same course to meet regularly. Our focus has been on connecting the parts of our system—what I think of as deliberate interdependence—rather than expanding our system, trusting that attention to the relationships of which our system is comprised will create richer opportunities for experience and reflection over time.

Part of our reflection process has been to consider what it means to be part of Providence College: how we maintain and build relationships across sometimes divergent values and conflicts and how we change and compromise while developing and maintaining our authenticity and integrity. We have been constantly reminded, on and off campus, that politics and power are real; and we have come to understand that the challenges we face on campus mirror in important ways the challenges of the communities and community organizations with which we work. Positive change in our college and in the communities with which we work requires systems thinking and managing complexity. It requires power mapping, understanding and engaging self-interest, and devising strategies for both bottom-up and top-down change. But it begins with thinking about relationship and community: how we are connected to one another, and the kind of community we want to become.

Our PSP curriculum has benefited, I think, by not looking to resolve differing perspectives about the meanings of service and service-learning. Rather than try to work toward a singular theoretical and methodological framework, we have concentrated on supporting ongoing dialogue about what service, service-learning, and civic engagement mean and how they are to be experienced. We have become increasingly committed to trusting experience in our curriculum and in our teaching. As a result, our interests have been increasingly drawn to community projects that deliberately test the boundaries of our thinking, emphasize co-creation and learning among faculty, students, staff, and community partners, and experiment with institutional relationships and change. Increasingly, we are imagining the boundaries between campus and community as permeable, and this perspective is surfacing in clear and often generous ways new dimensions of the ethical puzzle of relationship that is at the heart of community, service, and learning in higher education.

## References

Astin, A., Vogelgesang, L., Ikeda, E. K., and Yee, J.A. (January 2000) *How Service Learning Affects Students: Executive Summary*. Los Angeles: UCLA Higher Education Research Institute. Retrieved from http://gseis.ucla.edu/heri/PDFs/rhowas.pdf.

Astin, A. and Astin, H.S. (1996). *Guidebook for a Social Change Model of Student Leadership*. Los Angeles, CA: UCLA Higher Education Research Institute.

Battistoni, R.M. (1998). "Making a Major Commitment: Public and Community Service at Providence College." Zlotkowski, E. Ed., *Successful Service Learning Programs: New Models of Excellence in Higher Education*. Boston: Anker, p.169–88.

Battistoni, R. (2010). *Core Competency Self Assessment Instrument*. Providence, RI: Archives of the Feinstein Institute for Public Service.

———. (2011). *Exit Interviews of PSP Majors and Minors*. Providence, RI: Archives of the Feinstein Institute for Public Service.

Battistoni, R. and Longo, N. (2011) . "Putting Students at the Center of Civic Engagement." Saltmarsh, J. and Hartley, M. Eds., *"To Serve a Larger Purpose" Engagement for Democracy and the Transformation of Higher Education*. Philadelphia, PA: Temple University Press, pp. 199–216.

Bellah. R., Madsen R., Sullivan W., Swidler A., and Tipton S. (1985). *Habits of the Heart: Individualism and Commitment in American Life*. Berkeley: University of California Press.

Berry, W. (1987). *Home Economics*. San Francisco: North Point Press.

Capstone Seminar in Public and Community Service ( 2000, 2001, 2002, 2004, 2007, 2008, 2009, 2010). *Philosophies of Service*. Providence, RI: Feinstein Institute for Public Service Archives.

Chickering, A. W. and Reisser, L. (1993). *Education and Identity*. San Francisco: Jossey-Bass Publishers.

Chodron, P. (1994). *Start Where You Are: a Guide to Compassionate Living*. Boston, MA: Shambhala Press.

Coles, R. (1983). *The Call of Service: A Witness to Idealism*. Boston, MA: Houghton Mifflin.

Colby, A., Damon. W. (1992). *Some Do Care: Contemporary Lives of Moral Commitment*. New York: The Free Press.

Daloz, L.A., Keen C.H., Keen, J.P. and Parks, S. (1996). *Common Fire: Leading Lives of Commitment in a Complex World*. Boston, MA: Beacon Press.

Day. D. (1952). *The Long Loneliness*. New York: Harper Row.

Delve, C. and Mintz, S. (1990). *Community Service as Values Education*. New York: Jossey-Bass.

Dewey, J. (1938). *Experience and Education*. New York: The Macmillan Company.

———. (1927, 1954). *The Public and Its Problems*. Athens, OH: Swallow Press.

Elgin. D. (1998). *Voluntary Simplicity*. New York: William Morrow Publishers

Enos, S. and Morton, K. (2003). Developing a Theory and Practice of Campus- Community Partnerships. In Barbara Jacoby, ed. *Building Partnerships for Service-Learning*. San Francisco: Jossey-Bass.

Faculty Senate, Providence College (June 6, 2010). *Senate Bill 09–10/01/15, Changes to the Core Curriculum*. Retrieved from http://www.providence.edu/NR/rdonlyres/D98AB89F -D310–4D6B-97D5-D64B0F1804F3/19897/CoreCurriculum_Approved_050510.pdf.

Feinstein Institute for Public Service (June 6, 2010). Major Requirements. Retrieved from http://www.providence.edu/Feinstein/Department/Major.htm.

Freire, P. (1970). *Pedagogy of the Oppressed*. New York: Continuum.

Gandhi, M. (1993, 1928). *The Story of My Experiments with Truth*. Bok, S. Ed. Boston: Beacon Press.

Greenleaf, R.K. (1970). *The Servant as Leader*. Westfield, IN: Greenleaf Center for Servant Leadership.

Grove, M. (2006). *Conversations with Public and Community Service Majors and Alumni: The Articulation of Values in Education, Life and Work*. Providence, RI: Archives of the Feinstein Institute for Public Service.

Horton, M., Kohl, J. and Kohl H. (1997). *The Long Haul: An Autobiography*. New York: Teachers College Press.

Hudson, W. and Trudeau, R. (1995). An Essay on the Institutionalization of Service Learning: The Genesis of the Feinstein Institute for Public Service. *Michigan Journal of Community Service Learning*, 2(1), 150–58.

Hutchings, P. and Wutzdorff, A. (1988). *Knowing and Doing: Learning Through Experience*. New York: John Wiley and Sons.

Illich, I. (1990,1968). To Hell with Good Intentions. In Kendall, J. ed., *Combining Service and Learning: a Resource Book for Community and Public Service*. Raleigh: National Society for Internships and Experiential Education, *1*, 314–320.

Jentleson, B.C. (2011). *Better Together: A Model University-Community Partnership for Urban Youth*. New York: Teachers College Press.

Kendall. J. ed. (1990). *Combining Service and Learning: A Resource Book for Community and Public Service*. Volumes 1–3. Raleigh, NC: National Society for Internships and Experiential Education.

King, M.L. Jr. (1990). *Testament of Hope: The Essential Writings and Speeches of Martin Luther King, Jr*. New York: HarperOne.

Kohlberg, L. (1984). *The Psychology of Moral Development: the Nature and Validity of Moral Stages*. (*Essays on Moral Development, Volume 2*). New York: Harper Collins.

Kolb, D.A. (1984). *Experiential Learning: Experience as the Source of Learning and Development*. Englewood Cliffs, NJ: Prentice-Hall.

Kretzman, J. and McKnight, J. (1993). *Building Communities from the Inside Out: A Path Toward Finding and Mobilizing a Community's Assets*. Evanston, IL: Institute for Policy Research.

Kupiec, T.Y. (Ed.). (1993). *Rethinking Tradition: Integrating Service with Academic Study on College Campuses*. Providence, RI: Campus Compact.

Longo, N.V. (2007). *Why Community Matters: Connecting Education With Civic Life*. Albany, NY: SUNY Press.

McKibben, B. (2007). *Deep Economy: The Wealth of Communities and the Durable Future.* New York: Times Books.

McKnight, J. (1995). *The Careless Society: Community and Its Counterfeits.* New York: Basic Books.

Morton, K. (1995). The Irony of Service: Charity, Project and Social Change in Service Learning. *Michigan Journal of Community Service Learning, 2*(1), 19–32.

———. (1996). Issues Related to Integrating Service-Learning Into the Curriculum. In Jacoby, B., ed. *Service Learning in Higher Education.* San Francisco: Jossey-Bass, pp. 276–96.

———. (May, 1998). *PSP 101 Content Analysis of Syllabi, Fall 1994–Fall 1997.* Providence, RI: Archives of the Feinstein Institute for Public Service, Providence College.

———. (June 2011). Interview with Jim Tull; personal notes.

Morton, K., and Saltmarsh, J. (1997). Addams, Day, and Dewey: The Emergence of Community Service in American Culture. *Michigan Journal of Community Service Learning, 4,* 137–49.

Morton, K. and Callahan, J. (2009). Reflections on University-School Partnerships at Providence College's Feinstein Institute for Public Service, in Kelshaw, T., Lazarus, F. and Minier J., eds. *Partnerships for Service Learning:Impacts on Communities and Students.* Bolton, MA: Anker Publishing.

Morton, N. (1985). "Beloved Image," *The Journey is Home.* Boston: Beacon Press.

Newman. F. (1985). *Higher Education and the American Resurgence.* Princeton, NJ: Carnegie Foundation for the Advancement of Teaching.

Norberg-Hodge, H. (1992). *Ancient Futures: Learning from Ladakh.* San Francisco: Sierra Club Books.

Norberg-Hodge, H., Gorelick, S., and Page, J. (2011). *The Economics of Happiness.* Berkeley, CA: International Society for Ecology and Culture.

Palmer, P. (1997). *The Courage to Teach.* New York: Jossey-Bass.

Parks, S. (1999). *The Critical Years.* New York: Jossey-Bass.

Putnam, R. (2001). *Bowling Alone: The Collapse and Revival of American Community.* New York: Simon and Schuster.

Registrar, Providence College. (2011). PSP Majors and Minors by Year. Files of the author.

Research Committee. (May 1994). *Proposal for Academic Programs, Feinstein Institute for Public Service.* Providence, RI: Archives, Feinstein Institute for Public Service, Providence College.

Schön, D. (1983). *The Reflective Practitioner: How Professionals Think in Action.* New York: Basic Books.

Senge, P. (1990). *The Fifth Discipline: the Art and Practice of the Learning Organization.* New York: Doubleday.

Stoecker, R., Tryon E.A., and Hilgendorf, A. (2009). *The Unheard Voices: Community Organizations and Service Learning.* Philadelphia: Temple University Press.

de Tocqueville, A. (2003) Kramnick, I. Ed. *Democracy in America.* New York: Penguin Classics. (Original work published 1835, 1840.)

United Nations. (1948). *Universal Declaration of Human Rights.* New York: General Assembly of the United Nations. Retrieved from http://www.un.org/en/documents/udhr/index.shtml.

US Catholic Bishops. (1986). *Economic Justice for All: Pastoral Letter on Catholic Social Teaching and the U.S. Economy.* Washington DC: United States Conference of Catholic Bishops.

Weisman. A. (1998). *Gaviotas: A Village to Reinvent the World.* White River Junction, VT: Chelsea Green Publishers.

Wheatley, M. (2002). *Turning to One Another: Simple Conversations to Restore Hope to the Future.* San Francisco: Berrett-Koehler Publishers.

Wheatley, M. and Frieze, D. (2011). *Walk Out Walk On: A Learning Journey into Communities Daring to Live the Future Now.* San Francisco: Berrett-Koehler Publishers.

Wolfe, Alan (1989). *Whose Keeper: Social Science and Moral Obligation.* Berkeley: University of California Press.

# CHAPTER 6

# The Politics of Engagement

*Mary Beth Pudup*
University of California, Santa Cruz

At its founding, the University of California, Santa Cruz, shunned academic convention in favor of intellectual experimentation and innovation. Traditional academic departments were eschewed; instead, "boards of study" and residential colleges organized faculty and students around multidisciplinary common interests. Because students were the product of an enviably well-funded K–12 public education system, narrative evaluations were allowed to substitute for traditional letter grades. It was the early 1960s, after all. California's postwar economic prosperity still had no horizon and could underwrite the manifest optimism of the state's legendary Master Plan for Higher Education (Shrag 2004). California possessed abundant resources and faith in the future, not only to expand its eponymous university system, but also to permit the fledgling Santa Cruz campus to chart its own path in undergraduate education.

One of its bold experiments was an interdisciplinary program—the campus's first—called Community Studies, premised on the novel idea that undergraduates could gain academic knowledge from extended, full-time immersion in community work away from campus. This was long before the words "service" and "learning" or "civic" and "engagement" fused into meaningful phrases and, significantly, also before the rampant proliferation of undergraduate internship programs. The Community Studies experiment was notable, too, for its emphasis on social justice: students' community work was an explicit engagement with pressing social problems caused by unequal access to power and resources in society. Because such problems have complex histories and theoretical explanations, academic course work necessarily complemented the field study. The goal was a seamless integration of theory and practice, a phrase aptly describing the founding epistemology and pedagogy of Community Studies.

In the 40-plus years since its founding, thousands of students have matriculated successfully through Community Studies. In a survey conducted in 2005, department alumni reported lifelong civic engagement and connected it directly to their undergraduate major. Almost 100 alumni had founded nonprofit organizations, and scores more served on nonprofit boards or as community volunteers. Others served in government (including in elected office), and many more followed politics at all levels, developed informed opinions, and voted regularly. Along with a proud record of alumni achievement and civic engagement, the new century witnessed burgeoning enrollments and demand for the Community Studies major and new investments in a novel graduate program. Within the short span of five years, however, Community Studies was brought to the brink of closure. Ironically, this decline took place as the national movement for campus-based civic engagement gathered significant momentum, as did a revival of experience-based learning through off-campus internship programs.

This chapter develops an account of the rise and decline of Community Studies at UC Santa Cruz, one of the nation's pioneering experiential education social-justice-oriented academic departments. I first discuss the social milieu which gave rise to the department's formation in the late 1960s and then describe its distinctive three-part core curriculum. The chapter then shifts to explaining the department's precipitous decline after 2005. The proximate cause of its demise is California's deep, protracted budget crisis. While not discounting the significance of the fiscal crisis, which has had devastating effects across all sectors of public higher education in the golden state, I emphasize other factors, in effect addressing why the budget ax fell where it did: on a successful, long-standing, and much emulated experiential education program dedicated to progressive social change. I argue that although Community Studies enjoyed status as an academic and administrative unit of the campus, that is, as a freestanding department, its status was never secure. From the start, critics inside and outside the university equated the department's model of extended community-based field study with political troublemaking by radical student activists. This criticism persisted even as 1960s-era social movements receded into history, and even as field studies became virtually indistinguishable from the newly popular service-learning. Community Studies never stopped being a political target and, as such, was always somewhat risky business for the university. I suggest that the advent of new community engagement programs on campus, many with a social-justice orientation, made it possible for administrators to eliminate Community Studies and still trumpet the institution's commitment to community engagement. I conclude by suggesting that the Community Studies experience offers a cautionary tale for academic civic-engagement programs, which may also become political targets and are subject to shifting institutional priorities.

## The times, they were a changing: the birth of Community Studies

Social and political ferment was as much a part of the 1960s in California as its vaunted, and majority white, suburban prosperity, and that ferment shaped academic programming at Santa Cruz, as it did on campuses nationally. Within higher education, social movements coalescing around issues of civil rights, free speech, anti–Vietnam War activism, feminism, and ethnic cultural nationalism—to name but a few—stimulated demands that universities do more than bear witness to and analyze social change. "Upset by the abstract academicism of their professors and demanding relevance in their studies, many students turned to the 'real world' by translating off-campus activity into field study, i.e., remaining enrolled but obtaining academic credit for the activity beyond the campus" (Friedland and Rotkin 2003, p. 43).

Until the 1960s, academic field study had remained largely the province of graduate education in professions like social welfare, business, and nursing or in social science disciplines like anthropology and sociology. The era's social movements stimulated wider acceptance of undergraduate field study and conferred academic legitimacy on field studies of an explicitly social-change nature. Perhaps not surprisingly, "experience was idiosyncratic" (Friedland and Rotkin 2003, p. 44): some field studies were all about community work and had no specific academic demands; others had an academic component but lacked an institutional campus presence apart from one-on-one interactions between sponsoring faculty and students.

From the start, UC Santa Cruz students had eagerly embraced off-campus experiential education and field study in the spirit of experimentation that pervaded the campus upon its founding in 1965. While generally supportive of student initiatives, some faculty worried "that the potential for experiential learning was being dissipated in uncontrolled experimentation…such as raft-floating down the Mississippi" to recapture the experience of Huck Finn (p. 45). In a moment of historical serendipity, the wish to harness the academic potential of experiential education at Santa Cruz dovetailed with Cornell University sociologist William Friedland's sabbatical leave at nearby Stanford University during 1967–8. Friedland had founded Cornell's Migrant Labor Program, a year-long course focused on understanding farm-labor conditions in upstate New York. The centerpiece of Cornell's program was a summer field study in which students worked side-by-side with migrant farm laborers. Before doing their summer field study, students enrolled in a spring-semester preparation course modeled after graduate training in anthropology and sociology. In the fall semester following their field work, students participated in a seminar and wrote analytical papers based on their experience. The Cornell Migrant Labor Program offered a total package of undergraduate experiential education: rigorous academic expectations coupled to student immersion in a "real world" social-change situation.

The final piece of historical conjuncture that brought William Friedland to Santa Cruz to launch Community Studies was the late 1960s "urban crisis initiative" pursued by the University of California's governing Board of Regents in response to the insurrections that were roiling cities throughout the state and nation. UC campuses were exhorted to create programs that would respond directly to the urban crisis and received seed funding for program development and faculty recruitment. Community Studies was conceived as an undergraduate major that would fulfill this mandate, and Friedland was recruited to Santa Cruz to establish the program.

At its inception, Community Studies was modeled after Cornell's integrated three-part curriculum consisting of preparation, field study, and analysis. Unlike the Cornell program, however, in which all students worked on migrant-farm-labor questions, Community Studies students determined their own field-study locations. Another distinguishing feature of Community Studies intended to demonstrate its academic rigor was a required senior thesis based on significant original research. The three-part curricular model of preparation, community-based field study, and reflection/analysis has endured since the department was launched in 1969, even as individual core curriculum courses have been revised.

### Core curriculum: preparation. immersion. reflection.

As an interdisciplinary department, Community Studies developed its own philosophical underpinnings and modus vivendi in the absence of disciplinary conventions to supply curricular structure and coherence. [1] "Theory and practice" perhaps best captures its first principles. A guiding epistemology in Community Studies is that theory and practice are barely separate moments in the overall production of knowledge and exist in dialogical relationship with each other. Social theory is a discursive construction of social life whose meaning and relevance are continually "tested" by the unfolding of history. Likewise, social life is guided by institutions, organizations, and programs thoroughly (if unwittingly) steeped in (often competing) discursive constructions of society (Wagner 2001). Community Studies encourages ongoing mutual interrogations of the theoretical implications of practice and the practical implications of theory. Above all was the guiding philosophy that knowledge produced in and about society should always aim to improve society.

The sequential core curriculum begins with enrollment in a topical "gateway" seminar (CMMU 100 A–Z) focused on a key social-justice issue embodied within the substantive scholarly work of department faculty such as health-care inequalities; economic justice; immigration and social justice; public health, resistance, and social movements; agriculture and food justice; gender and sexuality; social documentation; and cultural politics. In choosing a gateway seminar, students signal their commitment to pursuing its focus throughout the major and, in particular, to undertaking a field study with an organization working on related issues. For example, students enrolled in the health-care inequalities gateway seminar would pursue a health-related field study and complete supporting course work, students enrolled in the agriculture and food justice seminar would pursue a food and/or agriculture–related field study, and so forth.

The gateway seminars were introduced as a major curriculum revision in 1995–6, replacing a generic "theory and practice" course through which the entire faculty rotated. The seminars were designed to strengthen the connection between faculty research and teaching within Community Studies. Because the major had a process-oriented core curriculum, faculty had taught comparatively few courses that were directly related to their scholarly research. Over time, this was considered a hindrance to their research productivity. The gateway seminars were designed to also address two critical student needs: (1) in-depth study of theory and history in an important domain of social change; and (2) connection with a faculty advisor possessing scholarly expertise supporting the student's field study and overall academic plan.

Following the gateway seminars is a relatively new (2010) core curriculum addition, a large cohort-sized lecture course entitled "Social Movements, Communities and the Third Sector." The improbable decision to augment the core curriculum amid a period of budget austerity reflected a tremendous pent-up demand for intellectual innovation. This was felt by a newer cohort of department faculty who were less tied to 1960s-era social movements (in terms of personal experience and graduate training) and more intellectually attuned to a poststructural emphasis on how systems of knowledge/power are produced and contribute to social inequality and cultural oppression (Joseph 2002). There was a recognition that while field studies typically took place within nonprofit- (or so-called third-) sector organizations with varying degrees of attachment (or commitment) to social movements, the core curriculum had not evolved to reflect the emergence of what has been portrayed, unflatteringly, as "the nonprofit industrial complex" (Incite!, 2007).

The new course was designed to address the fact that students were not receiving appropriate instruction about the institutional realm in which they were immersed for six months on field study. Nonprofit organizations in the social-service sector, though outside the realm of social movements, had become key sites for shaping political subjectivities (Wolch 1990, Poppendeick, 1998), in keeping with the Foucauldian insight that prisons, schools, and clinics are sites of both discipline and resistance (Foucault 1994, 1995, 2006). Interdisciplinary scholars of democracy and democratic practices have noted that "therapeutic" educational and clinical encounters are sites of real politics, and should not be disregarded as only acting in the realm of service delivery. Barbara Cruikshank (1999) speaks directly to the intellectual discussions in Community Studies that prompted development of the new core course:

> Democratic theory, with important exceptions, counts voting and open rebellion as "political" actions, for example, but neglects or dismisses the constitution of citizens in the therapeutic, disciplinary, programmatic, institutional, and associational activities of everyday life. Dismissing these activities and their locations as administrative, social, "prepolitical" or "de-politicizing" reduces democratic criticism to documenting the exclusion of certain subjects from the homogeneous sphere of the political, from the places and powers of citizenship.

By the end of the twentieth century, undergraduate field study increasingly involved placements that were in some sense therapeutic or educational, or that otherwise filled in public sector gaps, from participation in harm reduction / HIV programs to teaching kids "how to eat" in farm-to-school programs to gardening as a source of "empowerment" to "job skills" for at-risk youth. Field-study placements were all but indistinguishable from community-based internships associated with emergent service-learning programs. This is not to suggest that the Community Studies department had abandoned (consciously or unconsciously) its first principles, turned its backs on policy issues, racism, structural inequality, noninstitutional social movements, traditional social movements, or capitalism writ large—far from it. Instead, the pedagogical argument for the new course centered on exploring how structural inequalities intersect with the therapeutic encounter (Lyon-Callo 2008).

The final piece of "preparation" within the three-part curriculum model is CMMU 102, "Preparation for Field Study."[2] Critical to the success of the field study, and to students' overall experience in Community Studies, this core course combines the study of the ethical, intellectual, and practical dimensions of field work with methods-related instruction and assignments including interview techniques, field-note strategies, and organizational analysis (Shaw 1996, 1999). Over the years CMMU 102 has undergone several metamorphoses in response to changing resource endowments and institutional priorities, from a team-taught seminar with a required part-time field study to a large, cohort-sized lecture and section course employing both graduate teaching assistants and undergraduate (i.e., graduating senior) mentors.

If the three-part sequential core curriculum is the heart of the Community Studies major, the six-month, full-time field study can be thought of as the "core of the core." The field study has always been the signature piece of Community Studies. In exit surveys completed by graduating seniors and in two alumni surveys, students and former students uniformly reported that full-time field study was a highly valued part of their undergraduate education and, moreover, was of lasting significance in shaping their lives.

The academic goals of the full-time field study are inseparable from those of the entire major. Community Studies seeks to develop a dynamic critical awareness of the relationship between the theoretical and practical issues involved in social change, and of the wider global contexts in which social justice is pursued. The field study is the principal curricular site for bringing theoretical and historical knowledge into dialogue with direct experience. Accordingly, the field study is a site of genuine knowledge production and not simply a place where academic ideas are "tested" or "applied." Required reflective writing and analysis are the key strategies for transforming experience into knowledge. Students maintain daily field notes recording their direct experiences in the field-study organization as well astheir emerging conceptualizations about the organization's work and the wider domain of social justice in which it is located. Students reflect upon their academic learning in light of their experience, and vice versa. Field notes are submitted periodically for review and commentary. The other written assignments consist of two essays, a rubric-driven organizational analysis (after the first quarter), and a comprehensive reflection essay (after the second quarter).

Field study begins in the summer after CMMU 102 (typically between the junior and senior years) and extends through the end of fall quarter, for a total of two quarters of full-time academic credit over six consecutive calendar months. The length of the field study distinguishes Community Studies from other undergraduate programs incorporating field study or internships. Six months/two quarters is a long time in the life of an undergraduate student. Periodically, the department considered abbreviating the field study to a single academic quarter (three months). Because students are fully enrolled for academic credit while on field study and thus paying tuition, there was a real concern that some students might be excluded from pursuing the major, that is, that six months represented a financial hardship or was otherwise a "turnoff." Far from being "too long," students returning from the field affirm time and again that their experience deepened significantly during the second three months.

Accumulated evidence suggests the field study's six-month length was actually essential to its success as a site of knowledge production because it permitted students to settle into their field studies and deeply engage in the work of the organization and world of ideas. Students could move beyond first impressions and observations of events to reflections and analyses of enduring processes. For their part, when organizations were assured of students' presence for six months, they were more likely to develop the kind of trust necessary to include them in longer-term projects and planning. Both student learning and organizational investment in student learning expanded significantly during the second quarter of field study—after most other summer interns were back on their campuses.

Students are directed to organizations whose missions address the needs of disenfranchised populations and who work directly in and with those communities (Gunn 2004). Such organizations must also be able and willing to provide students with opportunities to engage in meaningful and academically enriching work assignments. Routine office work may be part of students' responsibilities but cannot constitute the major focus of his or her work. Students are told that no one should be above stuffing envelopes (including executive directors), but also that no one's work should be exclusively stuffing envelopes either. Over the long run, field studies have divided more or less evenly among placements in Santa Cruz County, elsewhere in California and the United States, and outside the United States. International field studies have concentrated in Latin America.

Academic supervision of the full-time field study has shifted in tandem with changes in resource endowments and campus priorities. Until the 1990s, all faculty directly supervised students over the entire six months; students chose a field-study advisor who seemed the best fit with their overall academic plan. So long as the major remained comparatively small, this meant each faculty supervised from 8 to 10 students over a six-month period by reading and offering comments on field notes and papers. The growth of the major during the 1990s coincided with rising campus expectations for faculty research productivity that conflicted with faculty commitments to summer field-study supervision. A new model of field study supervision thus was established in which the field-study coordinator assumed responsibility for direct student supervision. Since its founding the department had employed a field-study coordinator (the equivalent of a full-time lecturer) in an academic (as opposed to an administrative) staff position. Shifting responsibility to the academic staff person who offered to take on the new duties seemed like a logical and appropriate move. Faculty advisors have continued to approve field-study placements and remain connected with students through periodic, structured communication over the six-month period.

One of the strengths of the Community Studies curriculum is that it gives equal weight to the learning associated with preparation *before* and reflection *after* the field study. Post-field-study analysis and reflection have always been a defining feature of the program. Upon their return from the field, students participate in a seminar entitled Analysis of Field Materials (CMMU 194), the final piece of the core curriculum. This course has several ambitions. Paramount among them is encouraging students' thoughtful intellectual reflection about their field-study experiences. Students regroup with their cohort and exchange insights and knowledge. Finally, CMMU 194 is the forum for students to make significant progress on or actually complete their senior capstone requirement.

Until the mid-1990s, all Community Studies majors were required to produce a senior thesis. Most assumed a traditional written form, although considerable variety emerged over the years, with projects involving documentary audio, photography and video projects; fiction collections; and student-directed seminars. The typical thesis project (whatever its form) is initiated in the capstone course (CMMU 194) and is completed during the following quarter, when students work individually with their faculty advisors.

During the mid-1990s the department amended its thesis-requirement policy and created an alternative senior essay option in recognition of the fact that a thesis could be an insurmountable hurdle for some students who would be prohibited from graduating despite outstanding work elsewhere in the curriculum. Initially, most students continued to favor thesis writing, but over the years the balance shifted decidedly in favor of the senior essay. This has meant that many students are able to graduate upon completing the capstone course in which they write their senior essays—an increasingly desirable option as tuition costs escalate. What is remarkable is that despite their smaller scale, senior essays are of a generally high caliber. Students develop an impressive body of knowledge in their passage through the core curriculum and are uniformly eager and able to produce a superb record of their academic experience.

The Community Studies department curriculum, in sum, has retained an essential core structure across four-plus decades of profound social, economic, and cultural change—both on campus and in the wider world. In amending the curriculum over the years, department faculty have responded to three types of changing circumstances, singly or in combination with each other. Perhaps first and foremost have been the vagaries of California's state budget, which parallel cyclical and structural changes and crises in the overall economy. A second source of curricular change has been specific, programmatic mandates at the campus level, irrespective of budget conditions—for example, the mandate that all departments offer new kinds of general education courses. Finally, the Community Studies curriculum has changed as a result of established review processes, including periodic external reviews and internal assessments conducted in the course of regular department curriculum planning.

## Trouble in Paradise

What could go—or be—wrong with an academic department whose thoughtfully organized curriculum places students for six months in social-change organizations and integrates that experience with substantive, methodological, and analytical course work, and, moreover, that boasts of alumni achievement in several fields of professional endeavor attributed by the alumni themselves to their undergraduate major? Given the rapid descent of Community Studies after 2005 to the brink of closure in 2012, the obvious answer is quite a bit can go wrong and, moreover, did. How can we understand the apparent demise of Community Studies at the very moment civic engagement was gaining ground on US campuses and increasing numbers of students were augmenting their classroom learning with off-campus internships?

The department's demise is attributable to a critical mass of problems that concatenated during the new century's first decade. Some were associated with enduring skepticism about the academic mission of Community Studies and can be considered accumulated, available combustible material needing but a spark to ignite into a full-blown legitimacy crisis. Short-term problems constituted considerably more than a single spark; rather they were more like a spreading wildfire. These included institutional changes favoring more conventional academic structures, greater emphasis on faculty research productivity, and, increasingly, externally funded research. In effect, as the campus was "regularized" (the actual word used within the central administration), it became more risk averse. An insurgent conservative politics of neoliberalism within the wider society targeted public institutions of higher education and also stoked the campus embers. These changes all brought significant heat to Community Studies. California's protracted budget crisis was the conflagration engulfing the entire University of California system, with especially deleterious effects at Santa Cruz. The following discussion elaborates these causes.

### Learning or trouble making?

Even in the early years when the campus enthusiastically embraced curricular innovation, some departments and individuals were "puzzled by the idea of institutionalizing academic credit" for the full-time field study in the Community Studies major because, as noted earlier, they "considered the field experience simply as 'troublemaking'" (Friedland and Rotkin 2003, p. 47). The field study was a target for criticism from off-campus constituencies, as well. Department founder William Friedland recalled that during the early 1970s, the Santa Cruz chancellor had to defend the Community Studies department against complaints from the CEO of a California supermarket chain about students' participating in a boycott picket while doing field study with the United Farm Workers. The chancellor apparently rejected the complaint on the grounds that the students were acting responsibly within the organization they had chosen for field study as part of their university-level education.

Community Studies survived this and other early challenges to its curricular legitimacy. Rather than preliminary hurdles to lasting institutional stability, however, such challenges established a pattern of skepticism—and some outright hostility—that recurred throughout the department's entire history. Experiential education requires a leap of faith that undergraduate students can gain knowledge—intellectual knowledge—by participating in nonacademic activities away from the college campus and without the presence of fully credentialed professors to guide them every step of the way. In my own experience as department chair, I came to realize some faculty and administrators are simply unwilling or unable to make that leap of faith, particularly on the issue of faculty presence and direct guidance of the learning process. There is evident shock and disbelief that undergraduate students can be trusted to carry lessons from the classroom into a nonclassroom setting and, absent a faculty person, sustain the learning process. As one former dean put it to me, "How can students be learning if a there is no faculty present?"

Such lingering skepticism on campus gave rise to something like a Greek chorus whose negative commentary about the Community Studies curriculum, and the field study in particular, routinely surfaced during two kinds of moments in the life of the campus. First were moments of budget crisis, which inevitably targeted Community Studies as a "logical" place to cut resources, because, while it was impossible to imagine a University of California campus without a history or a sociology department, no campus "needed" a Community Studies department. Second have been moments of administrative transition when newly appointed deans and other central campus administrators had to overcome their unfamiliarity and/or skepticism about the field study.

It would be *faux-naïf* to pretend that questions about Community Studies and the full-time field study arose and persisted entirely because of its experiential education model, however. From its inception, students were encouraged to select field studies "with a social change component, to find situations where change was an explicit aspect of the organization or community to which they went... there is little doubt that students overwhelmingly selected field locations geared at progressive social change" (Friedland and Rotkin 2003, p. 45). Plainly stated, it was not the experience per se that raised the critics' hackles, but the apparent politics of the engagement.

Within Community Studies, the field study was not framed in terms of specific ideological commitments. Instead, with great deliberation, the department framed its social change pedagogy to be wholly consistent with the University of California's status as a land grant institution under the 1862 Morrill Act. Land grant universities across the nation had a well-established tradition of providing teaching, research, and especially the *extension of learning* to varied public constituencies, including farmers, ranchers, small businesses, and even large industries. Community Studies students "would explicitly be oriented to working with constituencies that had traditionally been underserved by the University of California, i.e., minority communities and groups, poverty programs, social experiments" yet still would be operating well within the Morrill Act framework (Friedland and Rotkin 2003, p. 45). If the State of California was willing to assist its influential agribusiness sector by investing university resources in the development of a tomato that could be mechanically harvested, then surely university resources could be invested in improving the lives of workers in the tomato fields.

Or so the thinking went. Such notions about widening public access to public resources were very much aligned with Saul Alinsky's model of community organizing, forged among Chicago's immigrant working class (Slayton 1988). Alinsky built coalitions among fractious neighborhoods by defining a common interest that overrode their ethnic and religious differences: namely, access to public resources. Alinsky embraced the mantle of "radical" and framed his work as furthering the democratic legacy of revolutionary heroes like Tom Paine (Alinsky 1969, 1971). Disenfranchised people could be organized and mobilized to hold the public sector accountable and claim their rightful share of resources and a seat at the decision-making table. Community Studies never explicitly modeled itself upon Alinsky principles. But its founding ethos of extending the university's public service mandate to historically underserved constituencies resonated with the main currents of community organizing theory and practice.

Not everyone shared this sanguine, if not downright patriotic view that Community Studies was widening the ambit of democratic participation in American society. The "troublemaking" label stuck to Community Studies and became a potent source of criticism of the department's and major's legitimacy. University academic-freedom protocols largely protected Community Studies from outright political attacks. Nonetheless, notions that the Community Studies field study was "really" about political organizing (troublemaking) and lacked academic rigor (if not academic content) remained a readily animated discourse and ineluctably shaped resource allocation and academic planning.

Given the ongoing skepticism about the academic mission of Community Studies, one may well ask how the department and major managed to survive at all. Community Studies was never an isolated outpost of social-change-oriented pedagogy. Though the program could often seem under siege, department faculty became active citizens of the campus, contributing to myriad academic initiatives, producing noted scholarship, winning awards, serving on committees, advising graduate students, assuming administrative roles, and generally imbricating Community Studies into the institution. In fact, founder William Friedland served as dean of Social Sciences for a brief period in the late 1980s.

Community Studies students also deserve considerable credit for their roles in blunting criticism and winning accolades for the department. Students engaged in part-time and full-time field studies in the local region became an important resource for local organizations and had a tremendous impact on the institutional landscape of social services and community organizations. Students' accumulated field study presence very much fulfilled the department's founding vision of the extended university. For many years, wise campus administrators knew whom to call when they needed to account for the university's contributions to the local community. A quick call to the Community Studies department would yield data about the thousands of hours of community-based work performed by Santa Cruz students, in the public interest, on behalf of people and organizations in the State of California. In addition, students won acclaim by successfully competing for campus scholarships and awards for their field study projects or senior theses. Students have been impressive ambassadors for Community Studies throughout its history.

## "Regularizing" Santa Cruz

While the campus could always justly boast of faculty scholarly achievement, the 1990s witnessed a new emphasis on raising Santa Cruz's profile as a research institution more closely and clearly aligned with other University of California campuses. The campus had earned a national reputation for its "uncommon commitment" to undergraduate education (particularly as part of a sprawling public-university system) but worried that this reputation overshadowed the campus's research ambitions and accomplishments. The more explicit emphasis on faculty research productivity was accompanied by expanded graduate education, as the 1990s witnessed the establishment of several new doctoral programs. In line with the campus priority that all departments embrace graduate studies, Community Studies planned and launched an innovative Master of Arts degree program in social documentation.

The "socdoc" program was designed to harness the power of media to produce representations of the very same community constituencies that had long been the focus of the undergraduate major. Several new faculty were hired to meet graduate program needs and accommodate burgeoning undergraduate enrollments.

Strenuous efforts to initiate traditional graduate programs were but one signal during the 1990s that the heady experimental days of the campus's founding were well and truly past. The decade witnessed a pervasive effort to "regularize" Santa Cruz by aligning its administrative and academic structures with those of the other University of California campuses. "Boards of study" (which in most cases had already ceased to be alternative structures) were eliminated in favor of conventional academic departments modeled after established academic disciplines, which were grouped into traditional academic divisions (physical and biological sciences, social sciences, humanities, arts, etc.). Residential-college affiliation among faculty was supplanted by department and disciplinary loyalties. A school of engineering was founded, marking a major new departure for a campus established around the liberal arts and sciences disciplines. By the late 1990s, the practice of individualized narrative evaluations—a signature Santa Cruz practice—had been eroded by the introduction of optional letter grades, and eventually gave way entirely when letter grades became the requirement and narrative evaluations the option. A network of social sororities and fraternities began taking members and contributing their characteristic rituals to campus social life. The iconic "Whole Earth" café was shuttered and replaced with a pizza restaurant within a new and improved student union complex. Finally, the banana slug campus mascot that once epitomized UCSC's indifference to many of the trappings of college student culture morphed from a slimy antimascot into a warm and fuzzy cheerleader giving the thumbs up at campus events.

## The times, they were a changing, *again*

These and other campus changes amounted to a heightened risk aversion to differences that can challenge an institution's reputation and legitimacy and impede its aspirations—in this case, the Santa Cruz quest to be recognized as a research university like its UC-system counterparts. Worry about the campus's institutional reputation was not ill-conceived, even though valid questions can be raised about specific changes. Beginning in the 1990s, Santa Cruz faced very real challenges to its funding and legitimacy, along with the rest of the public sector of higher education, as an advancing neoliberal political economy prioritized private sector initiatives over public ones in virtually every sector of social endeavor—including education. The most obviously quantifiable neoliberal shift has been the withdrawal of public financial support for public education systems at all levels. The decline of public financing amid rising privatization has stoked a new ethic in which institutions compete for scarce resources in what is now deemed an "education marketplace." The ascendant competitive ethic writ large in society finds its direct expression on campus when departments are forced to compete for never-enough institutional resources (such as faculty positions) and students are forced to compete for never-enough classroom resources (such as spaces in required courses).

Eroding support for public institutions of higher education extends beyond their funding, however, into the less quantifiable realm of political culture. The allocation of public resources reflects social values and perceptions, however imperfectly. Values and perceptions themselves reflect competing discursive constructions of the wider public sector: how the public sector and its role in society are defined, defended, and/or defamed. Support for public higher education among the general population depends crucially upon the extent to which institutions enjoy legitimacy: that is, they have clearly defined goals, work assiduously to achieve them and, in doing so, make the best use of public resources. An especially pernicious argument within neoliberal discourse has been that public education institutions fail in their most basic mission of serving the public interest because they are captive to narrow "special interests." Such claims undermine the legitimacy of public higher education and erode public trust, which in turn rationalizes reduced funding.

It is rarely possible to establish direct causal relationships between wider social changes like the advent of neoliberalism, and particular events like the closure of a specific academic program on a specific university campus. Yet the wider assault on public higher education contributed mightily to the legitimacy and funding crises experienced by Community Studies after 2005 when the Santa Cruz campus came directly into the crosshairs of conservative writer David Horowitz (Horowitz 2007 and 2010; Horowitz and Laksin 2009). Horowitz was—and is—a vociferous critic of the US professoriate for its supposedly pervasive liberal, left-leaning politics, which supposedly are foisted upon unwitting students in a classroom process more akin to indoctrination than education. As a self-styled defender of academic freedom, he launched the organization "Students for Academic Freedom," has published widely on the subject, is a regular on the lecture circuit, and because of his fearless provocations, has become a darling in certain media circles.

While allegations that professors inject left-liberal politics into their work is a staple of conservative criticism, Horowitz is distinguished by the consistent ferocity of his attacks, his commitment to political organizing around the issue and, no less, his unabashed practice of naming names. UC Santa Cruz was rudely introduced to these tactics in September 2007 when Horowitz named the campus "The Worst School in America" in the online journal frontpagemag.com and in various national media outlets (Clark 2008). While exempting science departments from the campus malaise, Horowitz bluntly argued that "inside the classrooms of its liberal arts division something besides the life of the mind is being nourished. In these environs, UC Santa Cruz is beyond any doubt the most radical university in the United States, its curricula anything but academic." The departments singled out for harsh opprobrium—raising questions about their curriculum, courses, and faculty—were interdisciplinary departments of American Studies, Feminist Studies, History of Consciousness, and perhaps inevitably, Community Studies—which he labeled "a training program in radical politics." The article deployed an attack strategy against UCSC already well honed by attacks against other public universities: parsing official class syllabi, departmental web pages, and course catalogs to allege violations of public regulations proscribing political indoctrination by faculty and protecting academic freedom of students.

The argument here is not that David Horowitz single-handedly took down Community Studies or any other department, although it is worth noting the coincidence that almost all the UCSC departments attacked by Horowitz have since experienced decline and/or outright closure. Most of his criticisms were old news, in fact. What *was* new and significant was that his criticisms were broadcast on global media platforms as part of a wider conservative political movement to undermine the legitimacy of public higher education *tout court*. Moreover, they appeared precisely as UCSC was going about the delicate exercise of distancing itself from certain aspects of its past to make way for its rebranding as a top-tier research university, replete with new private giving campaigns and a new website featuring a rolling sequence of approved images with the tagline "THIS is UC Santa Cruz." Horowitz's rantings never generated their desired official investigation into professorial misconduct, but neither were they officially repudiated. Unproven but not denied, Horowitz's invective against Community Studies occupied a strange liminal space with subtle yet quite powerful effects: reminding risk-averse campus administrators that for all the institution's changes and strenuous efforts of reintroduction, it still harbored a political liability in the form of Community Studies.

### State budget blues

The latter half of the first decade of the twenty-first century was an inauspicious moment for Community Studies to resurface as an institutional risk. Those years witnessed a period of administrative turnover with four different interim or permanent chancellors—one of whom died in a tragic suicide—and divisional deans. Throughout this turbulence, the campus continued the quest of elevating its research university stature and breaking into the National Research Council's (NRC) rankings of top doctoral-degree-granting departments. Such goals required that curricular planning and resource allocation assume greater strategic focus. Not every department would (or could) measure up and resource allocations would reflect this fact. A department like Community Studies with a popular and growing undergraduate major and innovative master's program might not cut it in a permanently changing institutional environment that had grown impatient with undergraduate-program idiosyncrasies and allegations of "troublemaking."

This grim scenario darkened considerably with each passing year amid California's worsening fiscal situation. Higher education is one of the few areas of discretionary spending in the state budget because unlike other sectors, even K–12 education, it is not protected by a specific spending mandate established through a citizens' initiative. The University of California budget was cut, cut again, and then again. On at least two occasions, it was cut midway through the academic year, a once unthinkably drastic and disruptive act. By 2011, state support was below 1997 levels, when the UC system as a whole was smaller and offered fewer degree programs to fewer students. The University abandoned the fiction that it didn't charge tuition, only "educational fees," and proceeded to increase tuition repeatedly, and in some years, more than once. By the beginning of the 2011–12 academic year, tuition and fees had increased ten times in the proceeding decade and had more than tripled the annual cost to students. Cuts to the Santa Cruz campus were especially draconian because the campus lacks revenue producing and/or revenue neutral ("self-support-ing") units like law or medical schools. The campus depends chiefly on the increas-ingly scarce resource: public funding.

It is hard to overstate the combined effects on Community Studies of the most serious budget crisis in the University of California's history and, at the local level, administrative turnover within an institutional context of realigned strategic priori-ties and heightened risk aversion. What during normal times are "regular" faculty departures because of retirement or tenure denial became crises as vacated faculty positions were transferred out of Community Studies to other departments deemed more strategically significant and used to write down the university's budget cut. For a few years, temporary academic staffing funds were sufficient to fill the gap between the department's curricular obligations and faculty resources, but by the end of the decade, temporary funds became scarce as well.

Community Studies entered a netherworld as key staff positions were perma-nently eliminated, and the presiding dean made it abundantly clear that faculty positions transferred out of the department would not be returned. The campus academic senate committee charged with overseeing undergraduate education sus-pended admissions into the major in spring 2010 out of concern that the depart-ment was no longer able to sustain its curriculum with available faculty. Under conditions where the department was losing resources and experiencing withering criticism, internal relations among faculty collapsed. Faculty associated with the department's graduate social documentation program (who had little connection with the Community Studies major) found a new department home for that degree program as other faculty transferred to greener pastures elsewhere on campus. Based on these departures, in spring 2011 the presiding dean submitted a plan to disestab-lish the Community Studies department as an administrative unit of the university and indicated his intention to follow up with a plan to discontinue the Community Studies major as an academic program.[3]

## Lessons from the Fall

The precipitous decline of Community Studies at UC Santa Cruz is obviously a singular event driven by myriad local factors, specific histories, and unique person-alities: in social science parlance, it is not generalizable. The department's demise is less a model for the fate of similar programs; rather, it is more a roadmap of warning signs and pitfalls. Specifically, the Community Studies experience offers cautionary tales about navigating institutional change and the inescapable politics of commu-nity work. The concluding section attempts to draw out such connections between Community Studies and the contemporary civic-engagement movement in higher education.

### Change happens

Institutional change is an obvious fact of life in higher education. Colleges and uni-versities are complex organizations riven by competing priorities and resource claims and expectations of and demands for continual innovation. Institutional change can follow carefully planned and prescribed paths, as when a campus develops and carries out strategic-planning initiatives. For example, the priorities of UC Santa Cruz were realigned consciously and significantly at the turn of the twenty-first century as the campus sought to shed its association as an undergraduate liberal arts school known for alternative programs and practices. Lacking a doctoral program (or even a path to creating one) and employing an experiential education model subject to ongoing skepticism, Community Studies became singularly identified with alternative undergraduate education at the time when the campus had set its sights elsewhere. Manifesting the past in an institution may be fine for cherished campus landmarks but bodes ill for academic programs. Even a program's best efforts to rebrand itself and demonstrate its relevance and excellence—all measures undertaken within Community Studies in response to the presiding dean's disestablishment plans—can fall on deaf ears when an institution has drawn new lines between its past and present.

Institutional change can also be opportunistic and shaped by emerging trends, if not fads, of institutional practices that often derive from imperatives in the wider society. Community Studies was founded during the late 1960s when society demanded the university become more engaged with life outside the campus boundaries. During the decades spanning the turn of the twenty-first century similar demands have been made on educational institutions at all levels to re-engage children and adolescents with the "habits of the heart" essential to rebuilding social capital (Putnam 2001, Bellah et al. 1985). Nothing less than the fate of American democracy is said to be at stake in the civic-engagement movement.

Such demands have given rise to a veritable civic-engagement industry devoted to encouraging—and often requiring—college students to become involved in communities near and far, through programs offering what has become known as "service-learning." In a tendency first observed by Alexis de Tocqueville about American social movements, civic engagement and service-learning have spawned national private- and public-sector organizations and partnerships seeking to heighten the impact of engaged activities dispersed across the vast institutional landscape of higher education. Perhaps the prime example is the Campus Compact formed in 1985 by the presidents of Brown, Georgetown, and Stanford universities. In 2011, the Campus Compact claimed membership of over 1,100 institutions of higher learning that accounted for over six million undergraduate students nationwide. While the Campus Compact rightly claims it is the "only national higher education association dedicated solely to campus-based civic engagement," its cause is widely shared among a host of other organizations, ranging from Association of American Colleges and Universities, which identifies civic diversity and global engagement as a core mission, to Learn and Serve America, a program of the federal Corporation for National and Community Service that establishes strategic priorities for service-learning and sponsors competitive grant programs.

Despite the impressive resources mobilized behind the campus-based civic-engagement and service-learning movements, there is no guarantee that these movements are gaining a permanent place within higher education. Much of the energy within the civic-engagement movement seems associated with relatively small liberal arts and community colleges, notwithstanding the institutional heft of the Campus Compact founders. Large universities have long promoted public service, and "civic engagement" may be just the current label given to this part of their institutional mission. It is an open question whether the civic-engagement movement can gain lasting traction without greater involvement by leading research universities, which tend to set the standards for higher education as a whole and place a significantly higher priority on faculty research productivity and excellence. Civic-engagement programs risk becoming tangential to the core missions (research and education) of the university (Fish 2008). At UC Santa Cruz, for example, top administrators did not renew the campus's membership in the California Campus Compact in 2010, citing limitations imposed by the ongoing budget crisis. The civic-engagement movement may lack staying power and service-learning programs may face waning institutional commitment should they become too costly relative to other mission-critical activities. Civic-engagement programs could also face competition from a movement in higher education promising "the next new thing." Such competition certainly played a role in undermining Community Studies.

### Brand management

Shifting campus priorities contributed greatly to the demise of Community Studies, but they do not tell the entire story. Given the department's long experience with social-change pedagogy, it is reasonable to ask about the extent to which, and how, the department applied its own expertise to its own situation and tried to adapt to changing institutional conditions. These questions are especially relevant because the rising civic-engagement movement (Skocpol and Fiorina 1999), on and off campus, might have provided a new lease on life to the Community Studies model of social-change-oriented experiential education. The short answer is that the department absolutely failed to learn from its own history and did not build on- or off-campus alliances with kindred programs. The longer answer explaining that failure illuminates both the department's difficulty in navigating an education marketplace increasingly crowded with civic-engagement options and the problematic nature of that marketplace itself (Brinn-Hyatt 2001).

While administrators wielding the budget ax have lamented how California's budget crisis forced their hand in closing Community Studies, they have been quick to offer assurances that students would be ably served by numerous other campus programs offering similar experiential education opportunities—and many social-justice opportunities, to boot. By the early 2000s, off-campus internship programs associated with individual majors and departments had become as popular at Santa Cruz as they were around the country. An array of student affairs programming augmented academic community-service opportunities, as well. The Student Volunteer Center had become an important hub of community service and civic-engagement activity replete with awards and recognition ceremonies. In 2001, the campus inaugurated an entire residential college dedicated to the theme of "social justice and community," which annually sponsors service-learning courses, a weekend practical-activism conference, an alternative spring break, and assorted speakers and events related to social justice throughout the academic year. A campus commitment to

civic engagement is also evinced in the recently revised general education requirements for undergraduate students that include service-learning.

The Community Studies department witnessed and worried about the creation
of courses, field-study programs, and entire majors that often duplicated some of
its own courses, practices, and/or curricular structure, to say nothing of its long-
standing focus on social justice. But the department never formally commented
or raised objections with the campus administration about the apparent—and
occasionally blatant—duplication of Community Studies. Overall, the department
eschewed taking action to distinguish the mission of Community Studies from
other the civic-engagement and service-learning programs sprouting up across campus. Perhaps more troubling, with a very few exceptions, the department did not
join forces and collaborate with or seek to establish a leadership role for itself among
the new social-justice-oriented programs.

How can such inaction be accounted for by a department known for its academic
activism? One simple reason is that until the prolonged budget crisis, plentiful campus resources allowed all such programs to grow and thrive: "Let a hundred flow-
ers blossom" captures that now distant moment. Those comparatively flush times
had permitted Community Studies to plan and launch its new graduate program,
which kept it plenty busy while social-justice-themed programming arose elsewhere
on campus. Institutional courtesy and custom restrain questioning the efforts of
colleagues who are launching new programs, however similar they seem to one's
own. Academic turf wars can be unseemly, perhaps especially when social justice is
a shared value.

By not intervening when new programs duplicated key features—and, in a few
instances, the entire structure of the Community Studies curriculum—the department created new vulnerabilities for itself. The proliferation of service-learning and
social-justice courses or programs blurred perceptions of Community Studies's academic mission. Community service programs advocated social justice and made
some of the same claims as the department about the importance of theory and
practice. Field-study programs proliferated and promised deep engagement with
community organizations. Under these conditions, it became plausible for students, and especially for administrative decision makers, to ask what distinguished
Community Studies from upstart campus service-learning, community engagement, and field-study programs—that is, aside from Community Studies' long
association with political activism and troublemaking.

Community Studies might have avoided its dire fate had the department proactively involved itself in guiding the development of service-learning on campus.
Similarly, Community Studies could have taken the lead in defining the campus's
involvement in the civic-engagement movement within higher education and, in
this way, made sure the department was included in new strategic moves rather than
responding to them *post hoc*. Put somewhat differently, the department could have
done a much better job of managing its brand, beginning with a basic recognition
that higher education was becoming crowded with programs doing or at least promising similar things as Community Studies, *even if in fact they only appeared to be
duplicating Community Studies*. That the department failed to build and maintain
campus alliances with kindred programs meant it could neither lead nor differentiate

itself from them. Latent hostility toward Community Studies, barely submerged during the best of times and reanimated by politically conservative attacks against the campus, at long last made the department seem dispensable (Bookwalter 2009). The (very likely) demise of Community Studies surely was not caused by the rise of new civic-engagement and service-learning programs on campus. But the changed campus landscape of community engagement opportunities has permitted an institutional retreat from Community Studies that would be unthinkable without the new programs.

## Making trouble after all these years

The wisdom of hindsight clearly indicates the department should have created new opportunities for itself as the campus leapt aboard the community engagement and service-learning bandwagons. Still, it is unclear whether such efforts would have succeeded given the wider institutional changes afoot, and especially given the long-standing animus toward the "troublemaking" field study and general derogation of the department—derogation which ignored every effort by the department and its supporters—students, alumni, community organizations, allied faculty—to save itself. In this regard, perhaps the final lesson to be drawn from the Community Studies experience is that politics are unavoidable and may get you in the end.

Community Studies channeled the zeitgeist of the 1960s by fusing social movement activism with experiential education and academically validating this fusion in a three-part curriculum. Given the array of issues at stake in the era's social movements and the university's role in promoting critical thinking, it was inevitable that Community Studies would develop a reputation for encouraging students to challenge institutional power wherever it resides: in corporate boardrooms, the halls of government, or the discursive domains of social institutions. The Community Studies model of organizing and mobilization inspired generations of college students to proudly adopt the Alinsky-style mantle of radical activism and seek resources and power for the disenfranchised and, above all, to transform institutions (DeFillipis et al. 2010). For 40 years, the university tolerated Community Studies, usually in a grudging way because the "radical activism" ostensibly practiced by students was easily recognizable as Morrill Act–inspired public service.

The advent of the civic-engagement movement offers the university a new model of public service that steers clear of associations with radical politics by emphasizing individual and private volunteerism as an antidote to social needs, which themselves are defined in individual and private terms. In the new civic-engagement model, college students work within institutional boundaries and offer civil society's principal resource—their volunteer service— and the promise of personal empowerment rather than institutional transformation. The civic-engagement and service-learning movements are no less a product of their time than Community Studies was, channeling the zeitgeist of an era when public service consists of private acts of charity.

For this reason, the contemporary civic-engagement and service-learning movements have become preferred alternatives to older models of campus-based community engagement such as the organizing and mobilization exemplified by Community Studies. Yet it remains to be seen if these contemporary movements will escape the risk-assessment calculations of university administrators who may become worried that "service" and "engagement" are just new words for "politics." This question is especially pertinent because the civic-engagement movement, including the blue-blooded Campus Compact, employs a discourse of social justice to characterize its goals. The nature and definition of "social justice" are rarely spelled out and are perhaps left deliberately vague, as is the very concept of civic engagement—though it includes arguably political work by students like voter registration. The Community Studies experience suggests it is impossible to avoid politics when pursuing social justice or performing public service. The experience of Community Studies also suggests how *that* can turn out.

## Notes

1. This discussion reflects the structure of the Community Studies undergraduate major circa 2009, immediately prior to the announced suspension.
2. Students also prepared for field study by completing three upper-level substantive courses directly related to their field-study and academic plan that could be taken in or outside the Community Studies department.
3. Under the policy and practice of shared governance within the University of California system, administrative and curricular decisions are the purviews, respectively, of the central administration and tenure track faculty.

## References

Alinsky, Saul. *Reveille for Radicals*. New York: Random House, 1969.
———. *Rules for Radicals*. New York: Random House, 1971.
Bellah, Robert N., Richard Madsen, William M. Sullivan, Ann Swidler and Stephen M. Tipton, *Habits of the Heart: Individualism and Commitment in American Life*. Berkeley: University of California Press, 1985.
Bookwalter, Genevieve. "Budget ax to fall on UCSC's popular and controversial Community Studies department." Santa Cruz *Sentinel*, posted online 04/07/2009 01:30:19 AM PDT at www.santacruzsentinel.com.
———. "Community Studies takes first cuts: UCSC staffers get pink slips in wake of $13 million deficit." Santa Cruz *Sentinel*, posted online 05/05/2009 01:30:45 AM PDT at www.santacruzsentinel.com.
Brinn-Hyatt, Susan. "From Citizen to Volunteer: Neoliberal Governance and the Erasure of Poverty." In Judith Goode and Jeff Maskovsky, editors, *The New Poverty Studies: The Ethnography of Power, Politics and Impoverished People in the United States*. New York: New York University Press, 2001, pp. 201–35.
Clark, James. "Conservative Activist David Horowitz Visits What He Calls the 'Worst School in America.'" *City on a Hill Press*, published June 5, 2008 at 12:00 a.m.
Cruikshank, Barbara. *The Will to Empower: Democratic Citizens and Other Subjects*. Ithaca, NY: Cornell University Press, 1999.
DeFilippis, James, Robert Fisher and Eric Shragge. *Contesting Community: The Limits and Potential of Local Organizing*. Piscataway NJ: Rutgers University Press, 2010.
Fish, Stanley. *Save the World on Your Own Time*. New York: Oxford University Press, 2008.
Foucault, Michel. *Discipline and Punish: The Birth of the Prison*. New York: Vintage Paperback, 2nd Edition, 1995.

————. *The Birth of the Clinic: An Archeology of Medical Perception.* New York: Vintage Books Edition, 1994.

————. *History of Madness.* New York: Routledge (lst edition), 2006.

Friedland, William and Michael Rotkin. "Academic Activists: Community Studies at the University of California, Santa Cruz." In Torry D. Dickinson, editor, *Community and the World: Participating in Social Change.* New York: Nova Science Publishing, July 2003.

Gunn, Christopher. *Third Sector Development: Making Up for the Market.* Ithaca: Cornell University Press, 2004.

Horowitz, David. *Indoctrination U: The Left's War Against Academic Freedom.* New York: Encounter Books, 2007.

————. *Reforming Our Universities: The Campaign For An Academic Bill Of Rights.* Washington, DC: Regnery Publishing, 2010.

Horowitz, David and Jacob Laksin. *One-Party Classroom: How Radical Professors at America's Top Colleges Indoctrinate Students and Undermine Our Democracy.* New York: Crown Publishing Group, 2009.

Incite! Women of Color Against Violence. *The Revolution Will Not Be Funded: Beyond the Non-Profit Industrial Complex.* Cambridge, MA: South End Press, 2007.

Joseph, Miranda. *Against the Romance of Community.* Minneapolis: University of Minnesota Press, 2002.

Lyon-Callo, Vincent. *Inequality, Poverty and Neoliberal Governance: Teaching Activist Ethnography in the Homeless Sheltering Industry.* Toronto: University of Toronto Press, 2008.

Peck, Jamie and Adam Tickell. "Neoliberalizing Space," *Antipode* 34, no. 3 (July 2002): 380–404.

Poppendieck, Janet. *Sweet Charity? Emergency Food and the End of Entitlement.* New York: Viking Penquin, 1998.

Putnam, Robert. *Bowling Alone: The Collapse and Revival of American Community.* New York: Touchstone / Simon & Schuster, 2001.

Shaw, Randy. *The Ac tivist's Handbook: A Primer for the 1990s and Beyond.* Berkeley: University of California Press, 1996

————. *Reclaiming America: Nike, Clean Air, and the New National Activism.* Berkeley: University of California Press, 1999.

Shrag, Peter. *Paradise Lost: California's Experience, America's Future.* Berkeley: University of California Press, 1998.

Skocpol, Theda and Morris P. Fiorina, editors. *Civic Engagement and American Democracy.* Washington DC: The Brookings Institution, 1999.

Slayton, Robert A., *Back of the Yards: The Making of a Local Democracy.* Chicago: University of Chicago Press, 1988.

Wagner, David. *What's Love Got to Do with It? A Critical Look at American Charity.* New York: The New Press, 2001.

Wolch, Jennifer. *The Shadow State: Government and Voluntary Sector in Transition.* New York: Foundation Center, 1990.

## CHAPTER 7

# Measuring the Impact of Community Service Learning

*Scott Seider and Sarah Novick*
Boston University

O pportunities for students to engage in community service and community service learning are increasingly prevalent on American college campuses. According to an annual survey of college freshmen by the University of California, Los Angeles (UCLA), 65 percent of American college students recently characterized their respective universities as offering opportunities for community service learning (Liu, Ruiz, DeAngelo & Pryor, 2009). Likewise, the Corporation for National and Community Service has reported that the number of college students participating in community service jumped from 2.7 million in 2002 to 3.3 million in 2005, a growth rate double that of adult volunteers during this same time period (Dote, Cramer, Dietz & Grimm, 2006).

Certainly, there have been a number of robust research studies of the effects of university-based community service learning upon both college students engaged in such service (e.g., Jones & Abes, 2004; Moely, Mercer, Ilustre, Miron & McFarland, 2002) and upon the community members with whom the students interact (e.g., Frumkin & Jastrzab, 2010). It behooves university faculty and administrators leading community service learning programs to be conversant in this literature; however, we also believe that these individuals must be critical consumers when it comes to the relevance of this research to their efforts. We offer this caution because, as prominent researcher James Youniss (Metz, McLellan, & Youniss, 2003) has noted, one of the challenges in drawing broad conclusions from the existing scholarship on community service learning programs is that both the "service" and the "learning" embedded in these programs can vary dramatically from program to program. Noting the broad range of service activities that can fall under the umbrella of community service learning, Youniss has noted that "It does not seem reasonable to expect that vastly different forms of service, such as tutoring peers, filing papers, or building houses for impoverished families, would affect adolescent participants in the same manner" (p. 189). In short, context matters.

For this reason, we believe it is crucial that university faculty and administrators leading majors, minors, and certificate programs in community service learning undertake their own evaluation of the impact of their programs upon their particular students and within the context of their particular community. In the remainder of this chapter, we seek to offer a tool kit for undertaking such an assessment. We deliberately use the phrase "tool kit" rather than "script" or "formula" to describe our efforts because, as noted above, we believe strongly that the evaluation of a particular community service learning program needs to be designed to meet the specific needs of that program. Toward that end, we have framed our tool kit around a number of questions we believe to be essential to developing a robust (and personalized) evaluation of one's program. To better illustrate the role of each tool within our tool kit, we draw upon, for examples, our own evaluation of a community service learning program at Boston College—the PULSE Program—during the 2008–09 academic year. Thus, before proceeding with our essential questions, we offer the briefest of overviews of the PULSE Program.

## The PULSE Program

The PULSE Program is a community service learning program that began at Boston College in 1970 with the dual goal of educating students about social justice and demonstrating the relevance of philosophy and theology to the "real world." As described on the PULSE Program website, the program's mission is the following

> to educate our students about social injustice by putting them into direct contact with marginalized communities and social change organizations and by encouraging discussion on classic and contemporary works of philosophy and theology. Our goal is to foster critical consciousness and enable students to question conventional wisdom and learn how to work for a just society.

Structurally, the PULSE Program functions as an independent program with a faculty director, assistant director, administrative support, and a nearly $1,000,000 endowment. However, the faculty members who teach in the PULSE Program are drawn from Boston College's philosophy and theology departments. In this way, the structure of the PULSE Program might be described as an *Ur-Department*—similar to the beginnings of many Women's Studies and African American Studies programs in higher education. By this we mean that these now well-established departments often began as interdisciplinary programs composed of faculty who held joint appointments in more traditional departments (English, History, Sociology, etc.) and only later achieved departmental status with their own unique faculty members (Butin, 2006).

Boston College students participating in the PULSE Program enroll in a year-long, 12-credit sequence in philosophy and theology entitled, "Person and Social Responsibility, I–II," which fulfills the entire Boston College core requirement in philosophy and theology (four courses). Students meet three times a week for class and participate in a weekly discussion section. While the content of the course varies somewhat across the 12 philosophy and theology faculty members who teach in the program, readings in all sections include works from the history of philosophy (e.g., Plato, Aristotle, Augustine, Boethius, Locke, Rousseau); from contemporary philosophers (e.g., Hannah Arendt, Michael Foucault, John Rawls, Charles Taylor); from classic and contemporary theologians (e.g., Augustine, C.S. Lewis, Dorothy Day); and from core theological texts (e.g., Old and New Testaments, Bhagavad Gita).

In addition to these academic courses, all Boston College students enrolled in the PULSE Program participate in a year-long service project at one of more than 50 social service agencies. Their work in these service placements ranges from tutoring urban elementary school students to volunteering at a suicide hotline to working in an emergency room to helping low-income families apply for affordable housing. Approximately 40 percent of the placements are in the field of education; 20 percent address issues of homelessness; 25 percent address issues involving health care or the elderly; the remaining 15 percent involve the corrections system, immigration, racism, and other social issues. Students devote 10–12 hours a week to their respective service placements (including travel time) for the entire academic year. The PULSE Program conceives of students' time at the service placement, not as a volunteer opportunity but as an additional learning platform, one that supplements and complements learning on campus. As such, the students are evaluated on their learning at their off-site placements; the evaluation represents 40 percent of their final grade for the course.

Every year approximately 500 Boston College students express interest in the approximately 400 places available in the program. These places are distributed via a randomized lottery based upon students' registration numbers. Students who are not selected to participate in the PULSE Program are placed on a wait list and are of course welcome to register for PULSE in a subsequent academic year.

### *The Tool Kit*

Having outlined the structure of the PULSE Program at Boston College, we seek in the pages that follow to offer a useful tool kit for faculty and administrators committed to assessing the effects of their own major, minor, and certificate programs in community engagement. We frame the take-aways as a series of questions we believe are worth considering prior to embarking upon any type of formal assessment of programmatic effects, and we use our own evaluation of the PULSE Program to try to illustrate the particular tools within the tool kit.

### Question #1: What is Your Program's Core Purpose?

One of the most robust evaluations of either community service or community service learning to date is Peter Frumkin and Joann Jastrzab's (2010) work on the effects of the AmeriCorps national service program. Although these researchers took a primarily quantitative approach to assessing the impact of AmeriCorps, they wisely began their evaluation by conducting 50 qualitative interviews with leaders in the field of national service. From these interviews emerged four different "visions or conceptions of the purpose and impact of national service" (p. 5). Here, we offer brief descriptions of these four different visions out of a belief that one cannot carry out an effective program assessment without tremendous clarity about the objectives one's program is seeking to accomplish.

Perhaps the most common objective underlying university-based programs in community service learning are to strengthen participating students' conception of themselves as citizens of a local, national, and international community and to increase their levels of civic engagement within these various communities. Actions that would constitute active citizenship could range from voting in a local election, to participating in a protest or boycott, to "liking" a particular candidate or social issue on Facebook. As Frumkin and Jastrzab (2010) note, "Citizenship is a complex concept in and of itself," and there are many different perspectives on the model of citizenship that should be driving a particular major, minor, or certificate program in community service learning. There is, of course, no single answer to the question, What does an engaged citizen look like? However, before evaluating a particular program's ability to foster more active citizens, faculty and administrators associated with the program must arrive at a clear and mutual understanding of the model of citizenship they wish their program to promote.

According to Frumkin and Jastrzab, a second group of leaders and policy makers involved in national service identified personal growth as the primary purpose underlying national service. This personal growth can take a variety of forms. For example, engagement in community service and community service learning often gives participants the opportunity "to cross paths with individuals they would otherwise never meet" (p. 10). For college students, participation in community service learning during a crucial period in their development of a mature adult identity community service learning can have a powerful effect upon their beliefs, values, and worldviews (Erikson, 1968).

Another group of leaders in national service focus less on the impact of community service learning upon students' perspectives and worldviews and more on its ability to open participants' eyes "to the full range of life choices that are available to them" (p. 11). These leaders also regard community service learning as a mechanism for "providing participants with training in both hard, technical skills and soft, interpersonal workplace skills" (p. 12). Clearly, a program that considers its primary objective to be personal growth or career development will want to choose a very different set of outcomes to assess than a program focused upon strengthening participating students' civic engagement. In this comparison, one can start to see why it is imperative to be clear about the purpose underlying one's program prior to embarking upon any attempt to evaluate its effectiveness.

The conceptions of public service we have just cited focused almost exclusively on the students or corps members carrying out the service. The final two conceptions of public service offered by Frumkin and Jastrzab take a perspective on service that more explicitly includes the communities and individuals served by the students or corps members. Specifically, one group of leaders and policy makers interviewed by Frumkin and Jastrzab characterized the primary objective underlying community service learning as the "forging of ties that bring people into contact with one another and create trust where once there was none" (p. 15). In other words, these leaders conceived of the service itself as less important than the bonds forged across traditional borders, such as age, race, class, immigrant status, and geography, which strengthen the sense of responsibility that Americans feel for fellow Americans regardless of those aforementioned differences (Giroux, 1992). Again, faculty leading a program in community service learning with the primary objective of forging such ties need to assess their program's outcomes quite differently than do colleagues leading a program focused upon personal growth or increased civic engagement.

Finally, a fourth group of leaders and policy makers in national service note that the AmeriCorps motto is "Getting things done." For these leaders, the primary purpose of public service is to provide a low-cost mechanism for addressing critical needs in low-income communities that otherwise might not be met. According to Frumkin and Jastrzab, this conception of the purpose underlying national service has meant that AmeriCorps has spent a significant amount of time and resources "counting the number of shrubs planted by a service project or documenting the number of tutoring hours delivered" (p. 20). Again, faculty leading a major, minor, or certificate program in community service learning for which "getting things done" is its primary purpose would want to choose an entirely different set of outcomes to assess its effectiveness than would faculty leading a program focused on social capital, personal growth, or active citizenship.

As noted above, we believe the first step toward assessing program effectiveness is clarifying the core purpose (or purposes) underlying the program. In sharing the four conceptions of public service offered by Frumkin and Jastrzab, we deliberately refrained from positing any sort of hierarchy. We neither believe nor claim here that a program striving to increase participants' civic engagement is necessarily better or worse than a program focused on personal growth or one focused on addressing critical community needs. Nor do we claim that a major, minor, or certificate program in community service learning can only focus on one of the above-mentioned objectives. We would, however, be skeptical about a program that claimed to put an equal emphasis on all four objectives—active citizenship, personal growth, social-capital building, and the meeting of critical needs. And, more importantly with respect to the focus of this chapter, we would be doubtful about the ability of any single evaluation to effectively report on that program's success across all four domains. In other words, we believe that even a program that legitimately focuses on several different objectives must make choices about what to focus upon in assessing its ability to meet these objectives.

We found ourselves faced with these very choices in spring 2008 as we began planning for our assessment of the PULSE Program. We met several times that spring with the director and assistant director of the PULSE Program with the goal of determining what the focus of our upcoming evaluation should be. Recall from earlier in the chapter that the mission of the PULSE Program is to "educate students about social injustice by putting them into direct contact with marginalized communities and social change organizations and by encouraging discussion on classic and contemporary works of philosophy and theology. Our goal is to foster critical consciousness and enable students to question conventional wisdom and learn how to work for a just society." On its face, this mission statement would seem to characterize the core objectives of the PULSE Program as most closely aligned with the second purpose laid out by Frumkin and Jastrzab (2010), namely, to offer Boston College students an opportunity for personal growth through their interactions "with individuals they would otherwise never meet" (p. 10).

With that core purpose in mind, we set out to design an evaluation tool that would allow us to capture the personal growth of PULSE participants—in other words, to capture the ways in which participating in the PULSE Program had impacted participating students' beliefs, values, and worldviews. Capturing these changes was of great interest to the PULSE Program's faculty and leadership, whose own academic training was in philosophy and theology. In fact, in previous years, students participating in the PULSE Program had completed course evaluations in which they had been asked to assess their personal growth along these lines and to report on their perceptions of the effects of the PULSE Program. For example, one question asked students to respond to the following statement: "Because of my PULSE experience, I have been able to clarify my values and beliefs." Certainly, there is value in better understanding how participating students describe and understand the effects of the PULSE Program upon them. However, in planning our own evaluation, we sought to take advantage of a number of existing (and validated) measures that could more directly assess PULSE participants' shifts in beliefs, values, and worldview. We describe these measures—and our process of choosing among these measures—later in the chapter.

Our assessment plan for making use of these measures was a relatively simple one. We administered a survey at the start of the 2008–09 academic year (Time 1) to all students participating in the PULSE Program as well as all students on the PULSE wait list. This "pre-PULSE " survey gave us baseline measures for all the students in our evaluation before the PULSE Program had actually started. We then administered an identical survey to these students at the conclusion of the 2008–09 academic year (Time 2), as the PULSE Program was coming to an end.

Comparing the changes between Time 1 and Time 2 for the PULSE students versus the wait-listed students gave us a strong sense of the impact of the PULSE Program upon participating students. One could make this comparison with a statistical analysis as simple as an independent samples t-test on one hand, or as complicated as fitting a multilevel regression model on the other hand. For program directors without extensive training in statistical methods, one could easily enlist a graduate student in mathematics or statistics as a paid consultant or for course credit.

In closing, then, we believe that the taxonomy of national service objectives put forth by Frumkin and Jastrzab holds great value for community service learning faculty and administrators who are reflecting upon the core purposes underlying their own efforts. That said, we also realize that national service does not align perfectly with the objectives of community service learning programs embedded within the university context. Our belief is that a significant portion of our readers will be particularly (though not exclusively) interested in the ability of their respective programs to foster the civic knowledge and engagement of participating students. Toward that end, the next question on which we focus is particularly relevant to that vision of community service learning; namely, What vision of citizenship guides your efforts to increase the civic engagement of your students?

## Question #2: What Vision of Citizenship?

Our study of the PULSE Program at Boston College sought to measure shifts in students' beliefs and attitudes through a quantitative pre–post survey tool. Of course, one's ability to capture such shifts is heavily dependent upon choosing the measures that align with what your program is seeking to accomplish. For this reason, prior to making any decisions about what types of questions to embed within a survey, it is worthwhile to think about the particular vision of citizenship nurtured by your program. One helpful mechanism for such reflection may be Kahne and Westheimer's citizenship trichotomy. Specifically, in a 2004 article published in the *American Educational Research Journal*, civic development scholars Joseph Kahne and Joel Westheimer lay out three different visions of citizenship that are often promoted by programs in community service learning or community engagement: the participatory citizen, the socially responsible citizen, and the justice-oriented citizen.

Programs that promote personally responsible citizenship seek to foster students who will act responsibly within their various communities through individual behaviors such as volunteering, recycling, or donating unwanted books to the public library. Programs focused on participatory citizenship, on the other hand, seek to nurture in their students a commitment to participating in the civic life of a community—voting, attending town meetings, campaigning for favored candidates, or running for a seat on the school board. Finally, programs that promote a justice-oriented conception of citizenship are engaged in highlighting for their students the political, economic, and social structures that contribute to inequity and then training students in collective strategies that can challenge this inequity.

Kahne and Westheimer posit no hierarchy among these three conceptions of citizenship. One is not framed as better than the others. However, the particular vision of citizenship nurtured by one's program should have a fundamental effect upon which measures are chosen to assess that program's effectiveness. It would be both unwise and ineffective, for example, to utilize the Skills of Political Analysis Scale (Colby, Beaumont, Ehrlich & Corngold, 2007) to assess the impact of a certificate program that frames community engagement primarily through a lens of personally responsible citizenship. In such a program, which focuses upon the civic role that students can play by engaging in individual behaviors such as volunteering or recycling, an assessment of students' political-analysis skills would simply not align with the objectives underlying the program's content and experiences. On the other end of the citizenship spectrum, it might be equally ineffective to utilize the Community Service Self-Efficacy Scale (Reeb, Katsuyama, Sammon & Yoder, 1998) to assess the impact of a community engagement program promoting a justice-oriented conception of citizenship. For such a program, focused upon the systemic and structural factors that contribute to social and economic inequity, the objective may be precisely that participating students come away from their service experiences feeling a *lack* of efficacy—and thus an awareness of the limits of direct service to address systemic inequality at its root.

Of the three conceptions of citizenship—participatory, socially responsible, and justice-oriented—Kahne and Westheimer characterize the justice-oriented vision as the least common among programs in community service learning, community engagement, civics, and citizenship education. In fact, they note that fewer than 10 percent of such programs are grounded in a justice-oriented conception of citizenship. However, the PULSE Program at Boston College—perhaps because of its placement within a Jesuit institution—seems to be situated squarely within the justice-oriented framework. Recall that the mission statement of the PULSE Program is to "educate our students about social injustice" and to "foster critical consciousness and enable students to question conventional wisdom and learn how to work for a just society." Recognizing this ideological foundation of the PULSE Program had a profound effect upon our decisions about which survey measures were most likely to capture the effects of the PULSE Program upon participating students. For example, because so much of the PULSE experience focused upon introducing students to systemic factors underlying economic inequality, we included a survey measure of students' beliefs about the causes of poverty, the National Survey on Poverty in America (NPR-Kaiser-Harvard, 2001); the Protestant Ethic Scale, a measure of students' belief in the veracity of the American Dream (Mirels & Garrett, 1971); and the Belief in a Just World Scale, a measure of students' belief in the justness of the world (Peplau & Tyler, 1975). We felt that students' responses to the items on these measures aligned directly with the PULSE Program's objectives.

At the outset of this chapter, we asserted that the tremendous variation among community service learning programs increased the importance of designing an evaluation particular to the students, community, and context of a given program. For that reason, we also want to acknowledge that Kahne and Westheimer's (2004) citizenship trichotomy may not be the right taxonomy for every faculty member or administrator contemplating the conception of citizenship fostered by his or her particular program. For such faculty and administrators, it may be worthwhile to consider the perspectives on service offered by two other contributors to this volume. Keith Morton (1995) characterizes community service learning as typically falling into the categories of charity, project, or social change; and Dan Butin (2007) offers a typology that conceptualizes community service learning programs as either technical, cultural, political, or antifoundational. From our perspective, more important than the particular typology selected is that one thinks deeply at the outset about the vision of citizenship at the foundation of your program and then selects measures best able to capture its effectiveness in promoting this vision.

### Question #3: What Do You Want to Assess?

If determining the conception of citizenship underpinning a program is the first step in developing a robust assessment of program outcomes, then a valuable second step is considering precisely what outcomes you want the assessment to capture. For example, your assessment measures could focus on attitudinal change: What impact does a particular community engagement program have upon students' enthusiasm for engaging in public service or their desire to pursue socially responsible careers? Attitudinal change is a valuable measure because of research that has found an individual's attitudes to have a strong relationship with that individual's actual behaviors (Kraus, 1995). In other words, one can feel reasonably confident that students who express a greater desire than their peers to engage in community service really are more likely than those peers to continue to engage in service upon graduation. Measures considered for our study of the PULSE Program that assessed attitudinal change included the Scale of Community Service Attitudes (Shiarella, McCarthy & Tucker, 2000) and the Political Cynicism Scale (Agger, Goldstein & Pearl, 1961).

Other community engagement faculty may be more interested in assessing the *skills* that their students have developed over the course of their participation in a particular major, minor, or certificate program. For example, perhaps a program has focused intently on developing students' ability to assess the authenticity and credibility of various sources of political information. Such a program might assess students' analytical skills through a measure such as the Skills of Political Analysis Scale (Colby et al., 2007). Another program might have focused upon developing students' ability to organize groups of community members and concerned citizens around social or political issues relevant to that constituency. Such a program might choose to assess students' ability at such endeavors through a measure such as the Skills of Political Leadership and Communication Scale (Colby et al., 2007).

Other community engagement programs might choose to assess participants' acquisition of specific content knowledge. For example, a community engagement course or program focused explicitly on issues of homelessness might choose to assess student learning through a measure such as Public Beliefs about the Causes of Homelessness (Lee, Jones & Lewis, 1990). A program focused on heightening students' engagement in contemporary social issues might utilize a measure such as the Current Events Knowledge Scale (Beier & Ackerman, 2001). A third program might assess students' developing knowledge of the purview and workings of various civic institutions such as the Supreme Court, Federal Reserve, or a local school board.

Still another set of faculty might choose to focus upon the impact of their respective community engagements programs on students' *behaviors*. These could range from increased participation in local and national elections to paying increased attention to various media covering important social issues. In between are a multitude of behaviors that include "liking" political candidates on Facebook, signing petitions in support of a particular social issue, campaigning for a political cause or party, putting a political candidate's bumper sticker on one's car, or responding to blog posts on political or social issues. As these last few examples demonstrate, the ubiquity of the Internet in the lives of many of our students has opened up dozens of new spaces and opportunities for civic engagement. A robust assessment of programmatic impact might do well to poll students about their engagement in such behaviors at the outset of the community engagement program and then again at its conclusion.

Assessing a program's impact on participating students' attitudes, skills, knowledge, and actions may be the most common type of assessment associated with community engagement programs in higher education; however, these are by no means the only aspects of the program worthy of assessment. Recall that, in their taxonomy of the purposes underlying national service, Frumkin and Jastrzab (2010) characterized one group of national service proponents as focused intently upon the ability of a particular service program to meet critical community needs. For a program focused primarily upon the "outputs" of community service learning, one can also strive to assess its impact on the community and community partners involved in the program. At the most basic level, a program might simply total the number of service-hours contributed by volunteers, estimate the value of that work to be, say, $15 an hour, and then report on either the number of person-hours or the value in dollars contributed by the program. Alternatively, one could focus on the actual products that result from those service-hours. A community service learning program involving service through Habitat for Humanity, for example, might choose to assess its efforts in terms of the number of houses built for low-income residents of a particular community. A community service learning program that staffs the Tuesday night dinner shift at a local soup kitchen might report on the number of meals prepared and served. As Frumkin and Jastrzab (2010) have written, "Service has long been about meeting critical public needs and filling gaps created by government and market failures. Volunteers are part of a system designed to deliver at low cost important public services that otherwise would not be available to communities" (p. 20). These researchers go on to characterize the person-hours contributed by volunteers, the financial value of those person-hours, and the products that result from such service as "the most visible and easily comprehensible artifacts within and outside the service movement" (p. 21). In other words, the outputs that result from a major, minor, or certificate program in community service learning are often the easiest metrics to assess and report upon.

Finally, one could also look for evidence of a relationship between participation in community service learning and other traditional university objectives such as academic achievement. At the most basic level, such an assessment could entail comparing the mean GPA of students participating in your program to that of your university's overall student body. It might also be useful to investigate whether participants in your community service learning program possess significantly higher overall grade-point averages at the conclusion of their involvement in the program than they did at its outset. For a research design like the one we used in our evaluation of the PULSE Program, one could compare the change in GPA of PULSE participants over the course of the academic year to that of their classmates on the PULSE wait list.

It is also possible that participation in community service learning diminishes students' likelihood of engaging in high-risk behaviors, such as binge drinking, and unethical behaviors, such as plagiarism. By collaborating with your university's office of student services, it may be possible to assess how the number of participants in your program who were implicated in such behaviors compares to the larger student body. Why focus on the potential relationships between community service learning and these other types of behaviors? Although opportunities for community service learning are often touted in university view-books and websites, the reality is that many such programs are significantly underresourced (Hartley & Morphew, 2008; Butin, 2006). Demonstrating the ability of community service learning programs to have positive effects, not only on students' conceptions of citizenship, but also on their academic achievement, health, and academic integrity could offer powerful arguments for increasing the resources allocated to such programs. For this reason, we are strong advocates of thinking outside the box when it comes to assessing the multiple and varied impacts of one's program in community service learning or community engagement.

In terms of our decisions about appropriate measures, recall from earlier in this chapter that our initial thinking about the PULSE Program led us to conclude that (1) the program's core purpose focused on providing participating students with opportunities to reflect upon their beliefs, values, and worldview; and (2) that the PULSE Program was informed by a justice-oriented vision of citizenship. Thus, we sought to choose existing (and validated) measures that aligned with the program's core purpose and conception of citizenship. In consultation with the PULSE Program's leadership, we ultimately settled upon the following measures:

1. Beliefs about Poverty in America Scale (NPR-Kaiser-Harvard, 2001)
2. Belief in a Just World Scale (Peplau & Tyler, 1975)
3. Conventional Electoral Activities Scale (Beaumont, Colby, Ehrlich & Tourney-Purta, 2006)
4. Expected Political Voice Activities Scale (Colby et al., 2007)
5. Public Service Motivation Scale (Perry, 1996)
6. Protestant Ethic Scale (Mirels & Garrett, 1971)

Our goal was to focus primarily on measures that would allow us to capture students' shifts in beliefs and values (e.g., the Belief in a Just World and Beliefs about Poverty in America scales) while choosing other measures that provide insight into the effects of these shifts in worldview upon students' commitment to various types of civic participation (e.g., the Expected Political Voice Activities and Public Service Motivation scales).

### Question #4: How Will You Assess?

Once you have considered the purposes underlying your program, the conception of citizenship the program seeks to instill within participating students, and whether your assessment efforts will focus on capturing changes in students' attitudes, values, skills, behaviors, academic achievement, or some other outcome, the final question for consideration is *how* you will assess what you want to assess. In this final section of the chapter, we offer some guidance on this question.

### *Pre-post surveys*

Paper-and-pencil (or on-line) surveys may not provide a "thick" or deeply nuanced window into the effects of your program, but they are a relatively cost-effective tool (in terms of both financial resources and time) for gaining a bird's eye view of your program's effects. Moreover, there are already hundreds of established measures that have been developed and validated by experts in educational measurement that can hone in on specific outcomes related to your program—for example, feelings of community service self-efficacy, commitment to future participation in public service or politics, acquisition of skills in working to effect change. An important aspect of all of these existing survey measures is that they do not simply ask the participating students their *opinion* of the impact of the program upon their sense of self-efficacy or motivation to engage in community service. Rather, they seek to more directly assess changes in attitude or skill-level by asking students a series of questions at the outset of the service experience about their current beliefs or behaviors, and then asking students these same questions again at the conclusion of the service experience. The shift in students' responses to these survey items from the beginning to the end of the program is one way of describing the impact of the community service learning program upon participating students.

As for where to find these existing survey measures, there are links on both the Bonner Foundation (www.bonner.org) and the National Service learning Clearinghouse (www.servicelearning.org) websites to a series of resources for assessing programs in community service learning and community engagement. These resources have been developed or compiled by highly respected organizations such as the National Campus Compact, the Center for Information and Research on Civic Learning and Engagement (CIRCLE) and the Corporation for National and Community Service and can be extremely useful to faculty and program directors seeking out existing measures to assess community service learning outcomes. Another useful resource for those seeking measures to evaluate community service learning is Robert Bringle's 2004 book, *The Measure of Service learning: Research Scales to Assess Student Experience.*

In our own evaluation of the PULSE Program at Boston College, our use of pre–post surveys demonstrated the PULSE Program to have a powerful effect upon Boston College students who participated in the program. Specifically, in comparison to their peers on the wait list, PULSE participants demonstrated statistically significant increases in their public service motivation and expected political involvement (Seider, Rabinowitz & Gillmor, 2012). Participating students also demonstrated increased skepticism about the veracity of the American Dream and an understanding of poverty that placed greater emphasis upon structural and systemic factors (Seider et al., 2010a, 2010b). Finally, our analyses demonstrated that Boston College students who participated in the PULSE Program concluded the academic year with a greater interest in both philosophy and theology than their peers who had not been able to participate in PULSE (Seider & Taylor, 2011; Seider, 2011a).

We also had a number of interesting findings when we utilized our pre–post surveys to compare different types of participants *within* the PULSE Program. For example, we found that business majors participating in the PULSE Program demonstrated smaller shifts in their beliefs about the causes of poverty than their peers majoring in the humanities, social sciences, and natural sciences (Seider et al., 2011b). We also found that the PULSE participants engaged in community service involving adults demonstrated greater increases in their public service motivation than did PULSE participants engaged in community service involving youth (Seider, 2011b). Finally, we found that students whose parents were highly enthusiastic about their participation in the PULSE Program were the most likely to demonstrate increases in their public service motivation and expected political participation over the course of the program (Seider, 2010c).

We have thus far sought to illustrate the role of pre–post surveys in evaluating a community service learning program by describing a number of the measures for which Boston College students participating in the PULSE Program demonstrated statistically significant changes (e.g., public service motivation, belief in the American Dream, etc.). However, it is also worth noting that *nonsignificant findings* are also highly valuable to faculty and administrators committed to understanding the workings of their program. For example, while we have already noted that participants in the PULSE Program demonstrated statistically significant increases in their expected political voice over the course of the program, it is also important for us (and for PULSE's leadership) to reflect upon why PULSE students did not show similarly significant increases in their expected participation in conventional political activities such as voting. In other words, it would seem that the PULSE Program increased participants' commitment to engage in some forms of political participation (e.g., signing an on-line petition), but not others (e.g., running for a local elected position). Perhaps these differences are entirely aligned with the PULSE Program's mission, but there is certainly great value in thinking through these types of nonsignificant findings as well.

### Correlation versus causality

A pre–post survey is a reasonably effective mechanism for measuring shifts in the attitudes, beliefs, or skills of participants in a community service learning major, minor, or certificate program. One potential limitation of a pre–post survey assessment in isolation is that one cannot conclusively demonstrate that the changes captured by the survey tool are the result of the community service learning program. For example, imagine that you administer Mark Pancer's Youth Social Responsibility Scale (Pancer, Pratt, Hunsberger, & Alisat, 2007) at the beginning and conclusion of a course or program in community service learning, and the participants in the program demonstrate significant increases in their sense of responsibility for the well-being of fellow citizens. How can one be certain that these shifts in social responsibility are due specifically to the teaching, learning, and experiences embedded within your program and not simply to the experience of being in college or even the increased maturity that comes with the passage of time? Especially when one considers that a robust body of research has demonstrated that college students become more committed to humanitarian issues over the course of their college careers, it cannot simply be assumed that positive changes in social responsibility (or any other measure) demonstrated by your students are necessarily the result of your program (Pascarella & Terenzini, 1991; Sax & Astin, 1999; Tanner, 2006).

Perhaps the most effective mechanism in the community service learning context for contending with the question of causality is a wait-list control or delayed-control research design. Our earlier description of our evaluation of Boston College's PULSE Program is a good example of a wait-list control design in action. Recall that 500 students expressed interest in participating in the PULSE Program, but only 400 could be admitted. The remaining 100 students were relegated to the PULSE wait list. By including the students on the wait list in our assessment of the PULSE Program, we were able to demonstrate that the attitude shifts in students in the PULSE Program were due specifically to their involvement in PULSE, and not simply to their enrollment in college, attendance at a Jesuit university, or development into older and wiser young adults. We did this by comparing the changes in attitude of the students in PULSE to the changes in attitude of the students on the wait list. Since the students on the wait list had also expressed interest in participating in the PULSE Program (but were unable to do so), we can argue that the difference in the changes exhibited by these two groups of students is directly attributable to the PULSE Program.

A wait-list control design works well from a research or program-evaluation standpoint. On the other hand, faculty or administrators leading a community service learning program are understandably reluctant to prevent interested students from participating in their program and reaping the benefits of this participation. For this reason, perhaps the ideal option from both the programmatic and program-evaluation standpoints is the delayed-control research design. In the delayed-control design, all interested students are able to participate in the community service learning program, but not all students get to start the program at the same time. Specifically, the students interested in participating in a given program are divided into two cohorts, and the students in one cohort simply begin the program a semester or a year behind their classmates. In that way, the delayed cohort can serve as a control group in your assessment efforts and, in so doing, contribute to your ability to demonstrate that the changes in attitudes or actions of the students in your community service learning program are caused by the program itself, and not simply the effects of being in college more generally (or simply time and maturity).

### Collecting longitudinal data

Perhaps the greatest limitation in the existing research on higher education programs in community service learning and community engagement is the scarcity of longitudinal data collected from students participating in such programs. It is relatively easy to survey students at the beginning and conclusion of their participation in a particular program, but such short-term data can only provide insights into short-term shifts in beliefs, attitudes, and actions. Perhaps, for example, college students experience surges in their sense of social responsibility or self-efficacy as they come to the end of a particular community service learning experience, but does that sense of social responsibility or self-efficacy persist in the months or years after the program ends? Do the effects of the program fade away or, perhaps, grow stronger with time? There have been distressingly few attempts to answer these questions—distressing because, of course, what those of us engaged in this work hope for is a *long-term* impact upon our students' beliefs about citizenship and commitment to civic engagement. Whether or not our programs are having that long-term effect remains largely an unanswered question.

The other reason collecting longitudinal data from students beyond their completion of our major, minor, or certificate program is that many types of behavioral changes related to greater civic engagement are not likely to be captured by short-term assessment measures. For example, we can ask students in short-term follow-up surveys about whether they *expect* to participate in protests or demonstrations in the future, campaign for a political candidate or cause, or run for a local political position themselves. However, it is impossible to argue with certainty that a young adult's expectations for the future will play out precisely as predicted. For this reason, it would be extremely valuable for faculty and administrators engaged in majors, minors, or certificate programs in community service learning to track program alumni and ask them to periodically complete a short assessment of their current levels of civic engagement.

### Qualitative assessment

The traditional focus of program evaluation has certainly been on quantitative surveys like those in the preceding section. However, we would argue that for faculty and administrators interested in assessing the effectiveness of their particular program, qualitative assessment strategies such as interviews, focus groups, and participant observation may be equally or even more valuable sources of data. In our earlier description of our evaluation of the PULSE Program, we characterized our pre–post survey data as offering a broad sense of *what* effect the PULSE Program was having upon participating students; however, these data were not capable of helping us to understand *how* and *why* the PULSE Program was having these effects.

It was with the goal of better understanding the *how* and the *why* that we also made the decision to carry out qualitative interviews with 30 Boston College students participating in the PULSE Program. We interviewed these students toward the end of their participation in the PULSE Program to learn more about how *they* described and understood the impact of the PULSE Program upon their beliefs, attitudes, values, skills, and actions. We also asked them to share the written assignments they had authored for the courses that were a part of their PULSE experience. Comparing our analyses from these three different types of data is referred to as "triangulation" and is a highly effective method of evaluating *what* effect a program like PULSE is having upon participating students as well as *how* and *why* the program is having the effects that it is (or isn't).

So what precisely did these qualitative inquiries buy us? We discovered through these qualitative interviews that students largely credited their shifting beliefs about poverty to conversations with men and women at their service placements that highlighted the barriers to escaping poverty. Take, for example, Selena Rambaud, whose service placement was at an all-women's homeless shelter.[1] Selena explained of the women she encountered there: "I always thought if they just worked hard and got a job, they would be fine. Just seeing the women who have jobs who still can't do it; it has definitely changed my view [of poverty]." Likewise, we learned that one way in which the PULSE Program increased participants' interest in theology was by highlighting the theological underpinnings of public service. For example, PULSE participant Felicia Santos explained that one of her favorite texts from the PULSE syllabus was Father Michael Himes's (1995) *Doing the Truth in Love*. According to Santos, "He talked about God not as a noun but as a verb— the fact that relationships are God and interactions and volunteering. We can't blame God for all the problems [in the world]. We are co-creators with him, so you can't despair with everything that is going on in the world—you have to help it, you have to alleviate it." For Santos and many other students, the PULSE Program heightened their interest in theology by demonstrating that theologians have something to say about the role of service in making the world a more equitable one.

We also discovered through our qualitative interviews with PULSE Program participants from the School of Management that many perceived there to be a tension between what they were learning in PULSE and in their business courses. As one student, Joe Antonucci, explained, "It is kind of like a little bit crazy because it's totally the opposite. It's like philosophy and theology versus the cut-throat business world." Finally, we learned through both our qualitative interviews and through students' written work that those with parents leery of their participation in the PULSE Program missed out on opportunities to reflect with valued mentors about what they were observing and learning. For example, Boston College freshman Annie Bartone explained that "My parents have trouble understanding why I do this....So I rarely find myself talking about it because we often get into fights." These students' descriptions of their experiences within the PULSE Program, and of their perception of the program's effect upon their beliefs and values, put valuable "meat" upon the bones of the quantitative survey data described above.

Perhaps the best example of the importance of our qualitative data relates to our findings about the effects of the *type* of service in which PULSE students engaged. Specifically, our quantitative survey data revealed that Boston College students engaged in adult-oriented placements (i.e., volunteering in homeless shelters, soup kitchens, prisons, rehabilitation centers, etc.) showed greater shifts in public service motivation than their classmates engaged in youth-oriented placements (i.e., volunteering in tutoring centers, school, and community centers). This finding was not an intuitive one to us—in other words, we didn't immediately understand why the two types of service placements differed in this respect.

Fortunately, our qualitative interviews with PULSE participants shed light on a subtle difference between the adult-oriented and youth-oriented service placements. Specifically, our interviews revealed that the students engaged in youth-oriented service placements such as tutoring had entered into these service placements with sky-high expectations about what they could accomplish with their tutees in a relatively short period of time. For example, the following explanation by one student, Eddie McCabe, is representative of a number of the college students engaged in youth-based service placements. According to McCabe, "At first I was expecting to send these kids to college, put them on the honor roll, but then I realized the motivation level for these kids wouldn't always allow that, so during the winter I kind of found myself really discouraged and not really looking forward to PULSE anymore."

In contrast to McCabe and the other students involved in youth-based placements, the Boston College students who chose adult-based placements entered into them with much hazier expectations about what they would accomplish. The majority had never before visited a homeless shelter, soup kitchen, or prison and, as a result, their expectations for the experience focused on the impact of the service placement upon their own personal development. For example, Alice McGonagle explained that, as she began her service placement at a suicide hotline, "I just think I hoped to become more aware…of the things that people go through. I kind of wanted to put myself into the experience of people who haven't been able to live the life that I have." Seemingly as a result of this focus on personal development rather than concrete outcomes, the students engaged in adult-oriented placements came away from their participation in the PULSE Program far more satisfied with their service experience than the students engaged in youth-oriented placements. Importantly, this greater satisfaction seemed to leave the participants in adult-based service programs more eager to participate in community service and community service learning opportunities going forward.

In this example from our PULSE Program evaluation, our qualitative data allowed us to see what our quantitative data did not; namely, that there was *not* some intrinsic aspect of the adult-based service placements that made them more conducive to community service learning than youth-based service placements. Rather, the difference between these two types of service experiences was the mindset with which the PULSE participants entered into them. As a result of this insight, one of our recommendations to faculty and administrators leading the PULSE Program was to explicitly engage their students headed for youth-based service placements in preservice reflection about what they expect to accomplish; what obstacles might prove challenging; and what types of outcomes constitute success. Conducting this kind of preservice visioning could go a long way toward mitigating the frustration expressed by many of the PULSE students engaged in youth-based service placements, and this take-away emerged directly from our qualitative interviews.

### *Participant observation*

While interviews with participating students (and supervisors, clients, and community members) are a highly effective tool for collecting qualitative data, there are certainly other useful methods as well. For example, there is tremendous value in carrying out participant observation both at the sites in which students are engaging in service and in the discussion sections and seminars in which they are connecting these service experiences to academic curriculum and content. Participant observation entails visiting and observing in these spaces as the students carry out their everyday roles and responsibilities and documenting one's observations and insights through detailed field notes. These field notes can later serve as a valuable source of qualitative data. Take, for example, one finding from our evaluation of the PULSE Program that led us to regret *not* having engaged in participant observation during the program's weekly discussion sections. Specifically, our quantitative survey data revealed that students of color in the PULSE Program reported a weaker sense of community in their weekly discussion sections than did their white classmates. In qualitative interviews, a number of students of color described their reluctance to participate in discussions of race and race-related issues when these topics arose in their PULSE discussion sections. These explanations were invaluable, but an even more direct form of data would have been participant observations in the discussion sections themselves. During such participant observation, we could have explicitly tracked who did and did not contribute to various types of class discussions with an eye toward differences in participation by race/ethnicity but also gender and other demographic variables as well.

## Innovative inquiry

Qualitative interviews and participant observation may represent the most common types of qualitative inquiry, but a number of researchers are experimenting with more innovative forms of inquiry as well. For example, photovoice is a qualitative methodology which was originally developed by researchers Carolyn Wang and Mary Ann Burris (Wang & Burris, 1994). In this methodology, the participants in a study are given cameras and asked to photograph experiences that they perceive to be indicative of their learning, beliefs, or values (the focus of the photographs varies with the focus of the evaluation). The researchers then conduct an analysis of the photographs and the themes emerging from the photographs, as a mechanism for assessing the impact of the particular learning experience upon participating students. Similar to participant observation, this methodology, too, seems to offer the advantage of not simply asking service learning participants to describe what they perceive themselves to have learned; rather, the participants *demonstrate* their learning more directly.

Finally, there is tremendous energy and momentum behind a new form of program evaluation that proponents refer to as Youth Participatory Action Research (YPAR). Participatory action research is based upon the premise that societal structures privileging the perspective and values of certain groups of citizens over others are often reproduced by a research design in which "expert" researchers study a group of (often marginalized) individuals but give them no control or stake in the results of the research. Toward this end, participatory action research engages individuals who are typically the *subjects* of a research project in framing the research questions of importance to *them*, collecting data to address these questions, and then interpreting the results.

In the community service learning context, a YPAR design would entail asking the students participating in the service (or the community members interacting with these students) to play a leading role in determining the focus of a program evaluation, decide upon the appropriate data to collect, carry out the collection of these data, and then analyze and present the data. Faculty and administrators serve as partners and resources to the students as they carry out this research, but the interests, perspectives, and voices of the students lead the way. Of course, it is worth noting that faculty and administrators of a particular program in community engagement can gain enormous insights into the workings of their program via the topics for research that the students within their program choose as the focus of their participatory action research. Specifically, faculty and administrators can gain a deeper understanding of the facets of community service learning and community engagement that are most sentient to their students and can then evaluate whether or not these facets align with the program's stated objectives, the objectives of the faculty leading the program, and the mission of the larger university.

## Conclusion

In highlighting the work of university faculty and administrators leading majors, minors, and certificate programs in community engagement, the present volume seeks to offer a compelling argument for the institutionalization of community engagement within the university and also to provide valuable resources for faculty and administrators committed to developing such programs themselves. The lead editor of this volume, Dan Butin (2006), has long argued that a number of factors are necessary if community engagement is to gain legitimacy as an academic discipline within the academy. One of those factors is the institutionalization that lies at the heart of this volume, and a second involves the development of a robust theoretical framework that PULSEs as the foundation for this burgeoning field. We would argue that a third factor in this pathway toward community engagement enjoying a full and permanent place within the academy is robust evaluation of the effects of our course work and programming upon both participating students and the surrounding community. It is not sufficient to simply *assume* that our programs in community engagement are achieving their intended outcomes, or to base such conclusions upon anecdotes or even student self-report. In this chapter, we have sought to offer a resource for faculty and administrators committed to robust assessment and evaluation of their existing programs with the belief that such assessment will not only be of value to these programs, but will also PULSE the broader movement as well.

## Note

1. All students in this chapter are referred to by pseudonyms

## References

Agger, R., Goldstein, M., & Pearl, S. (1961). Political cynicism: Measurement and meaning. *The Journal of Politics, 23*, 477–506.

Beier, M. & Ackerman, P. (2001). Current-events knowledge in adults: An investigation of age, intelligence, and nonability determinants. *Psychology and Aging, 16*(4), 615–28.

Beaumont, E., Colby, A., Ehrlich, T., & Torney-Purta, J. (2006). Promoting political competence and engagement in college students: An empirical study. *Journal of Political Science, 2*(3), 249–70.

Bringle, R., Phillips, M. & Hudson, M. (2004). *The measure of service learning: Research scales to assess student experience.* Washington DC: American Psychological Association.

Butin, D. (2006). The limits of service learning in higher education. *Review of Higher Education, 29*(4), 473–98.

———. (2007 November-December). Focusing our aim: Strengthening faculty commitment to community engagement. *Change: The Magazine of Higher Learning,* 34–7.

Colby, A., Beaumont, E., Ehrlich, T., & Corngold, J. (2007). *Educating for democracy: Preparing undergraduates for responsible political engagement.* San Francisco: Jossey-Bass.

Dote, L., Cramer, K., Dietz, N., & Grimm, R. (2006). *College students helping America.* Washington, DC: Corporation for National and Community Service.

Erikson, E. (1968). *Identity, youth, & crisis.* New York: W.W. Norton.

Frumkin, P. & Jastrzab, J. (2010). *Serving country and community: Who benefits from national service?* Cambridge, MA: Harvard University Press.

Giroux, H. (1992). *Border crossings: Cultural workers and the politics of education*. New York: Routledge.

Hartley, M. & Morphew, C. (2008). What's being sold and to what end? A content analysis of college viewbooks. *Journal of Higher Education, 79*(6), 671–691.

Himes, M. (1995). *Doing the truth in love: Conversations about God, relationships and service*. Mahwah, NJ: Paulist Press.

Jones, S., & Abes, E. (2004). Enduring influences of service learning on college students' identity development. *Journal of College Student Development, 45*, 149–66.

Kahne, J. & Westheimer, J. (2004). What kind of citizen? The politics of educating for democracy. *American Educational Research Journal, 41*(2), 237–69.

Kraus, S. (1995). Attitudes and the prediction of behavior: A meta-analysis of empirical literature. *Personality & Social Psychology Bulletin, 21*(1), 58–75.

Lee, B., Jones, S., & Lewis, D. (1990). Public beliefs about the causes of homelessness. *Social Forces, 69*, 253–65.

Liu, A., Ruiz, S., DeAngelo, L., and Pryor, J. (2009). Findings from the 2008 Administration of the College Senior Survey (CSS): National Aggregates. Los Angeles, CA: Higher Education Research Institute, UCLA.

Metz, E., McLellan, J., & Youniss, J. (2003). Types of voluntary service and adolescents' civic development. *Journal of Adolescent Research 18*(2), 188–203.

Mirels, H. & Garrett, J. (1971). The Protestant ethic as a personality variable. *Journal of Consulting and Clinical Psychology, 36*, 40–44.

Moely, B., Mercer, S., Ilustre, V., Miron, D., & McFarland, M. (2002). Psychometric properties and correlates of the civic attitudes and skills questionnaire (CASQ): Measure of students' attitudes related to service learning. *Michigan Journal of Community Service learning* (Spring), 15–26.

Morton, K. (1995). The irony of service: Charity, project, and social change in service learning. *Michigan Journal of Community Service learning, 2*(1), 19–32.

Myers-Lipton, S. (1998). Effect of a comprehensive service learning program on college students' civic responsibility. *Teaching Sociology, 26*(4), 243–258.

NPR-Kaiser-Harvard. (2001). "National Survey on Poverty in America." http://www.kff.org/kaiserpolls. Retrieved October 1, 2009.

Pancer, S., Pratt, M., Hunsberger, B., & Alisat, S. (2007). Community and political involvement in adolescence: What distinguishes the activists from the uninvolved? *Journal of Community Psychology, 35*(6), 741–59.

Pascarella, E. & Terenzini, P. (1991). *How college affects students*. San Francisco: Jossey-Bass.

Peplau, L., & Tyler, T. (1975). *Belief in a just world and political attitudes*. Paper presented at the meeting of the Western Psychological Association. Sacramento, CA.

Perry, J. (1996). Measuring public service motivation: An assessment of construct reliability and validity. *Journal of Public Administration Research and Theory, 6*(1), 5–22.

Reeb, R., Katsuyama, R., Sammon, J., & Yoder, D. (1998). The community service self-efficacy scale: Evidence of reliability, construct validity, and pragmatic utility. *Michigan Journal of Community Service learning, 5*, 48–57.

Sax, L. & Astin, A. (1999). Long-term effects of volunteering during the undergraduate years. *Review of Higher Education, 22*(2), 187–202.

Seider, S., Gillmor, S., & Rabinowicz, S. (2012 ). The impact of community service learning upon the expected political voice of participating college students. *Journal of Adolescent Research, 27*(1), 44–77.

———. (2010a). Community service learning and conceptions of poverty among American college students. *Analyses of Social Issues & Public Policy, 10* (1), 215–36.

————. (2010b). Complicating college students' conception of the American Dream through community service learning. *Michigan Journal of Community Service learning, 17*(1), 5–19.

Seider, S. (2010c). The impact of parental support upon the community service learning experiences of American college students.Presented at *Annual Conference of Association for Moral Education*. November 2010, St. Louis, MO.

Seider, S. (2011a). Deepening college students' interest in religion and theology through community service learning. *Teaching Theology & Religion, 14*(3) 205–25.

Seider, S. (2011b). The impact upon college students of community service learning involving youth vs. adults. Presented at Annual Meeting of *American Educational Research Association*, April 2011, New Orleans, LA.

Seider, S., Rabinowicz, S., & Gillmor. S. (2011a). The impact of philosophy and theology service learning experiences upon the public service motivation of participating college students. *Journal of Higher Education, 82*(5), 597–628.

————. (2011b). The impact of community service learning upon the worldviews of business majors vs. non-business majors at an American university. *Journal of Business Ethics, 98*(3), 458–504.

Seider, S., & Taylor, J. (2011). Broadening college students' interest in philosophical education through community service learning. *Teaching Philosophy, 34*(3), 197–218.

Shiarella, A., McCarthy, A., & Tucker, M. (2000). Development and construct validity of scores on the community service attitudes scale. *Education and Psychology Measurement, 60*(2), 286–300.

Tanner, J. (2006). Recentering during emerging adulthood: A critical turning point in life span human development. In J. Arnett and J. Tanner (eds.). *Emerging adults in America: Coming of age in the 21st century.* Washington DC: American Psychological Association.

Wang, C., & Burris, M. (1994). Empowerment through photo novella: Portraits of participation. *Heath Education & Behavior, 21*(2), 171–86.

# CHAPTER 8

# Building in Place

*Talmage A. Stanley*
Emory & Henry College

## In the Valley of the Holston

From nearly any point on the campus of Emory & Henry College, persons can see the mountains from which the Holston River descends.[1] The Holston's North Fork flows from the ridges and limestone ledges of Bland County, under the southern lee of Burke's Garden and Clinch Mountain. The first tentative streams of the Holston's South Fork surface beneath the rhododendron and hardwoods on high ridges between Washington and Grayson counties, from springs that come from the rocky faces of Whitetop and Mount Rogers, the highest mountains in Virginia, and from the seeps and creeks on the side of Iron Mountain. Emory & Henry is located in the valley of the Holston's Middle Fork, which rises at the base of Walker Mountain, 35 miles east of the college.

Beyond this watershed, to the north and west, is the Allegheny Plateau with its confusing maze of streams and narrow hollows where the limestone bedrock gives way to shale and seams of bituminous coal. To the south and east, are the Blue Ridge Mountains, their peaks often obscured in fog banks. Together, the geographies of the Holston watershed and the areas just beyond it constitute the central and southern portions of the Appalachian region.

Engraved on the landscape of this region are the stories of the natural environment—geologic time, tectonic shifts, seas rising and falling, mountain formations and erosions, complex ecosystems, and the traces and memories of a once-vast expanse of hardwood forests that stretched beyond the horizon in every direction.

There is the long history of the built environment—the human response to the demands and opportunities of climate, topography, and hydrography. It's the legacy of the first people in this place, who took shelter in caves and beneath overhanging rocks, and later, the tribal peoples, who built villages along the river banks. Following the valleys and watercourses, stretching across the ridge tops, were travel routes for tribal warring parties, diplomatic emissaries, and trading missions. This landscape offers up the history of a temperate and fertile place in which the native peoples and the generations of Europeans to come after them realized that nearly anything could be grown here, and in a plenteous abundance. Across this landscape, there are the elegancies and functionalities in the design and architecture the Anglo-European farmers produced in response to this bountiful land.

Into this built environment are also carved the legacies and scars of the misuses and devastations and the downright ugliness humans have wrought across the landscape. At points, the forks of the Holston pass denuded hillsides made sterile by emissions from chemical plants, and there are long stretches where the waters have been made lethal from manufacturers that used for decades this river to dispose of heavy metals. Set within this built environment is the story of how small-scale agriculture—a network of family farms and connections of kin and neighbors forged in shared work—has been so crippled and weakened that we now grow virtually nothing here.

Infusing this place are stories of people's long habitation together. They are stories of prolonged tribal conflicts as well as of competing bands and groups of native peoples stepping back from warfare over who would control these resources, determined to hold this good and fertile place in common between them. This landscape carries the stories of the movements of Europeans into the region, of the systematic and violent replacement of one way of life with another, the drawing of maps and the giving of land grants, the founding and building of towns. From the time of both the tribal cultures and the European settlers who followed them, there are stories of conquest, slavery, war, and the myriad troubles and sufferings to which such evils always give rise. There is the story of American industrialization, beginning in the eighteenth century, and with it the stories of those who understood this place only as fuel for the American economic engine, who saw the value of this place and the worth of its people as only what the market affixed to the goods and products produced here.

This place, with its mountains blue in the distance, also offers stories of ordinary people who have labored for justice, who have stood against oppression, and who routinely make choices for civic leadership and building strong communities. Here are stories of people choosing to abide in a place that the wider culture no longer acknowledges as valuable. In their civic work, they have written on this place their struggles with the difficult issues of changing demographics; economic, financial, and workplace instability; environmental distress and sustainability; and the need to meet food, shelter, and health-care disparities.

The totality and complexity of this three-part interaction of the natural environment, the built environment, and human culture and history, and the stories etched into this place, call into question traditional models of education and long-held assumptions about what it is that constitutes effective citizenship (Johnston, 1991, p. 97). These stories remind us that this place is rife with conflicts and contradictions, raising questions about citizenship and justice for which there are no right or easy answers. In this place, traditional understandings of citizenship fall short, ineffectual before the prevailing realities of conflicts, questions, and the examples of citizens who have written by their civic choices stories of honesty and courage. This place compels us to challenge and resist the thoughtless and damaging glibness of a civic-engagement pedagogy that is satisfied with short-term partnerships naively touted as transforming society, an understanding of citizenship that ignores the ways American and global economic structures devalue places and people, and a pedagogy that does not build in place.

If, however, this place challenges traditional models of citizenship and education, it also holds out the promise of an educational model that takes seriously the whole way of life of a place, offering new insights into the critical and shared importance of place, education, and citizenship. Building in place, the teaching and practice of a citizenship of place, opens a deeper appreciation of how truly complex effective citizenship is, and what educational institutions might be required to do to equip a more effective and participatory citizenry.

### Building in this Place

Emory & Henry was established and became a participant in this place's stories and conflicts in 1836 when civic and religious leaders founded an institution intended to educate leaders for the new American republic. Implicated in the most profound moral and social contradictions of human history, the founders chartered Emory & Henry as an institution of the Methodist Church, calling for teaching and learning that would join faith and civic service. That faith was for whites only, and that education was for white men only. The first buildings erected on this campus represent the best of indigenous, nineteenth-century architecture in this place. They were constructed using slave labor. Those founders located the college adjacent to the Great Wagon Road, over which settlers were streaming into the new territories of the northwest and southwest to build new lives, to claim for themselves the promises of the new democracy and, paradoxically, to wrest those territorial lands from the native peoples who had long claimed them. Along this same road were herded long coffles of women, children, and men, chattel for the burgeoning plantation economy of the Deep South. The founders intended that the new college, with its access to this principal highway, would serve both the immediate area and the wider republic. Citizenship in that republic was severely limited by race, sex, education, and property.

In the social processes that form this place, Emory & Henry has changed in many ways, dismantling the barriers that first shaped the education it offered. The college has served as the region's common ground, offering welcome and opportunity to this place and its people. Emory & Henry has long defined itself by the education it extends to first-generation college students, many of whom come from this region and without the college's intervention could never have achieved a college education. For all of its history, Emory & Henry has been about the work of educating public-school teachers, ministers, doctors, lawyers, other professionals, and civic leaders who have gone on to serve in the places they have settled.

In other ways and at other times, Emory & Henry has aligned itself with forces and interests, cultural values, and educational practices that have systematically silenced or ignored the lives and experiences of many people and places. Over the years, there was a general public impression of Emory & Henry as an elitist institution, equipping young people for effective leadership but also preparing them to leave the region. Among many who did not have access to college education, there was the feeling that Emory & Henry had distanced itself from the travails of the people and places around it. There have also been times when the college and its people have stood as brave witnesses for new understandings and new social orders, arguing for and supporting the work for tolerance, change, and justice, both in the college and in the wider world.

Throughout the 1970s and 1980s, this work of brave and challenging witness gained new focus through the teaching of Dr. Steve Fisher. A scholar-activist, Dr. Fisher called his students to question and contend against the systems of power and privilege that were at the root of the conflicts and forces helping to shape and limit this place. Beginning in the early 1980s and drawing from Paulo Freire's pedagogical models and the work of Noam Chomsky, Francis Moore Lappe, Parker Palmer, and bell hooks, and such Appalachian scholar-activists as Helen Lewis and Dick Couto, Dr. Fisher increasingly called his students to bring to the classroom their own stories and those of their families. Before service-learning and civic engagement were fashionable trends in American higher education, Dr. Fisher was finding ways to implement these practices in his classrooms putting his students to work in this place, sharpening the effectiveness of his classrooms.

In 1996, Emory & Henry College applied for and received a major grant from the Jessie Ball duPont Fund to further integrate into its mission the teaching and engagement that had come to define Dr. Fisher's work. The core insights underwriting the duPont proposal were that service is more complex and more important than volunteerism or charity; that service is integral to education; that service, participatory citizenship, policy making, justice, and democracy are deeply intertwined and profoundly interdisciplinary. The grant made possible the development of an interdisciplinary degree program, Public Policy and Community Service, at first housed within the Political Science Department and a decade later becoming its own academic department. The grant also provided for the establishment of the Appalachian Center for Community Service.

The duPont proposal was the culmination of a long planning process involving faculty, staff, students, and representatives from outside the institution. This committee laid the foundation for the degree program and the Appalachian Center. Because the work a duPont grant would support ran counter to most traditional approaches to education, and because such an undertaking required advocates and practitioners from across the institution, the planning involved persons who were enthusiastic about its possibilities and those who were skeptical, even hostile, to any idea that would challenge the familiar ways of higher education. Emory & Henry is an institution defined in its commitment to traditional, classically focused liberal arts education, and many members of the faculty viewed with doubt and suspicion a process that, it had been made clear, would undertake to dismantle divisions that have defined higher education.

Such reservations speak of the frequent rigidity of traditional disciplinary departments, the antipathy toward interdisciplinary scholarship, as well as a view of citizenship as expressed only through voting, political participation, and keeping abreast of current events. There was the criticism that a college like Emory & Henry could not offer a program in public policy because it lacked the resources and the status of a research university to produce sweeping quantitative research, or the writing of white papers, or the support of policy institutes and think tanks. Many colleagues looked warily at a degree program that had community service as one of its components; a number of faculty members believed that service was not a venue for critical thinking or effective teaching. These critics maintained that the Public Policy and Community Service program, while perhaps valuable for a certain category of students, was too soft, too nontraditional for students with the skills and abilities to be serious academics. Any effort to link education with service, citizenship, and public policy was questionable.

In thinking through the many components of a proposal for a new and unconventional academic program and at the same time charting the focus and mission of the community service center, the planning committee worked collaboratively, dividing duties among its members, routinely reporting to and updating the campus community, asking for input and counsel from all quarters. All of this was instrumental in bringing credibility and integrity to the idea of a civically engaged curriculum. When it came before the faculty for final vote, the plan had been fully vetted and every voting member of the faculty had had ample opportunity to express all concerns. With grudging approval from a slender minority of faculty members but with enthusiastic support from many more, the plan passed the faculty with unanimous consent. The duPont proposal carried with it the full weight of this support and was clearly consonant with Emory & Henry's mission and legacy.

The proposal also had significant internal integrity. In structure and in process, in theory and in practice, the means and ends were one, and they were consistent with the program's goals. The degree program's objectives were focused on providing students with the interdisciplinary tools and skills for effective engagement in public policy and community building, and gave practical meaning to the pedagogical philosophy that puts the teaching of citizens and the formation of character and community at the center of a liberal education. The proposal to the duPont Fund had argued that such an educational practice would provide a firm grounding in the interdisciplinary and interrelated concepts of citizenship, service, and in the democratic processes of policy making, justice, and the recognition of contributions made by diverse peoples in a democratic society.

Setting the proposal apart from every other program or department at the college and many across higher education at the time was the inclusion of a service-learning component. The proposal called for service not just in support of this education, but also as a full expression of it. Every course in the new major was to integrate into its curriculum a service component designed to enhance classroom teaching, challenging students with demanding responsibilities and at the same time offering tangible and substantive good to the places in which the students would work.

At the core of the degree program is the precept that public policy is the means by which a nation or a community lives out its values, its priorities, and its ideologies; the means by which it makes regular and routine its self-understanding. Necessarily ingrained in every public policy are the contradictions, conflicts, and inconsistencies of the people of a locality, state, or nation, particularly when policy formation is reserved as the purview of the few and only large research universities are the practitioners of policy research and advocacy. In such instances, public policy reinstates the values of the market economy, often to the detriment of individuals and places little valued in that economy. The Emory & Henry program premises policy making and policy advocacy as the responsibilities of all citizens, putting into action and sustaining the values and insights that have been forged in service and an encompassing citizenship of place.

In its initial years few students came to Emory & Henry expecting to select Public Policy and Community Service as their major area of study; most were unaware there was such a program. Efforts to develop strong relationships with admissions personnel and representatives were necessary and ongoing, educating them about the strengths of the program and the profile of students who might be most interested in it. We have found a way to speak of the goals and scope of the Public Policy and Community Service program so that persons who are not familiar with it can easily grasp its significance and potential. Moreover, faculty and staff associated with the program have had to think of themselves as recruiters; there could be no division of labor or responsibilities. Now, some 15 years into the program, even though it has gained considerable national attention, faculty still make telephone calls, write letters, speak with prospective students and their families, and attend many admissions events, encouraging prospective students not just to select Public Policy and Community Service as their major or minor but also to consider taking a class during their first year. In many cases, students who take the introductory course as an elective in their first year determine to pursue it as their major focus area.

The Public Policy and Community Service program enacts a coherent developmental model, the cornerstone of which is relational learning, with all of the courses interlocking and in full conversation with each other through ongoing themes, ideas, concepts, and questions. This model rests upon what Paulo Freire describes as the problem-solving model of education, dismantling barriers between classroom and place, creating a learning space in which students and teachers are co-learners and co-educators together (Freire, 1970, pp. 57, 66–74). Students move through the curriculum as a cohort, taking most of their courses together. Over their four years in the program, they develop strong relationships with each other and the teaching faculty, learning how to trust their colleagues enough to depend on them, to be collaborators and partners, to be teachers and students of each other, to learn to know and appreciate the others' stories and perspectives. Participants must learn to deal with their differences, to negotiate and work through a range of conflicts. This is neither simple nor easy, and introduces a new and often difficult dynamic into the learning environment that can take months and years to resolve, if resolution is even possible.

Bringing their own lives and stories into the classroom, through their readings and their questions of their colleagues, students empower each other to move from considering the problems they encounter in their service as always matters of individual choices, individual responsibility, and individual blame, to the lived results of societal structures and historical movements and questions (Mills, 1959, pp. 3–22). In the places in which they serve, from the civic partners who are also their teachers, students learn to challenge a vision of citizenship that focuses on voting and electoral participation as the only means of democratic expression. They come to question values that suggest being successful in America implies moving away from places American culture devalues. Whether they choose to major in Public Policy and Community Service or take only a course or two, many students come to claim for themselves a vision of participatory democracy in which citizens are individually committed and collectively engaged. Students also learn that this multivoice, dynamic classroom and civic work are representative of the caliber of work that must be undertaken in public life if ours is to be a participatory democracy fostering the common good.

Because of the suspicion among educational traditionalists about the program's academic rigor, the degree program has demanding reading and writing expectations; students wrestle with material that is more often found in graduate-level courses. Writing in a daily journal, asking students to struggle with questions for which there are no answers, and to strive to find the connections between their personal stories, the work they are doing in the places in which they are engaged, and the classroom conversations are expectations of all courses in the program. In courses with a heavy civic-engagement component, there are necessarily some modifications of traditional classroom expectations, such as requiring fewer formal research papers or seminar presentations, but these modifications are kept to a minimum. Students often complain of the amount of work associated with a degree in Public Policy and Community Service.

As a means of structuring the program's curriculum, the developmental model means that in the program's introductory course, students undertake service that offers opportunities for one-on-one work with persons served. Students learn the importance of the relational model for understanding the intersection of education, service, and larger questions of power. Joining their classroom learning with the one-on-one service experiences, they confront the failure of individual and singular approaches to addressing systemic issues. In the Community Organizing course, students collaborate in teams, taking on larger projects that require people to work together. They learn the process of negotiation and consensus building; they come to understand that democracy is not always an individual undertaking and that all effective, sustainable, democratic change in any place derives from people who have organized to make change happen. They also learn to discern and to question the ideological and cultural barriers to thinking collectively and organizing for effective citizen action in the American context. Offering other disciplinary perspectives and constituting the major's core curriculum are also courses in other departments: political science, economics, environmental studies, sociology, psychology, and geography.

Later in the sequence, students build on and apply classroom learning and service experiences in courses in sustainable development, social and cultural identity, civic methodologies, and politics and public policy. In these courses, students' civic engagement in this place is as teams or as a class in support of major initiatives, and the outcomes and goals may extend beyond the semester. In the senior practicum and senior project, the program's capstone experiences, the civic engagements are individually defined, but students meet weekly with the learning collective they have built and strengthened over four years of shared experiences, to grapple with questions of justice, identity, service, citizenship, and public policy as they confront them in their placements. In all the service-learning experiences, students are engaged in efforts that their civic partners have identified and helped to design, which are connected to the curriculum of the individual course and coordinated through the Appalachian Center in support of long-term regional and local partnerships.

Simultaneous with the launch of the major in Public Policy and Community Service, the planners called for the development of the Appalachian Center for Community Service to build a culture of service on the Emory & Henry campus. The goal was to centralize and coordinate all aspects of service then taking place at Emory & Henry, to create and sustain new programs and initiatives, and to weave service into the fabric of the whole way of life of this institution. The Appalachian Center would oversee service-learning opportunities related to the degree program, and also provide faculty-development opportunities and logistical support to integrate service-learning across the Emory & Henry curriculum. The center's mission was to bring this institution to serve the needs of the people of this region and to dismantle the barriers between this college and this place. Central to this mission, the center challenges and dismantles traditional divisions of curricular and co-curricular service. Therefore, in both theory and practice, at every level, the degree program and the other initiatives coordinated through the Appalachian Center offer an education that brings students into the reality of relationships and conflict, a thoroughgoing examination of what it means to be an effective citizen of this or any place, at the same time learning that one important means of giving expression to the education that shapes them is service.

There were no maps and blueprints for the centralized, cohesive, relational model of service and civic engagement envisioned for the Appalachian Center and the degree program in Public Policy and Community Service. Few such centers then existed; there were even fewer academic degree programs of this type, and none were in rural areas. There were some ideas about the direction better relationships between the college and its neighbors might take, but there were only limited examples of institutions that had overcome their elitist reputations to acquire the sense and bearing of a responsible public citizen. Although the collaborative planning process had produced a visionary structure, the committee could not foresee all that would be required to bring that structure into a living reality with creative force. Despite the endorsement afforded the proposal when it came before the faculty and the support it received from across the campus, there was much debate, and no consensus on what this culture of service should, could, or would entail.

The duPont grant provided limited funds for hiring a person to coordinate the development of the Appalachian Center for Community Service. A tenth generation Southwest Virginian and a 1983 graduate of Emory & Henry College, in 1996, I was just finishing my PhD in American Studies at Emory University. The position described in the duPont proposal called for a volunteer service coordinator who would facilitate both curricular and co-curricular service, oversee service-learning placements, and direct the Bonner Scholars Program.

My dissertation had been a study of place and culture in twentieth-century America, seen through the lens of my family's struggle to enter the American middle class in the coalfields of Appalachia. At that time, the terms and concepts "place" and "politics of place" did not occupy much space in common or in academic parlance, and they certainly did not figure in discussions of service-learning and civically engaged pedagogy. The dominant and emerging usage, the newest academic fashion, was community service.

Although the planning committee provided the structure and the goals, both the Public Policy and Community Service program and the Appalachian Center required a compass point that would ground and structure the work and its long-term direction. In January 1997, less than four months after the launch of the Appalachian Center and the major in Public Policy, I articulated an understanding of what a place-based model of education and service would be at Emory & Henry College. The Bonner Foundation had asked all the schools in its affiliated network to produce a document outlining how best to expand the scope of the Bonner Scholars Program in that school. Writing the Emory & Henry document gave me an opportunity to move beyond a narrow focus of Bonner to articulate a unified vision for the Appalachian Center and the degree program in Public Policy, and the principles and philosophies, values and vision that are its heartbeat. Building on the structure called for by the original planning committee and endorsed by the duPont Foundation, I put forward what a deep attentiveness to this place might teach about educational practice and the art and craft of citizenship. Just as the mountains rising to the east of the college mark the boundaries of the Holston watershed, the writing of this internal document was a watershed event, defining who we were to be and what we could and would do in this place.

This watershed document called the college to build in *place*—to build and sustain in this place a program that springs from and is part of its fibers and sinews. This document also called for the college to *build in* place: to integrate this place into the way it taught, into the values it espoused, into what it sought to accomplish as an institution for teaching and learning. It called Emory & Henry to come to an awareness of itself as an institutional, public citizen of this place. Much as the tributaries and headwaters of the Holston arise from within this place, to build in place requires that the history, stories, experiences, and social processes imbued across this landscape, beginning with the very foundations of the earth and continuing into tomorrow, shape every aspect of this pedagogy.

As the lodestar of this building, place came to function in two ways. Place is this particular place with its distinctive stories and histories, its contradictions and conflicts. Place is also a general theoretical concept, offering a civic, intellectual, and ethical framework informing and shaping one's life choices, thinking, and citizenship; a collection of values and perspectives, tools and insights, methodologies and skills students take with them when they graduate. Two responsibilities, two callings, and two understandings of place, simultaneously undertaken, joined in deep and important ways, both equally never finished, both consuming and dynamic, and both with lessons for American higher education.

Informing both of these functions of place and both of these ways of building is the understanding that all persons have the gifts, talents, abilities, passions, and a vision to make a difference in the lives of others and in the life of their places, quite apart from any value or worth that accrues to them in the market economy. Some will see this as social capital as Richard Couto defines the term (Couto & Guthrie, 1999, pp. 36–69). Moreover, persons do not have to wait until they graduate from college or have advanced education or enough money to make this difference; they can enter immediately into this work. Indeed, such is the very stuff of citizenship and service-learning. If this is true of people, it is also true of places as socially constituted; if people can have social capital, so too can places. Every place has the potential to be a safe, healthy, and good place for all its people, regardless of that place's role in the economic exchange, the value attached to that place in the market economy, or the social conflicts that have roiled it.

Whether we are students, faculty, or civic partners in our places, one of the first things this educational process asks is that its participants begin to make the distinction between service and charity. Although it is now an assumed to be commonplace among service-learning practitioners, a developmental model that is relational and accepting of conflict and that begins from the point where persons are, asks its participants to understand first the connection between service and education. Whether inside the academy or without, service confronts issues of power, questions of justice, and the enduring realities of conflict. Service understands that all places are constituted in analogous processes, and that the needs of the people in any place are connected to larger questions, global forces, and issues. Service in a place provides the opportunity for us to move beyond the narrow limits of our private world or neighborhood, raise questions of power and privilege, and become aware of our own deep complicity in systems of oppression and destruction. Service is a force for building common ground between divided and disparate peoples, offering lived experiences from which persons can build and sustain coalitions, confront societal and individual conflicts, and organize to achieve systemic solutions to real problems, creating opportunities for citizens to be agents of social change. Service learns from this place and from any place in which it is undertaken. Service is necessarily complex, multilayered, interdisciplinary, and ongoing, just as is this or any place.

Building in place at Emory & Henry requires that the college's service partnerships not be with a single agency or organization. Instead, the partnerships necessary for building in place are between a place and its people in a long-term relationship so that they can identify needs and issues and capitalize on assets and resources, defining strategies and solutions from within the place and that are consonant with that place. Partnerships that build in place struggle with systemic forces to address systemic needs and issues, recognizing that to do so involves reaching across the single issues and narrow focus that define any one agency or organization, any one approach, drawing on wide collaborations and an embracing common ground.

### Radical Particularity

In discussing the political and intellectual legacy of Raymond Williams, the geographer and cultural critic David Harvey attributes to Williams what Harvey describes as a militant or radical particularity, knowing a place in its fullness, with its contradictions, its conflicts, its questions, knowing what it means to be a citizen in that place (Harvey 1996, pp. 19–45). Building in place, practicing a pedagogy and a citizenship of place, are practices requiring radical, militant particularity focused on the interaction of the natural environment, the built environment, and the human culture and history over the millennia. At Emory & Henry, we have built and continue to build in this place, but our work of radical, militant particularity is defined in partnerships with three specific places: Meadowview, in the Valley of the Holston in Washington County, Virginia; Fries, on the New River in Grayson County, Virginia; and Caretta, in the Big Creek watershed of McDowell County, West Virginia, just across the Virginia–West Virginia border.

In his novel, *Jayber Crow*, Wendell Berry describes the town of Port William. "In the eyes of the powers that be, we Port Williamites live and move and have our being within a black period about the size of the one that ends a sentence. Thousands of leaders…entire administrations, corporate board meetings, university sessions, synods and councils of the church have come and gone without hearing or pronouncing the name of Port William" (Berry, 2000, p. 139). The same can be said, in fact is said, of Fries, Caretta, and Meadowview. Marsha Timpson, a lifelong resident of McDowell, once told me, "America would rather not have to deal with us" (Timpson, 2007). She was speaking of Caretta and McDowell County, but her thoughts have their echoes in Meadowview and Fries. These three places offer ways of seeing much of what has transpired in this landscape and America over the last century and a half and ways of exploring what it means to be an effective citizen in the twenty-first century.

They are places "from which capital has moved on," taking with it power, prestige, and the attention of American culture (Harvey, 1993, pp. 3, 5, 7). Until the 1960s, Meadowview, in Washington County, was the commercial center of a great agricultural region—producing dairy products, beef, pork, wool, poultry and eggs, apples, wheat and small grains, corn, and burley tobacco. A shipping center, the town of Meadowview was economically vibrant with stores, restaurants, craft artisans, and services. By the turn of the new century, all of that was gone and the Meadowview Town Square was lined with abandoned and collapsing buildings. In 2010, as many as 67 percent of households qualified as low or moderate income, and over 50 percent of the children in the Meadowview Elementary School qualified for free and reduced-price lunches.

In 1948, McDowell County, West Virginia, had a population of over 100,000 people. At the mid-point of the twentieth century, McDowell was one of the wealthiest counties in the United States, its wealth built on its coal resources. In the 1930s, boosters described McDowell as the billion-dollar coalfield. By 2010, its population was less than 20,000 people. When measured by median household income, in 2010 McDowell ranked as the eighth poorest county in the United States; 46 percent of its children lived below the poverty line. Caretta is located in the southernmost portion of the county, in the area most economically distressed.

Fries, on the New River, came into being as a cotton mill town. From 1903 through 1988, the Washington Mills was the largest employer in Fries, providing jobs for generations of families. The mill closed in 1988, and by 2010, 542 people were living in Fries. With an aging populace, Fries counted 20 percent of its total population living below the poverty line, but 30 percent of its children.

Both Fries and Caretta were company towns, towns in which the industrialists that built them controlled them lock, stock, and barrel until the mines and the mills and the town along with them were sold to another company. When profits declined, when the American economy yet again restructured itself, capital moved on, leaving behind the place and its people. Meadowview was not a company town, but the same economic shifts and forces that made Fries and Caretta redundant and lessened their importance and value, accomplished the same results here.

The work of building in place teaches us that these three places, and any place, need people who are prepared to see and to understand the world from the perspective of that place, to have a deep attentiveness to all its realities. I have been involved in work in McDowell County, West Virginia, for almost twenty years. Sometimes at night, I can close my eyes and see the serrated bluffs and cliffs along the ridge tops. Sometimes, when I close my eyes, I can see coal slurry impoundments, with millions of tons of rock and dirt, and billions of gallons of tarry and smoking sludge, collecting behind earthen dams, looming over towns and neighborhoods, the wastes of our efforts to satisfy an insatiable national and global thirst for cheap fuel. Sometimes, I see the former company towns, and hear in the dialects that are so familiar to me, the stories of those places. Some of those towns were washed away in the floods of July 2001 and May 2002, and the towns and places I can see are gone forever, the dialects are of people that can no longer live in McDowell. This is part of what it means to build in place and what it means to be attentive to the particularity of this place. This is what makes place-based work so elusive and never fixed, always evolving and deepening, always maturing, because places are so. Nothing in most graduate programs and even less in American academic culture teaches this attentiveness. I have learned it from the places in which I live and work. This attentiveness is a value and a way of being that only our places can teach us over a very long time. Our responsibility as citizens is to learn this attentiveness to the particularity of our places. Our responsibility as teachers is to create opportunities for students to see and understand the values and acquire the skills that lead to such attentiveness, to such particularity, to this building in place.

These places have challenged me to move beyond the cliché of social justice to create spaces in classrooms and service experiences for students to grapple with this concept with a radical, militant particularity, finding ways to apply the concepts of social justice and work toward realizing it. In this, we have together come to appreciate Paul Theobald's concept of *intradependence*, which he defines as "exist[ing] by virtue of the necessary relations *within a place*" (Theobald, 1997, pp. 7–31, emphasis original). Theobald's intradependence echoes the same ideas that Wendell Berry suggests, "There are moments when the heart is generous and then it knows that for better or worse our lives are woven together here, one with one another and with the place and all the living things" (Berry, 2000, p. 210). These places are teaching us that weaving together, intradependence, justice, are built and enacted within lived relationships with the natural environment, with other individuals, with groups, but also in relationships with the history and culture of a place, as well as with the distant future of a place. Living by virtue of the necessary relations within a place is what makes justice social; all that constitutes a place serves as the standard and measure of justice. Ideas, actions, policies, habits, assumptions, politics, processes, decisions, and approaches that together or individually expand, encourage, enrich, enliven the weaving together of relationships necessary within a place are just. Those ideas, actions, policies, habits, assumptions, politics, processes, decisions, and approaches that together or individually discourage, damage, or destroy the relationships necessary within a place, are not just.

This place, in connection with every place, becomes the standard of justice, raising questions, offering ideas, troubling all easy assumptions. That a person in suburban Washington, DC, can have access to affordable electricity for all manner of technological applications seems a good thing, perhaps outside the arena of social justice. That the means of production of that affordable electricity are mountaintop removal in McDowell County, West Virginia, and that there are both profound environmental and social issues involved in this process make it an issue of social justice in Northern Virginia and in McDowell County and throughout Appalachia and America.

These places teach me, in ways subtle and opaque, and in ways direct and pellucid, that building in place is the way of deep questions. People in Fries, in Caretta, in Meadowview will say we do not need your answers, we need citizens who can struggle with tough questions; we need citizens and partners with the capacities to put down roots, to understand, and take the long, long view. Do not send us answers, they say, send us people, young people, who have the capacity to hear our stories, endure the conflicts, keep silent when silence is called for, and understand the questions. These places teach that the academy's power and assumptions lead its people to think and to live as if they will change the place; serve it, perhaps, but be the final and authoritative answer to the issues faced in that place. The academy often appears on the scene with all the answers, never having heard the questions. The painful truth is that there is little difference between that approach and the power that mill owners and mine owners exerted in Fries or in Caretta; they grow from the same consciousness.

These places teach that building in place means that our relationships in a place must be reciprocal. My Meadowview neighbor plows my garden. When his wife's brother died, we took a pound cake by the house. What service-learning professionals may call reciprocity, others usually call neighborliness. This neighborliness means that in the processes by which we address the central issues of our places, we of the academy must be changed and our power must be challenged in the lived relationships in a place. My friends in Caretta, Meadowview, and Fries tell me that one of the means that educators work to maintain their power and to deny a mutual neighborliness is the use of jargon. I have seen this. Academics are masters of jargon—CBR, action research, place-based work, service-learning, community service learning, academic service-learning, participatory evaluation. Our places teach us that such language, such jargon is both pretentious and dishonest. We must find a language that speaks less of the academy's power and more of the place. If what we want to say, if what we want to undertake is important enough to be heard, to be joined, it is important enough to be put in such language that the people of a place can know our meanings. The particularities of these places teach that building in place is a question of accessibility and relationship, of fairness and justice—of neighborliness.

In contemporary public life, politics is too often a debate over the one right answer, the narrow ground that an individual or a group must claim and defend against all others if victory is to be declared. Politics has become a series of campaigns to own the narrow space of the one right answer, vanquishing the claims or questions of all others. Meadowview, Caretta, and Fries teach us that the defining conflicts of a place are about questions and issues for which there is no single right answer. An education and a citizenship built in place, and defined in radical particularity, struggles with the difference between the right answers and the honest responses. The academy is about the right answer—give the right answer, you will pass the quiz; give the right answer, you will get tenure; give the right answer, you will fix the problem and then can move on, and we teach our students so. Sometimes, we must give the right answer, as when authorities hold grant funds until we firmly outline in prescribed language and terms what our vision is for our place. More often, however, what are most needed in a place are the honest response and the ability to discern the differences between the honest response and the right answer. The academy and its members must develop the courage to create learning spaces, whether involving service-learning or not, in which silence is allowed and the honest response, often stumblingly articulated, perhaps even inchoate, perhaps wrong or unconventional in a traditional class-room, is accepted and honored.

This interweaving, this intradependence, this understanding of justice as social, this commitment to difficult questions and honest struggles give rise to civic choices that often run counter to mainstream American culture that sees as flip sides of the same coin upward professional and economic mobility and geographic mobility. These places are teaching us to challenge the values and structures that have encouraged the academy to produce a wandering, nomadic professoriate and administrative class that often devalue or dismiss a citizenship of place or the processes of building in place. The academy has taught us to value more highly appointments in elite colleges and universities, located far away, both geographi-cally and emotionally from places like Fries or Caretta or Meadowview—where schools are better, where there are more cultural opportunities, where good coffee and good music go hand in hand. Building in this place has required us to leave the vacuum tube of the Interstate that runs between the fashionable places and their universities and colleges and make the ethical choices to dwell and abide and practice our citizenship in places with little significance in the market economy (Berry, 1993, pp.168–73).

This work of building in place and the success of the proposal for the major are due in large measure to the continuity of key faculty and staff. Dr. Fisher had lived and worked across this landscape for over 20 years when the college formed the planning committee that built the foundation of this place-based education. I have now been at the college for 15 years, and my roots are generations deep in this region. Both Dr. Fisher and I have made decisions to stay, to abide here, when other positions beckoned. Although Dr. Fisher retired in 2006 after 35 years of teaching, he remains here, this was the place that defined his lifework. The success of programs, the growth of a culture of service on this campus, have significantly benefited from faculty and staff who abide, who are committed to the long, hard journey of building in this place.

This continuity has also meant that after 15 years of building in place, we have come to the end of the easy answers. If the Emory & Henry program were one from which key faculty and administrators were frequently moving to other institutions, if other persons were frequently arriving with new packages of ideas, theories, and practices, the degree program and the center would be continually reshaped and reinvented, shining with the newest fashions in civic engagement, the most up-to-date jargon. In this process, the work of building in place would lose the continuity and stability necessary for knowing and understanding the stories and conflicts of this place and people; with every new hire, the stories must be relearned; the relationships, rebuilt; the particularity, re-discerned. Our continuity has made possible many successes, more than would be possible otherwise, but the Emory & Henry degree program and Appalachian Center must now confront questions many other programs with a more transitory or nationally focused leadership have not yet confronted. The questions we face in these places are too difficult, the global structures and their local expressions too impervious to challenge, and the progress we have made seems too meager for us to say honestly that we are changing the world or that we have transformed forever concepts of citizenship or the academy's self-understanding.

Our continuity has also produced an awareness that the language we use to speak of place and citizenship, the values we say are at the core of this building in place, are losing their relevancy to new student generations at Emory & Henry and even to those faculty members who are coming to us just out of graduate school. For too long we have been content to build in place with students who self-select to be engaged in this education, students who are like us in thinking and vision, and students whom we like. As does every campus, Emory & Henry has students who profess an ideology of civic engagement and are adept at providing the expected answers, but who choose not to assume the responsibilities of citizenship. What then is the responsibility of service-learning and civic engagement? If our responsibility is the education and equipping of an effective and participatory citizenry, what then is our responsibility to these students who are also citizens with all the rights and privileges and obligations of citizenship? To say that sometimes education takes root only years later, or that we cannot take responsibility for those who refuse responsibility for themselves, seems somehow wrong or lazy or woefully complacent when set in the particularity of the places with which we are joined in partnership and the issues and questions prevailing in those places.

If our abiding here, if building in these places, has brought us to confront the end of the easy answers, a point at which our relevancy might be slipping, these places, this building in place, has also brought us to a new understanding of what citizenship means and what is required to equip persons for it. Global citizenship, citizenship in the American republic of the twenty-first century, must also be a citizenship of place—whether that place is Caretta, or Meadowview, or Fries, or the Upper West Side of Manhattan, or the Watts neighborhood of Los Angeles, or the Lower Ninth Ward of New Orleans. This is a citizenship of questions and honesty, of abiding, of service, of intradependence. American higher education must find ways to make relevant this concept and to equip our students for this citizenship. In this, again, the places in which we live and teach, the places in which we build, places imbued with stories and conflicts, are our teachers, requiring of us careful, honest listening, born of and returning to a radical particularity.

## Note

1. Portions of this essay are from keynote addresses I have delivered, *Building In Place,* at the North Carolina Campus Compact Civic Engagement Administrator Conference, May 26, 2010, at Barton College, Wilson, North Carolina, and *Places Your G.P.S. Can't Take You,* at the Gulf-South Summit, March 2–4, 2011, at Roanoke, Virginia.

## *References*

Berry, Wendell. (1993) *Sex, Economy, Freedom & Community.* New York: Pantheon.

Berry, Wendell. (2000). *Jayber Crow: The Life Story of Jayber Crow, Barber, of the Port William Membership, as Written by Himself: A Novel.* Washington, DC: Counterpoint.

Couto, Richard and Guthrie, Catherine, S. (1999). *Making Democracy Work Better: Mediating Structures, Social Capital, and the Democratic Prospect.* Chapel Hill: University of North Carolina Press.

Freire, Paulo. (1970). *Pedagogy of the Oppressed.* Trans. Myra Berman Ramos. New York: Herder and Herder.

Harvey, David. (1993). "From Space to Place and Back Again: Reflections on *The Conditions of Postmodernity,*" in Jon Bird, ed. *Mapping the Futures: Local Cultures, Global Change.* London: Routledge, pp. 3–28.

Harvey, David. (1996). *Justice, Nature, & the Geography of Difference.* Oxford: Blackwell.

Johnston, R. J. (1991). *A Question of Place: The Practice of Human Geography.* Oxford: Blackwell.

Mills, C. Wright. (1959). *The Sociological Imagination.* New York: Oxford University Press.

Theobald, Paul. (1997). *Teaching the Commons: Place, Pride, and the Renewal of Community.* Boulder, CO: Westview.

Timpson, Marsha. (2007). Interview with Talmage A. Stanley. Tape and transcript held by the author.

## PART II

## Reflecting on the Future of Community Engagement

# CHAPTER 9

# A New Hull House? The Monumental Challenge of Service-Learning and Community Engagement

*Peter Levine*
Tisch College, Tufts University

This book tells rich and moving stories about students who venture into the communities around their campuses, in places like Providence, Rhode Island; Bland County, Virginia; and Santa Cruz, California, to work with faculty and community partners on common issues. As they start off, they may hear their professors say (or tell themselves): "Never doubt that a small group of thoughtful, committed citizens can change the world. Indeed, it's the only thing that ever has."[1]

Those sentences, usually attributed to Margaret Mead, are inspirational—but false. One *should* doubt that small groups can change the world, for the vast majority fail. Small groups are certainly not the only agents of change: what about governments, armies, markets, professions, and corporations? Finally, even when they do succeed, citizens are not always beneficial. Lenin, Mussolini, Mao, and Hitler started with bands of committed companions who spent a lot of time thinking before they made the world much *worse*.

Thus, small groups of committed students and faculty or community partners face an intellectual task. They must decide whether a group such as themselves can possibly change the world; and if so, how. They must also decide whether the change that they would cause is good.

Fifty years ago (early in the Kennedy administration), many such groups would have aligned with a political movement that provided them with values, diagnoses, prescriptions, strategies, networks, inspirational stories, living leaders, candidates and party slates, regular news reports, organizational supports, cultural expressions (from songs to clothes), and potential career paths.

Some young activists might have associated themselves with Marxism in one of its versions, from revolutionary communism to Liberation Theology or European-style social democracy. Today, Marxism lives on college campuses only as scattered reading assignments.

Other groups would have aligned with the liberalism of the New Deal and New Frontier. Liberal values have actually grown more popular among young Americans, but liberals are now basically in a defensive or conservative posture, dedicated to protecting or modestly expanding the laws and institutions that were built between 1932 and 1968 (Levine, Flanagan, & Gallay, 2009).

Still others would have joined the civil rights movement, then at its apogee and heading toward triumph and disintegration. Rachel Carson's *Silent Spring* was published in 1962, and some students would have gravitated toward the nascent environmental movement, widely seen as in crisis in 2012. Just a year later, Betty Friedan published *The Feminine Mystique*, and by then, some young people were beginning to create Second Wave feminism. But in 2008, just 14 percent of Americans (of all ages) said that they considered themselves feminists (Penn, Schoen, & Berland, 2008).

Finally, a few activist students and faculty would have endorsed the libertarianism of Barry Goldwater and Milton Friedman. That movement remains vital today and deserves respectful attention, but it draws only a small minority's support.

Perhaps the authors of this book regard the decline of organized systems and ideologies as welcome news. Stanley (Chapter 8) advocates "militant or radical particularity, knowing a place in its fullness, with its contradictions, its conflicts, its questions, what it means to be a citizen in that place." That is an implicit critique of any ambitious, widely applicable theory. Morton (Chapter 5) notes that the curriculum at Providence College "introduces a relational and experiential complexity." Community Studies at UC-Santa Cruz has been criticized for an allegedly leftist orientation, but Pudup (Chapter 6) insists that "the field study was not framed in terms of specific ideological commitments."

By the same token, the authors cited most frequently in these pages are proponents of pragmatism, of learning from particular and personal experience, and of open-ended conversations. John Dewey is mentioned in three contexts, Paolo Freire four times, Parker Palmer twice, and C. Wright Mills three times. In my view, these authors do not propose political theories as much as they invite readers to develop their own; they are primarily concerned with *processes* of deliberation and inquiry. The one ideology that is discussed frequently in these pages is "neoliberalism"; it emerges as a shadowy enemy without a specific parallel on the left. Stanley imagines the voice of communities around his institution saying: "We do not need your answers, we need citizens who can struggle with tough questions, we need citizens and partners with the capacities to put down roots, to understand, and take the long, long view. Do not send us answers, they say, send us people, young people, who have the capacity to hear our stories, endure the conflicts, keep silent when silence is called for, and understand the questions."

I am sympathetic to this kind of pragmatic, local, experiential, experimental, bottom-up, open-ended politics. Perhaps Dewey (1927) was right that no institution can claim "inherent sanctity." There are no general principles, no "antecedent universal propositions." The nature of the good society is "something to be critically and experimentally determined."

That may be true, but it sets a very difficult agenda. It is much easier to participate in politics and civil society if one can employ ideological heuristics and join large movements that have already developed both theories and practices. Making a decision from scratch about each policy and situation is hard for anyone, but it is hardest for the young and the poor. For people who do not (yet) have much education, experience, or leisure, an ideology is a valuable shortcut that enables them to cast a vote or make a consumer decision without having to deliberate endlessly. We know from survey data that Americans who have ideological or partisan commitments vote at higher rates than other people, which suggests that ideology is a resource that can compensate for a lack of time and education (Abamowitz, 2010).

If we ask students or anyone else to make decisions about each separate issue, place, and policy instead of choosing among parties or ideologies, the cognitive demands will rise and the rate of participation will fall. Indeed, during the Progressive Era (1900–14), reformers tried to de-emphasize ideology and partisanship by creating ideologically neutral newspapers, allowing the people to vote on separate candidates and referendum questions instead of choosing between the major parties, and promoting open deliberation. Voter turnout plummeted from 73 percent in 1900 to 49 percent in 1920, and the active electorate narrowed to a more educated and wealthier slice of the population (Levine, 2000).

The authors of this volume are radically ambitious, hoping to increase the scale and frequency of civic engagement while also eschewing ideologies and avoiding large political movements. Unfortunately, the academic world that stands behind them is not well organized to help "small groups of thoughtful and committed citizens" make wise decisions.

First, social scientists, recognizing the relatively small impact of deliberate action by voluntary groups, devote most of their attention to large processes and institutions: states, markets, elections. This emphasis reflects hard-nosed realism, but it means that for people interested in how to maximize their impact as members of small groups, the literature is surprisingly scanty.

Second, scholarship is not as helpful as it should be for deciding whether any given change is beneficial. Social scientists are often uncomfortable with values, treating them as opinions to be studied or as biases to be minimized and disclosed—not as propositions to be defended with arguments and critically assessed. In fields like philosophy, theology, and political theory, values are openly debated. But scholars in those fields tend to be quite uninterested in strategy. I think of a philosopher colleague who recently made a forceful argument in favor of greater equality in education. When a reporter noted that the American people tend to disagree, my colleague replied, "I've given up on the public" (Kahlenberg, 2011). That is an example of a sophisticated and probably valid theory that is attached to no political strategy whatsoever.

It is hard to think of contemporary writers who combine empirical rigor, strategic acumen, and moral persuasiveness in work of broad relevance. That is why this book makes so few references to living intellectuals, other than a few proponents of localism and personal integrity.

The challenge implicit in these chapters is huge: to decide how to improve the world when it is getting worse in so many ways, when there are no satisfactory Big Ideas or attendant political movements, and when academia is not oriented to assist intellectually. But a crisis is also an opportunity. If we lack compelling political/intellectual movements and our major institutions are broken, then we had better begin building examples of ethical and effective civic work at the grass-roots level. If our intellectual life is fractured in ways that reduce its value for active citizens, then we had better find settings that reintegrate scholarship and address serious problems. Certificates, majors, and minors in community engagement may be just such settings.

Movements of much greater scale and impact may ultimately emerge from such projects. Consider, for instance, American liberalism in its heyday around 50 years ago. It then had everything that an ideology should: millions of active adherents, heroes and leaders, supportive organizations (from the AFL-CIO to the ACLU), legislative victories and an unfinished legislative agenda, empirical theories and supportive evidence, and moral principles. The principles could be summarized as the famous Four Freedoms that President Roosevelt had announced in 1941 (freedom of speech and expression; freedom of religion; freedom from want; and freedom from fear); but we could spell them out a bit more, as follows. The individual liberties in the Bill of Rights trump social goods, but it is the responsibility of the national government to promote social goods once private freedoms have been secured. The chief social goods include minimal levels of welfare for all (the "safety net," or Freedom from Want), equality of opportunity (achieved through public education, civil rights legislation, and pro-competitive regulation in the marketplace), and consistent prosperity, promoted by Keynesian economic policies during recessions.

These ideas had empirical support from sociology and economics and could be developed into a whole philosophy. Franklin Roosevelt constructed a temple to Thomas Jefferson because he wanted to show liberalism's debts to that enlightenment philosopher; the interior of the Jefferson Memorial in Washington, DC, is bedecked with quotes favorable to the New Deal. Other parts of the liberal synthesis can be traced back to Jefferson's less popular contemporary, Alexander Hamilton. John Maynard Keynes, Louis Brandeis, Gifford Pinchot, and Felix Frankfurter were more proximate intellectual sources. We could understand the New Deal as a development of Victorian liberalism that added arguments in favor of federal activism to combat monopoly, environmental catastrophe, and the business cycle.

But I do not believe the New Deal originated in theory. I would explain its origins in an entirely different way: as the "scaling up" of concrete examples and experiments that were undertaken originally in a highly pragmatic vein. Think, for example, of Jane Addams in 1889. She is a rich and well-educated person who has no possibility of a career (because she is a woman) and who is deeply troubled by poverty in industrial cities. She is impressed by the concrete example of Toynbee Hall, a settlement house in London. She and Ellen Gates Starr move into a house in a poor district of Chicago without a very clear plan for what to do. They launch projects and events, many of which have a "deliberative" flavor—residents come together to read challenging books, discuss, and debate. They work in a pragmatic intellectual milieu that encourages people to set assumptions aside. They engage with some of the most formidable thinkers of the era, from Tolstoy to Dewey, and make Hull House a seminar room as well as a service center.

Out of the pragmatic, problem-solving discussions in Hull House come a kindergarten, a museum, a public kitchen, a bathhouse, a library, numerous adult education courses, and reform initiatives related to politics and unions. Some 2,000 people come to Hull House every day at its peak, to talk, work, advocate, and receive services.

In the 1920s, when progressive state governments like New York's start building more ambitious social and educational services, they fund settlement houses and launch other institutions (schools, state colleges, clinics, public-housing projects, welfare agencies) modeled on Hull House and its sister settlements. Then, when Roosevelt becomes president and decides to stimulate the economy with federal spending, he creates programs like the Works Progress Administration (WPA) that are essentially Hull House writ large. At this point, tens of millions of people can take the relatively simple political act of voting for the president who had brought them the WPA; mass mobilization supports small-scale democratic experimentalism, and vice versa.

It is that kind of ending we should be aiming for. I do not mean a replica of the New Deal, for our problems are entirely different. I do not necessarily mean a center-left political movement. But I do mean a *political* movement (or a healthy competition among several such movements) that originates in a combination of direct, hands-on experience and really serious intellectual work. Perhaps the cases described here will one day serve as early chapters in the history of that democratic revival.

## Note

1. On the quotation and doubts about whether Margaret Mead really said it, see Nancy C. Lutkehaus, *Margaret Mead: The Making of an American Icon* (Princeton, NJ: Princeton University Press, 2008), p. 261.

## *References*

Abramowitz, A. (2010). *The disappearing center: Engaged citizens, polarization, and American democracy.* New Haven, CT: Yale University Press.

Dewey, J. (1927). *The public and its problems.* New York: Henry Holt.

Kahlenberg, R. (2011, October 17). Calling Philosophers of Education. *Blog of the Century.* Retrieved on October 17, 2011 from http://botc.tcf.org/2011/10/calling-philosophers-of-education.html.

Levine, P. (2000). *The new progressive era: Toward a fair and deliberative democracy.* Lanham, MD: Rowman & Littlefield.

Levine, P., Flanagan, C., & Gallay, L. (2009). *The millennial pendulum: A new generation of voters and the prospects for a political realignment.* Washington DC: New America Foundation Monograph.

Lutkehaus, N. (2008). *Margaret Mead: The Making of an American icon.* Princeton, NJ: Princeton University Press, 2008.

Penn, Schoen & Berland Associates (2008, November 5–6). Retrieved on September 1, 2011 from http://www.tdbimg.com/upload/pdfs/TheBarrierThatDidntFall.pdf.

# CHAPTER 10

# Disciplining Higher Education for Democratic Community Engagement

*Ariane Hoy\*, Mathew Johnson\*\*, and Robert Hackett\**
\* Bonner Foundation
\*\* Siena College

A s we write this response essay, the finishing touches are being put on a report to the US Department of Education entitled, "The Crucible Moment: College Learning and Democracy's Future," developed by the Association of American Colleges and Universities and key stakeholders to describe the current state of community engagement in higher education. That report, like this volume, is a call for renewed focus and energy to be placed on the seemingly stalled state of community engagement, civic engagement, and service-learning at institutions of higher learning. Many of the essays in *The Engaged Campus* call into question the sustainability and impact of our collective work to promote and put into practice the civic mission of higher education. As Butin argues well in the introduction to this book, the lack of ideological and theoretical frameworks—especially when we are working with institutions whose pièce de résistance includes defining disciplinary theories and epistemologies—is a barrier to our progress. Indeed, for this very reason many of the authors of this volume founded certificates, majors, and minors, in part to attain academic legitimacy for the important work of community engagement in their respective institutions. If the service-learning and community engagement movement has been stalled, we believe that the way forward is to break open these frameworks: curricular versus co-curricular; professor versus community partner; disciplinary versus experiential knowledge; classroom versus community learning; academics versus politics.

The creation of academic community engagement programs is often driven by an aim to provide students with clearer, more coherent academic pathways and to define recognizable academic structures that undergird faculty participation. The Bonner Foundation shared this aim in our 2004–08 project utilizing the Fund for the Improvement of Post-Secondary Education (FIPSE) funding to spur the creation of civic-engagement minors and certificates. Other aims include the desire for academic legitimacy (and its corollary, resources) and the desire to *further the field* by developing logical delimitations about what exactly "the field" is. Founding a program can also be fed by a desire to stake a disciplinary claim to a bound academic "field" and thereby position intellectual leaders in that "field," if even only at local institutions. While we agree with Butin's central call for more written work, more research, and more books like this one that draw together lessons from across the "field," we may interpret the need for "discipline" in a slightly different way— one that would drive institutions' accountability to the communities they serve and continue to realign and refine civic-engagement work to produce community and social impact.

A recent white paper entitled *Democratic Engagement,* by John Saltmarsh, Matt Hartley, and Patti Clayton (2009), suggests a key distinction for the next wave of community engagement in higher education. The authors suggest that the next wave involves a fundamental questioning and reorienting of the epistemological foundation of modern American higher education. Far from advocating the "disciplining" of a field, the authors suggest that a primary limiting factor in community engagement preventing the movement from reaching a deeper, more robust wave of practice and knowledge creation is *precisely* the way the academy *organizes and privileges certain knowledge over other knowledge*: faculty over student, faculty over staff, disciplinary over experiential, and most clearly, academy, in all its forms and representations, over community.

We contend that the theoretical and ideological core of community engagement already exists in a more-or-less organic and evolving fashion. Unlike a discipline, community engagement has several layers of core knowledge that include classical knowledge frameworks and theories associated with a discipline, but also include the process and practice knowledge better understood as "best practice," which often does not neatly fit into a classical disciplinary framework. In addition, community partners, when truly engaged as co-educators and teachers, deeply inform students' learning and application of knowledge, often through unstructured dialogue opportunities. As Keith Morton aptly describes in Chapter 5, "Process, Content, and Community Building", the academic program at Providence College sought to answer the question, "Citizenship for what?" They chose to define building community and relationship building as core aspects of the curriculum, drawing on the Deweyian notion of public life as something created through social imagination and action. Not only must structures that break the traditional barriers of academic and community be deliberately developed, but also the community may be read *as text*. This work, hence, often must be intentionally interdisciplinary and integrative, as well as reflective of the particular places and distinctions of both institution and community. Just as a generation earlier, Women's Studies, the full range of ethnic studies, and other curricular transformations, like "writing across the curriculum," welcomed and were sustained by a rich interdisciplinary community of practice that bled into and across the curricular and noncurricular life of the academy—changing the academy and the traditional disciplines—so, too, will the next wave of community engagement lead to transformation of higher education if it succeeds.

The chapters in this book describe many of the theories, perspectives, and experiences we need to chart our ascent to the next plateau. We see in our collective work and in these chapters five key themes to consider as we embark on the next wave of community engagement:

(1) We must *move beyond the course-based glass ceiling* of community engagement toward deeper, developmental, community engagement, engaging a broader range of students and practices.

(2) We must move beyond the limiting power of the current "academy as expert, owner, and creator of knowledge" epistemology of higher education to an epistemology that *values community and student voice as co-creators of knowledge.*

(3) We must more fully *engage faculty and staff in curricular and co-curricular integration* and therefore encourage an opening of the boundary between the two.

(4) We must *connect our work in lived campus-community contexts with the imperative of democratic engagement* that shapes our polity and policies on the local, state, regional, national, international, and even virtual level.

(5) We must *cultivate and utilize evidence-driven practice and community impact.*

## Beyond the Course-Based Model of Engagement:

### Intensive, Multiyear, Developmental Pathways

One definition of service-learning is "a course-based credit-bearing, educational experience in which students participate in an organized activity that meets identified community needs and reflect on the service activity in such a way as to gain further understanding of course content, a broader appreciation of the discipline, and an enhanced sense of civic responsibility" (Bringle & Hatcher, 1995). Most certainly, the service-learning movement must be recognized for helping to catalyze important transformations in the way we think of teaching and learning, with research that suggests its impact on student development. For example, Eyler and Giles (1999) demonstrated that one-semester service-learning classes had significant, consistent, and modest effects on student personal, civic, cognitive, and academic outcomes. A 2000 study of 12,000 college students conducted by Astin, Vogelsang, Ikeda, and Yee revealed that more than 75 percent of students had participated in some form of civic engagement during college, with 30 percent having participated in course-based service-learning and 46 percent participating in some other form of community service. Service-learning, like any movement, has faced challenges as it has neared a tipping point; indeed, its stalling may be due to its own definition as a course-based endeavor, one that doesn't mesh well with the ongoing developmental needs of the students, community partners, and faculty involved in complex projects to address community needs and achieve impact.

Our own perspective here is shaped by the connection of the work of the Bonner Program with Campus Outreach Opportunity League (COOL), founded in 1984 by Wayne Meisel and Bobby Hackett, who later brought to the Bonner network their experience motivating and organizing students to shape the national college service movement. From its inception, COOL named five qualities of effective community service that paralleled service-learning: (1) education and training, (2) meaningful action, (3) community voice, (4) student voice, and (5) reflection and evaluation. However, the aim was to affect community change first, not student learning of course material, with student idealism at the core. This early work shaped the developmental, student-led approach of the Bonner Program, one that is supported by research.

In Bonner programs students embark on a four-year developmental journey in which they *explore* a place and a social issue; gain *experience* through 8–10 hours of community engagement each week; become *examples* to peers through site-based, program, and campuswide leadership; and strive for *excellence* through the integration of their academic and co-curricular lives as they seek to understand and change the core systemic causes of community issues.

Key aspects of the *intensive, multiyear, developmental pathways* include placing students in site-based teams that create cohort-based planning, reflection, issue-based research, and leadership opportunities; professional development and training on a regular (weekly) basis to support ongoing growth of the students as professionals in their sites and as community engagement leaders on campus; intentional annual transitional experiences that harvest the knowledge gained by the student and engage students in planning the way forward in their community engagement; and intentional connection and integration of academic pursuits with community engagement throughout the multiyear experience.

This framework is fertile with opportunities for curricular pathways. Indeed, through our work with the nearly 20 campuses involved in the FIPSE grant to create civic-engagement minors, certificates, and academic programs, we were able to create a course scaffolding that parallels the one Butin describes, consisting of (1) a lead-in or gateway course; (2) courses addressing poverty, politics, and societal inequalities; (3) research courses and projects; (4) intensive internships either in courses or in summer programs; and (5) capstones. Where these programs have failed to gain traction, however, is in their failure to be feasible for busy, engaged students. In other words, students still have a major (sometimes two or three of them), and something has to give.

Unfortunately, most service-learning experiences are episodic, and not in ways that build upon each other. The longitudinal and alumni research of the four-year Bonner Scholars Program supports the power of a multiyear co-curricular model, but not the importance of service-learning courses. No significant associations were found between the number of service-learning courses and the opportunity for dialogue or opportunity for service. Keen and Hall (2009) write: "This finding suggest that the larger college experience, and not just one or more service-learning classes, may be essential to increase the chances that seniors will value dialogue and service opportunities to address social justice concerns" (p. 65).

In a longitudinal analysis of its four-year Bonner Scholar Program, the most important factor of its effectiveness is dialogue across difference, defined as both structured and unstructured dialogue with individuals served, peers, supervisors and partners, advisors and faculty. As Keen and Hall (2009) write in *Engaging with*

*Difference Matters: Longitudinal Student Outcomes of Co-Curricular Service-Learning Programs,*

> Academic, civic, and personal gains correlate with four years of involvement in Bonner Scholar Program activities. Most notable was development between the freshman and senior year regarding the importance of opportunities for dialogue and between the junior and senior years regarding skills needed to cross boundaries of difference. (p. 64)

In short, the senior year matters. Moreover, the important dialogue and social justice is associated with co-curricular, not curricular, service-learning.

In addition, a 2011 study of the 5,000 Bonner Program alumni reaffirms the importance of dialogue across differences, finding that structured reflection opportunities—which may occur not only in courses but also in co-curricular settings such as regular Bonner Meetings or in team meetings with partners at sites—have a magnifier effect on unstructured reflection. We are most interested in models that provide this powerful combination dialogue, in ways that include co-curricular and curricular settings through the senior year. In fact, this was part of the insight that led to the investment in working with campuses to create civic-engagement academic programs. While these programs did, in general, include a capstone course, in practice many of them have failed to enroll or retain many students; others have struggled to define clear pathways through the curriculum. Tracey Burke, Diane Hirshberg, and Tara Smith do an excellent job describing some of the complexities of this challenge in Chapter 1, "Theory Matters: Articulating a Theoretical Framework for Civic Engagement." They urge others to design an academic program around a clear set of learning outcomes and a conceptual framework, building shared understanding and opportunities for students to co-create knowledge. Our observation is that this is much easier to do when there is a strong, multiyear co-curricular program in place, one that can link at multiple points and in ways that support the discovery and application of knowledge in community contexts.

Finally, a closer examination of the purportedly high levels of student volunteerism raises some questions about the frequency and depth of students' experience in college. In the past three years, the Siena Research Institute at Siena College in Albany, New York, has developed the National Assessment of Student Community Engagement (NASCE). Siena is also home to a Bonner Leader Program (as well as a 25-member VISTA Fellows Program that engages members full-time with community partners). This assessment provides more data about the overall level of student engagement in terms of frequency, depth, and breadth. To date, more than 30 institutions have participated in the study, including a third that also host Bonner Scholar and Leader Programs, as well as many in the New York Campus Compact network. More than 14,000 undergraduates have completed the survey, making it the largest national data set exclusively focused on community engagement. While analysis of that data is just beginning, it is revealing some interesting factors, including several that debunk claims that students are highly involved in service and community engagement. While students may certainly participate in service on at least one occasion, the data suggests that *nearly half of students in the sample have not been involved in any activity whatsoever.* In addition, on most campuses, roughly 10 percent of students perform 80 percent of the community engagement. There is a 30-point drop in student participation from high school to college, and students also cite that they are dissatisfied with their own levels of participation. The top reasons they do not participate include a need to study and a need to work. In this era, effective programs perhaps should integrate both academic credit and financial support.

## Beyond the Traditional Academic Departmental Model

### Campus Infrastructure

The Bonner Program also aims to support the development of campuswide infrastructures that build, coordinate, and assess community engagement activities and initiatives across campus for students, faculty, and community partners. Drawing on both student affairs and academic (curricular and research) expertise, the most effective centers bridge the curricular and co-curricular silos that are present in higher education today. This bridging makes the intensive, multiyear, developmental pathways possible. As such, most effective centers capitalize on the student leadership that emerges from these pathways for campus-community initiatives, curricular development, co-curricular community engagement programs, and community-based research.

Center staff and faculty also work as expert brokers of the campus-community relationship, drawing on a full range of resources to sustain impactful relationships with community partners. Essential elements of an effective center include: a plan for strategic partner selection; a process for joint development of a multiyear partnership plan with community partners; processes for regular assessment of the relationship and for regular communication between the community partner and the center; an ethic that seeks to acknowledge and rebalance the power relationship between the academy and the community as much as is feasibly possible in each partnership by engaging partners as co-educators, co-researchers, and co-producers of knowledge. Like the work with students and faculty, this work is inherently developmental. The importance of departments and centers that play this role is illustrated well in several chapters. Besides Morton's Chapter 5, there is Keene and Reiff's "Contending with Political and Cultural Campus Changes" (Chapter 4). Another role that the center's staff play is as bridge between faculty and community. Center staff prepare faculty through faculty development and training for community engagement, *and* draw on the expertise of faculty across all disciplines to address community needs. In our observation, the most effective centers build multiple campus connections with a wide variety of academic and student support services programs. While some of these centers do build academic programs (majors, minors, or certificates), without strong attention to the fundamentals of the *intensive, multiyear, developmental pathway* and the other roles mentioned herein for the center, such programs often do not succeed in enrolling, retaining, and graduating students. Once again, the co-curricular structure for the program is critical here, and supported by assessment. First-year retention rates and graduation rates are higher for students in the Bonner Program than for the institution as a whole at all of the institutions.

As many authors in this volume attest, there are four key factors that shift the epistemology towards democratic engagement in the community: (1) strong center infrastructure, (2) the roles of staff and faculty as builders and facilitators of reciprocity, (3) the attention to power relations between the academy and the community, and (4) the continual valuing of community knowledge and student leadership.

### *Turning They into We*

**Developmental Community Partnerships**

In Chapter 8, "Building in Place," Tal Stanley describes the fundamental importance of the "three-part interaction of the natural environment, the built environment, and human culture and history" that defines Emory & Henry College and provides a core for its Bonner Scholar Program, Public Policy and Community Service major, and the broader work of the Appalachian Center. As Stanley writes:

> Building in place at Emory & Henry requires that the college's service partnerships not be with a single agency or organization. Instead, the partnerships necessary for building in place are with a place and its people in a long-term relationship to identify needs and issues and capitalize on assets and resources, defining strategies and solutions from within the place and that are consonant with that place. Partnerships that build in place struggle with systemic forces to address systemic needs and issues, recognizing that to do so involves reaching across the single issues and narrow focus that define any one agency or organization, any one approach, drawing on wide collaborations and an embracing common ground. (p. 162)

This philosophy is shared throughout the Bonner network. Each program and campus builds and manages multiple community partnerships over years of engagement. Because of the multiyear structure of student engagement, it is common (indeed, encouraged) that students return to the same nonprofit organization for two or more years, making it possible for those students to take on increasing levels of responsibility and complex capacity-building academic and co-curricular projects.

Currently, the 3,000-plus students participate in more than 866,631 hours of community engagement annually (roughly 280 hours each), with each campus generally managing 10–20 committed multiyear partnerships, and another 10–60 one-time and short-term projects. While we do not believe that student hours are a good measure of quality, they are important because they far exceed what may be possible in many service-learning courses (which often average 20–40 hours per semester) and create the occasions for *dialogue across difference and meaningful interactions with mentors*, two essential factors of success. There are many programs in this volume that show similar levels of engagement, at least over one year, and this is a fact that shouldn't be easily overlooked. But, what's more interesting is the possibility of building and sharing evidence-driven practice for more effective service-learning and civic-engagement work through this intensive, multisite network of students, staff, faculty, and partners. Because these nonprofit and governmental agencies and their partnering institutions build developmental partnerships, they have the opportunity to build a full range of engagements—including direct service, community-based research, service-learning, resource generation, capacity building, and even public policy and model program research.

Partners report greater need for the capacity-building activities that only long-term intensive participating students can fulfill. In a recent survey of community partners from across the Bonner network, partners indicated major gaps in their need for more sophisticated forms of engagement. For example, while only 24 percent receive policy news and analysis support from campuses, 92 percent want these services. In addition, 89 percent want help with capacity building (such as board development, training, staff development, and technology needs), whereas only 19 percent report receiving this help. Moreover, 87 percent want institutions to play a role as conveners, for example, by bringing partners together to share best practices, but only 28 percent receive this help. Moreover, 88 percent want the institution to act as a community information hub, whereas 34 percent believe the campus is beginning to play this role. Because of this work, we have begun an initiative to integrate public policy research and issue briefs (i.e., that address topics like chronic homelessness, the achievement gap, green jobs, prison reentry) in ways that might build the collective knowledge of programs to best address community needs. We believe that higher education can play vital roles as information hubs, conveners, and network weavers for partners and communities.

Seider and Novick offer some important insights and distinctions in their essay, "Measuring the Impact of Community Service Learning." In particular, they note the use of the 2004 article by Joseph Kahne and Joel Westheimer that poses three views of citizenship: participatory, socially responsible, and justice-oriented. The Bonner Program, in fact, uses this article as part of its developmental training of students to explore, over four years, their engagement and future pathways of citizenship. In fact, the alumni survey reveals that 100 percent of alumni report remaining civically engaged, with 90 percent voting in the last election and 49 percent volunteering in the past 12 months; choosing meaningful careers with 34 percent working in government, 33 percent in nonprofit agencies, 25 percent in for-profit careers, and 8 percent self-employed, which they cite is connected to their desire to effect change. It is precisely because of the field's ability to produce civic-minded professionals that perhaps we can begin to explore the complex interconnections of student and partner, faculty and alum, parent and policy maker.

Seider and Novick go on to explore the tensions between evaluations of student learning, tasks completed through service (*getting things done*), and other measures of social capital. While we agree that programs often face operational constraints that limit strategies for assessing community and program impact, once again, a developmental and long-term approach is a key advantage. Our programs and network are beginning to pilot strategies for linking ongoing program evaluation with deeper strategies for community impact assessment, which may be aided by the sharing of publicly available data and well-honed tools that have been developed and tested in nonprofits, government agencies and other research entities. On the local level, centers like the University of Richmond have begun dedicating staff time to deep-listening projects with community partners, with the eventual aim of surfacing intended outcomes and impact evaluation strategies. This work is part of a broader trend for evidence-based practice, one that even higher education associations like Imagining America and Bringing Theory to Practice have begun to echo and explore.

## *The Untapped Reservoir*

### The Civic Mission of Higher Education

Students don't often become sociologists, mathematicians, or physicists, but they do become community members and leaders. Indeed, the historic growth of community engagement in higher education is a direct outgrowth of its original civic mission that transcends discipline. To that end, recent research points to a vast untapped reservoir of students who are not being touched by that civic mission.

Far from being at a pinnacle, we believe that the national civic-engagement and service-learning movement is at a critical crossroads, one that we must cross with purpose. Collectively, and in part because of books like this and others, we finally have a solid foundation of program development and management, student development, and campus-community partnerships, that will enable us to get serious about long-term structural changes and community impact.

We recognize this big vision will require higher education to embrace work that some may deem *political*, one that will necessitate its members identifying themselves as being from and part of the community, be that of place or of a chosen identity. Indeed, as several of the authors in this book express, especially Mary Beth Pudup (Chapter 6) and Sherry Giles (Chapter 3), the work to create and sustain *just one* academic program is fraught with political dimensions. Giles, in "Negotiating the Boundary between the Academy and Communities," does an excellent job of providing a vision of how higher education, through its disciplines, might contribute to reshaping its own enterprise as she describes the impetus for a Community Justice major at Guilford College: According to Giles, the creators of the new major viewed it as grounded in a democratic thesis, "people coming together and trying to govern ourselves, rather than be governed by others." They crafted a curriculum and pedagogy intended to serve as "prerequisites for fundamental social change," educational experiences in which students could change from being "isolated, individualism-oriented people...to relate well enough to form a strong collective to create social change" (p. 56).

We believe that higher education is now more prepared to embark on the long-held vision—to fully embrace our civic missions by choosing to engage its most valued assets in service of the common good. The challenge is not to create a discipline in which a few or some students major; rather, we believe we must take what we know about creating institutions that fully integrate the values and structures for civic and community engagement to scale, across the curriculum and institution. We believe that as a field we are poised to tackle this crucible moment and, through it, to build pathways for higher education to contribute to the health and strength of our communities, nation, and world.

## References

Astin, A., Vogelgesang, L., Ikeda, E. K., and Yee, J. A. (January 2000). *How Service Learning Affects Students: Executive Summary.* Los Angeles, CA: UCLA Higher Education Research Institute.

Association for American Colleges and Universities and the Global Perspective Institute. (November 2011). *A Crucible Moment: College Learning and Democracy's Future.* US Department of Education.

Bringle, R. G. and Hatcher, J. A. (1995). A service-learning curriculum for faculty. *The Michigan Journal of Community Service-learning, 2,* 112–22.

Eyler, J. and Giles, Jr., D. (1999). *Where's the Learning in Service-Learning?* San Francisco: Jossey-Bass.

Eyler, J. S., Giles, D. E., Jr., Stenson, C. M., and Gray, C. J. (2001). *At a Glance: What We Know about the Effects of Service-Learning on College Students, Faculty, Institutions, and Communities,* 1993–2000. (3rd ed.). Washington, DC: Learn and Serve America National Service-Learning Clearinghouse.

Keen, C. and Hall, K. (2009). Engaging with difference matters: Longitudinal student outcomes of co-curricular service-learning programs. *The Journal of Higher Education, 80*(1) p.59–79 (January/February 2009).

Johnson, M. and Levy, D. (forthcoming). *A National Assessment of Service and Civic Engagement.* Siena Research Institute.

Saltmarsh, J., Hartley. M, and Clayton, P. H. (2009). *Democratic Engagement White Paper.* Boston, MA: New England Resource Center for Higher Education.

Saltmarsh, J. Hartley, M. Eds. (2011). *To Serve a Larger Purpose: Education for Democracy and the Transformation of Higher Education.* Philadelphia PA: Temple University Press.

# CHAPTER 11

# De Tocqueville Rediscovered:
# Community-Based Civic Engagement

*Elizabeth L. Hollander*
Tisch College, Tufts University

T wo and a half decades into the higher education civic engagement movement, as Dan Butin indicates in the Introduction to this book, there is concern that the movement has "stalled," partly because of imprecise and conflicting language and compartmentalized networks and a remarkably "apolitical agenda." In the view of this author, the "movement" has not exactly stalled. Rather, it has spread widely throughout higher education. Many campuses have service and/or service-learning centers. Service-learning is widespread in many disciplines. Membership in Campus Compact has grown to nearly 1200, and there is a proliferation of other organizations addressing civic engagement on every type of campus. Civic engagement has been "institutionalized" through accrediting requirements, a Carnegie Classification option, and a federal recognition program. Most recently, AAC&U and the Global Perspectives Institute have worked with the federal Department of Education to develop a report calling for more and better civic education of college students.

Why then, do some feel the movement is stalled? For some, as Butin references, it is because it has not accomplished the aim of transforming higher education but has, rather, been absorbed into current structures. For others, including this author, the concern is that the movement lacks a coherent articulated theory, especially regarding how communities and systems are changed. It remains, for the most part "apolitical," another concern for this author.

In reading the chapters in this book, however, I discovered that, at least in several majors described here, there is a dominant theory of change and a view of democracy. It is the power of citizens to make change at the most local level, the deTocquevillian notion that American citizens are, in the end, willing to organize themselves to accomplish what their governments are unable to provide. In the next few pages, I will attempt to sketch out how the larger movement grew without much coherent theory. Meanwhile, faculty on campuses countered the limits of unreflective volunteerism and university self-interest by teaching students how to engage in community improvement at the local community level.

The absence of rigorous theorizing about community change in the civic-engagement movement is not surprising when we look at its origins. Civic engagement in higher education started as a co-curricular, student, and college-president driven initiative. In response to claims that the college generation of the 1980s was self-centered and lacking in empathy (Bellah, 1985), students organized the Campus Outreach Opportunity League (COOL) in 1984, and college presidents organized Campus Compact in 1985. In the early years, the focus was on providing students with co-curricular opportunities for community service. Much of this service was of a one-on-one ameliorative nature, for example, serving in soup kitchens. There was neither a general emphasis on systemic change nor on political activism.

The funding of service by the Corporation for National and Community Service also reinforced the apolitical nature of the service movement. Those who received federal funds were, in fact, prohibited from even engaging in voter registration efforts. One of my "aha" moments in my early days at Campus Compact was being asked by my board chair Edward "Monk" Malloy, the president of Notre Dame, "How would you make the case for student civic engagement to a conservative Republican member of Congress as well as to a liberal Democrat?"

Faculty who were interested in engaged teaching and research, in the early days, came from the ranks of those who believed in the power of experiential learning. They found an organizational home in the Society for Experiential Education and in a group named the "Invisible College" (later renamed Educators for Community Engagement). By the early nineties, increasing attention was being paid to "service-learning" as a way to deepen students' systemic understanding of the conditions they were trying to ameliorate and as a way to connect classroom theory to the "real world." These efforts to deepen and spread the practice of service-learning were not focused on a particular discipline, but rather on promoting service-learning as a powerful pedagogy for all disciplines. The dominant theories were pedagogical (e.g., Paulo Freire and John Dewey).

Another driving force in the early days of the higher education civic-engagement movement was a rediscovery of the institutional role of colleges and universities as "anchor" institutions in their communities, especially those located in challenged urban neighborhoods. In many cities, "eds and meds," or college and universities and medical complexes had become the largest employers. Given their capital investment, they were not likely to move, and, therefore, they had a lot of motivation to work with their adjacent neighborhoods to improve local conditions. These efforts were led by a combination of presidential leadership (such as Evan Dobelle at Trinity College) and outreach centers such as the Netter Center at the University of Pennsylvania. (Presidents at the University of Pennsylvania have also been involved.) Sometimes these efforts are linked with the curriculum (e.g., the University of Wisconsin, Milwaukee) but often they are not (Trinity, for example, built three schools adjacent to its campus without involving the education faculty). These efforts (especially those in the inner city) often reflect the universities' self-interest in neighborhood safety, housing values, and quality commercial outlets, as well as expansion space. Power differentials between the university and their neighbors were endemic and a source of tension. A recent publication by Axelroth and Dubb (2010) provides a useful typography of the types of interventions by differing types of institutions.

Once again, given the origins of these efforts, they are rarely driven by a coherent theory of community improvement. Rather, the driving force is often the administrative leadership of the campus, such as the president and a vice-president of public affairs whose knowledge of the intricacies of urban development varies. In some cases, to be fair, such as the at University of California, Los Angeles, and the Netter Center, or more recently, Syracuse University, outstanding intellectual leadership in urban improvement has been harnessed to drive these efforts. In addition, HUD, the US Department of Housing and Urban Development, which funded these efforts in the 1990s (under the rubric of Community Outreach Partnership Centers) set very stringent partnership criteria for their funding designed to balance investments and decision making between the community and the campus.

### Gathering concerns about the state of the democracy

In 1998, the National Commission on Civic Renewal chaired by William Bennett and Sam Nunn published a powerful report entitled "A Nation of Spectators." Written by academics, the report decried the absence of civic participation in US democracy and called upon every sector *except* higher education to do something about it. The report notes the absence of participation in national political activities and high levels of distrust in government leadership, especially at the national level. At the same time, it points to the vibrancy of local citizen engagement as a source of optimism. Calling it a "new movement," the report cites such efforts as neighborhood organizing to improve safety and opportunities for jobs, youth volunteering, civic entrepreneurs, and the role of faith-based institutions in supporting families.

This analysis parallels this author's experience. I became very aware of the vibrancy of democratic engagement at the neighborhood and local government level, first as a local government official in Chicago in the mid-eighties, then as director of a foundation effort to improve government and as director of an urban center at a university in the nineties. Currently, I serve as a board member of the National Civic League (NCL) and Public Allies. NCL annually celebrates citizen engagement with government in their All American Cities awards, and many Public Allies are deployed to build the capacity of local neighborhood groups and nonprofit organizations to engage in community improvement. Across America, there is a quiet revolution of citizen engagement in local initiatives ranging from public safety to environment, to elder care and child support. Smart local governments are harnessing this "citizen power" to analyze local problems through dialogue, to put "eyes on the street," maintain trails and parks, look out for the housebound and create safe and productive spaces for children after school. Citizens are coming together to ask for more and better from their local officials and for help in the heavy lifting. Over the past decades these initiatives have continued to gain momentum as the trust in national institutions and national politics continues to decline.

It is important to note that this grass-roots citizen engagement was not at all on the radar of college presidents. In the early 2000s, Chris Gates, then president of the NCL, gave a speech to a Campus Compact presidential colloquium, and it was clear that the group was fascinated and totally surprised to learn of the vibrancy of grass-roots civic participation. They were more concerned about college student voting rates.

Even though college presidents are generally not up to speed on local citizen engagement, the civic-engagement movement in higher education, has, for the most part, helped students to engage at the most local level where democratic participation is more vibrant and results are more tangible. It has, on the other hand done little to overcome cynicism about larger institutions, and in fact, if we look closely, has reinforced the inherent injustice of such systems. One example is the mission statement from Guilford College major (emphasis mine).

> The mission of the major is to support students as they integrate scholarship from Social Theory with community engagement to develop knowledge and skills relevant to citizens organizing in communities and institutions, the roles of public service organizations, and the larger institutional structure of society, *understood as operating systematically to generate unjust inequality.*" (Giles, Chapter 3, this volume)

From the outset, in the civic-engagement movement, faculty and staff leaders have sought to teach students to understand the systemic causes of the social conditions that volunteerism was seeking to ameliorate (Morton, 1995). They have also sought to problematize the "service" paradigm and help students to recognize the capacities that exist in even the poorest communities. McKnight and Kretzman's (1996) "Asset-based community development (ABCD)" perspective on communities is, for instance, very often part of the training of student volunteers. These efforts resulted from an early understanding that one-off, drive-by community engagement could, in fact, reinforce students' stereotypes about poor people being responsible for their own poverty due to character flaws or lack of initiative.

From the beginning, studies showed that students who did serious reflection on their service experience, in or out of a class, gained significant understanding of the complexities of social conditions and the challenges in ameliorating them (Giles & Eyler, 1994). However, preparing students to take systemic action, especially through the traditional political routes of involvement in campaigns, lobbying, letter writing, and the like, have never been a dominant theme in the civic-engagement movement in higher education. During the late 1990s and early 2000s, the low level of voter turnout among young people became a concern and money and effort were put into rallying students to more traditional political activism (although in a very apolitical way, given the level of foundation funding). When students were challenged about their interest in service vis-à-vis political action, they responded with a very sophisticated statement of service as politics (Raill & Hollander, 1996).

As these efforts were codified into majors, it should not be surprising, then, that the majors are (as exemplified in this book), focused on learning how to effect change at the most local level, whether through community organizing, relationship building, therapeutic assistance, or even imagining and building "alternative" sustainable communities that operate, to the extent possible, without reliance on larger, unjust systems of distribution of wealth, economic opportunity, energy, education, and the like.

At Providence College, citizenship is not equated with a specific, discrete, definable body of knowledge but as something that is created through experience. To help students find the means to create citizenship experiences, the emphasis is put on building relationships with local communities and learning the skills of eloquent listening, power mapping, group process, crossing cultural boundaries, examining personal behavior and *values,* as well as developing systems thinking, organizational skills ( e.g., budgeting) and content knowledge of a particular issue. Included in the major is an opportunity to recognize that many systems "are nearing collapse and ask what an alternative future, based on values of community may look like" (Morton, Chapter 5, this volume).

Providence's major also stresses service as relationship, developed through experience.

> Service and citizenship are actions, framed by choices, themselves framed by values. Over time the content of the major and minor focused increasingly on experience and reflection with the reflection understood as a way of sorting out values, meaning, and action—the ingredients of personal practices of citizenship, and the bridge into effective public work. (Morton, Chapter 5, this volume)

The term "public work" is Harry Boyte's and is very relevant to the concept of citizenship inherent in the civic-engagement majors and minors examined in this book. Boyte (1991) uses the term public work to describe the actions of citizens working together to create something of "public value." Local efforts mentioned earlier in this chapter, such as community policing or block groups, are examples of public work.

The emphasis on local action in relationship with the local community is also a mainstay of the Emory & Henry's Public Policy and Community Service major. Their program

> premises policymaking and policy advocacy as the responsibilities of all citizens, putting into action and sustaining the values and insights that have been forged in service and encompassing citizenship of place. (Stanley, Chapter 8, this volume)

They contrast this approach with public policy that is reserved as the purview of the few and one in which large research universities are practitioners of policy, research and advocacy with the result that public policy "reinstates the values of the market economy, often to the detriment of individuals and places little valued in that economy." (Stanley, Chapter 8, this volume)

At Bryant University, the sociology and service-learning major is focused on helping students understand the connections between their individual lives and larger social forces. Based in sociology, this major draws from major social theorists such as

C. Wright Mills and takes students through a conscious journey of moving beyond self, and examining the limits of one-on-one service, to recognizing larger social forces and eventually finding ways to ameliorate them. The relationship to community starts with one-on-one helping and observing and moves to designing and implementing projects for nonprofits. Most recently, a Social Entrepreneurship track has been added. This is the one major described in the book that resides entirely in one discipline, making it easy to identify its underlying theories. C. Wright Mills's work is front and center.

But what is the theoretical base for the other majors described above? Providence College cites Frank Newman, Robert Bellah, Robert Coles, Alexis deToqueville, Ivan Illich, John McKnight, Wendell Berry, James Adams, John Dewey, and Dorothy Day. Wendell Berry is also cited in the Emory & Henry chapter, as are C. Wright Mills, Paul Theobold, Paulo Freire, David Harvey, and others, but it is not clear what literature the students read. At Guilford, the Community Justice Major is located within the Justice and Policy Studies department, which also houses the Criminal Justice major. There has been an attempt to increase its theoretical basis; however, the chapter does not describe which theories.

In discussing theory in the Community Studies program at UC Santa Cruz, it is emphasized that this interdisciplinary department developed its own philosophical underpinning that emphasizes the constant interplay between theory and practice in which they are testing each other's contribution to the development of knowledge aimed at improving society.

Chapter 6 describes the incorporation of a new course at UC Santa Cruz "attuned to poststructuralism's emphasis on how systems of knowledge/power are produced and contribute to social inequality and cultural oppression." The course includes an exploration of how structural inequalities intersect with the therapeutic encounter (Lyon-Callo 2008). The course reflects the younger faculty's interest in post modernist theory.

The very preliminary insight this small sample of campuses gives us into the theories driving the civic education of college students is intriguing. The challenges of an interdisciplinary major become evident. It would be interesting to have more detail on how these majors balance the mix of social, political, economic and environmental theory. I notice no mention of either political or economic theorists, but without syllabi to examine that may be incorrect. The powerful common element of these programs is that students are constantly exposed to experiences in which to test and think about theory, and to use reflection and capstone experiences to do so.

It is also very difficult to discern how much insight students get into the working of local, state, and particularly national government and how those policies impact community based efforts and visa versa. Is a widespread cynicism about national political life reflected in the emphasis on local democracy? I expect that there is an attempt to help students understand how grass-roots democratic engagement might eventually influence politics and policy making at various governmental levels. However, I sense an absence of insight into how governmental systems might themselves be influenced more directly.

Are the skills to influence government being taught in political science or public policy departments or classes? Are these classes integrated into civic-engagement majors but not highlighted in the discussions in this volume? Providence College, for example, describes their political science major as providing

> students with the tools for a careful and systematic study of politics.... Students are grounded in factual material about governments and politics, and in political philosophy as well. The department's program is also grounded in values: we study both what happens and what ought to happen in politics. (http://www .providence.edu/academics/Pages/political-science.aspx)

Does the emphasis on very local civic-engagement help explain why the civic-engagement movement has been so apolitical? Or does the apolitical genesis of the movement help explain why majors have developed with a local emphasis? In either case, it is worth examining, going forward, whether it might be helpful to pursue a greater balance between local citizen and nonprofit based efforts and governmental systems at all levels.

This author is not the first to raise this issue. Anne Colby and colleagues address it in their 2007 book *Educating for Democracy*. The author is influenced by her own history of college engagement, which included applying political and economic theory to civil rights activism. It is evident that, particularly at this point in our history, there is much to be cynical about, especially regarding our national political scene. I also recognize that campuses have good reasons to worry about "politicizing" their civic-engagement efforts for fear of losing funding, or of favoring one political point of view over another.

I would argue that it would be helpful for students to have exposure to political philosophers and political and economic and other theorists who have struggled, over the centuries, with the challenges of balancing individual and communal interests and with achieving just systems, consistent with democratic values. I saw such a program at a small, faith-based college on the West Coast when I conducted a review of their civic-engagement center. As part of that work I attended a sociology class on social theory, a political science class on theories of justice and a religious studies class on wealth and poverty in the bible. Each of these classes gave students exposure to a rich literature examining how societies are and can be structured. This provides a very interesting backdrop for students who, in their direct engagement with community, are encouraged, as in the majors described in this volume, to build community relationships, and act as "servant leaders."

It would also be helpful for students to have an idea of how government acts administratively as well as politically. There is a dearth of knowledge about what government actually "does." I'll never forget being told by a dean at a major midwestern university that its automotive engineering students had "no understanding that the government builds roads." Increasingly, it seems to this author the role of government is invisible and misunderstood. How else could people claim to want government off their backs, but say in the same sentence, "don't mess with my medicare?"

The field of civic engagement is maturing, and more and more campuses are instituting majors and minors. This is a ripe opportunity to examine in detail what students are being taught. We need to ask ourselves, as a field, whether our students need to understand the role that government plays at the local, state, national and international levels. Should they examine how government intersects with politics and citizen-based efforts at all these levels? Should they have an understanding of the levers for changing both government and politics? Can we provide them this knowledge along with a subtle introduction to local, place-based community institution building?

These are not easy questions. The editor and authors of this book have done the civic-engagement movement in higher education a service by providing at least a beginning understanding of the content of current civic-engagement majors. Without a detailed look at how civic education is actually being carried out, we do not have the tools to conduct a thoughtful self-examination of our goals, our theories, and our practice. This book should be the first of many to push the field toward a disciplined examination of civic education on our campuses.

## References

Axelroth, R., & Dubb, S. (2010). *The road half traveled: University engagement at a crossroads.* College Park, MD: The Democracy Collaborative.

Bellah, R., Madsen, R., Sullivan, W., Swidler, A., & Tipton, S. (1985). *Habits of the heart: Individualism and commitment in American life.* San Francisco, CA: University of California Press.

Bennet, W., & Nunn, S. (1998). *A nation of spectators.* Washington, D.C.: National Commission on Civic Renewal.

Boyte, H. (1991). Community service and civic education. *Phi Delta Kappan*, 765–67.

Colby, A., Beaumont, E., Ehrlich, T., & Corngold, J. (2007). *Educating for demoracy: Preparing undergraduates for responsible political engagement.* Stanford, CA: Carnegie Foundation for the Advancement of Teaching.

Giles, D. & Eyler, J. (1994). The impact of a college community service laboratory on students' personal, social, and cognitive outcomes. *Journal of Adolescence, 17,* 327–39.

Kretzmann, J., & McKnight, J. (1996). Assets-based community development. *National Civic Review 85,* 23–29.

Lyon-Callo, V. (2008). *Inequality, policy, and neo-liberal governance.* Toronto: University of Toronto Press.

Morton, K. (1995). The irony of service: Charity, project and social change in service-learning. *Michigan Journal of Community Service-learning, 2,* 19–32.

Raill, S., & Hollander, E. (1996). How campuses can create engaged students: The student view. *Journal of College & Character, 7*(1), 1–5.

# Contributors

## Editors

**Dan W. Butin** is an associate professor and founding dean of the school of education at Merrimack College. He is the author and editor of more than 60 academic publications, including *Service-Learning in Theory and Practice: The Future of Community Engagement in Higher Education* (2010), which won the 2010 Critics Choice Book Award of the American Educational Studies Association; *Service-Learning and Social Justice Education* (2008); and *Teaching Social Foundations of Education* (2005). Dr. Butin's research focuses on issues of educator preparation and policy, and community engagement. Prior to working in higher education, Dr. Butin was a middle-school math and science teacher and the chief financial officer of Teach For America. More of Dr. Butin's work can be found at http://danbutin.org/.

**Scott Seider** is an assistant professor of Education at Boston University, where his research focuses on the civic development of adolescents and emerging adults. He is the author of *Shelter: Where Harvard Meets the Homeless* (2010) as well as more than 40 journal articles and book chapters. He also serves on the editorial boards of the *Journal of Adolescent Research* and the *Journal of Research in Character Education* and as a contributing editor of the *Journal of College & Character*.

## Authors

**Tracey Burke** is associate professor of Social Work at the University of Alaska Anchorage. She has taught a social work/general education service-learning class in partnership with the Food Bank of Alaska for over five years, played a lead role in constructing UAA's Certificate in Civic Engagement, and is past chair of the Center for Community Engagement & Learning's Advisory Council. Dr. Burke holds the Higher Education seat on the State Commission for Community Service, ServeAlaska, and is the recipient of the 2011 Sellkregg Award for Community Engagement & Service Learning.

**Sandra L. Enos** is associate professor of Sociology and Coordinator of the Service-Learning program in Sociology at Bryant University in Smithfield, Rhode Island.

She earned her doctoral degree from the University of Connecticut. Former Project Director of The Project on Integrating Service with Academic Study at the national office of Campus Compact, she has a long career in the public and nonprofit sectors.

**Hollyce (Sherry) Giles** is an associate professor of Justice and Policy Studies at Guilford College, a liberal arts college of Quaker heritage in Greensboro, North Carolina. A psychologist by training, Giles teaches in the Community and Justice Studies major, which integrates scholarship in social theory with students' engagement with local communities. Her areas of scholarly inquiry and publication focus on the group dynamics of social change initiatives, and on community-based teaching and research.

**Robert Hackett** is the president of the Bonner Foundation.

**Diane Hirshberg** is associate professor of Education Policy at the University of Alaska Anchorage. She conducts research on indigenous education issues and school improvement and teaches in the UAA Honors College. Dr. Hirshberg has taught in the Certificate in Civic Engagement at UAA, is past chair of the program, and current chair of the UAA Center for Community Engagement and Learning Advisory Council.

**Elizabeth L. Hollander** served as the national director of Campus Compact from 1997 to 2006 and is currently a senior fellow at the Jonathan M. Tisch College of Citizenship and Public Service at Tufts University.

**Ariane Hoy** is a senior program office at the Bonner Foundation and the former executive director of the Campus Outreach Opportunity League (COOL).

**Mathew Johnson** is the director of academic community engagement and an associate professor in Sociology and Environmental Studies at Siena College. He also serves as a program and research consultant to the Bonner Foundation.

**Arthur S. Keene** is a professor in the Anthropology department at UMass Amherst where he has taught for the last 32 years. He is founder and director of the UMass Alliance for Community Transformation (UACT) and along with John Reiff is co-director of the UMass Citizen Scholars Program. Keene is currently collaborating with his undergraduate students on an ethnographic exploration of how the Millennial Generation learns.

**Peter Levine** is the research director of the Jonathan M. Tisch College of Citizenship and Public Service at Tufts University and director of the Center for Information & Research on Civic Learning & Engagement (CIRCLE). He is the author of eight books including *Reforming the Humanities* and *The Future of Democracy*.

**Elizabeth Minnich** is a senior scholar at the Association of American Colleges and Universities and the series editor of Temple University Press's "New Academy" series. She is also the author of *Transforming Knowledge* (2005) and dozens of articles on issues in higher education.

**Keith Morton** is professor of Public and Community Service Studies at Providence College, where he has taught since 1994. He is interested in the history of the idea of community, in how we learn from experience, and in community and youth development. Much of his community work is located in the Smith Hill neighborhood of Providence, Rhode Island, and he works closely with the nonprofit organizations Smith Hill Community Development Corporation, Southside Community Land Trust, and Institute for the Study and Practice of Nonviolence.

**Sarah Novick** is a doctoral candidate in Curriculum and Teaching at Boston University. She previously worked as an elementary school teacher in the New York City public schools. Her work has been published in *Educational Leadership* and the *Journal of College & Character*.

**Mary Beth Pudup** is associate professor of Community Studies at the University of California, Santa Cruz. Her research focuses on issues of economic justice, historical geography of the United States, and public policy.

**John Reiff** is Director of the Community Engagement Program of Commonwealth Honors College at UMass Amherst and is Faculty Supervisor for Civic Engagement overseeing the new UMass individualized civic-engagement major. He has taught service-learning since 1981.

**Tara Palmer Smith** is associate professor of English as a Second Language (ESL) at the University of Alaska Anchorage. She has taught the Introduction to Civic Engagement course for the Certificate in Civic Engagement numerous times, in addition to coordinating the ESL program. Ms. Smith has provided leadership for the Certificate assessment, UAA campuswide program assessment, and the campuswide E-portfolio initiative. She also served on the UAA Center for Community Engagement and Learning Advisory Council from 2005 to 2011.

**Talmage A. Stanley** lives and works at Emory & Henry College in Emory, Virginia, where he is Chair of the Department of Public Policy and Community Service. He also is director of the Appalachian Center for Community Service, the Bonner Scholars Program, and the MA program in Community and Organizational Leadership. He is active in civic affairs in Southwest Virginia and southern West Virginia. His book, *The Poco Field: An American Story of Place*, is available from the University of Illinois Press.

# Index